Sex Life

DOROTHY EINON & MIKE POTEGAL

Sex Life

Happier relationships and better sex through frank accounts of couples' love lives

Illustrations by
BRUCE HOGARTH

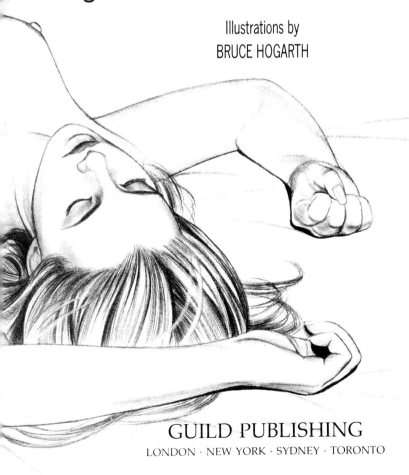

GUILD PUBLISHING
LONDON · NEW YORK · SYDNEY · TORONTO

This edition published 1990 by Guild Publishing
by arrangement with Bloomsbury Publishing Limited
Copyright © Dorothy Einon & Mike Potegal, 1990
© Duncan Petersen Publishing Ltd 1990

Conceived, edited, designed and produced
by Duncan Petersen Publishing Ltd,
5 Botts Mews, London W2 5AG

Filmset and originated by SX Composing Ltd,
Rayleigh, Essex

Made and printed in Britain by The Bath Press, Bath, Avon

Editorial director
Andrew Duncan

Assistant editor
Fiona Hardwick

Art director
Mel Petersen

Designer
Beverley Stewart

CN 8667

This is a book about sex as it occurs in *life* – an every day, yet extraordinary part of our experience. Each section is a blend of explanation, advice, opinion and curious facts stitched into an account of an individual sexual relationship. We hope that the result shows with great vividness how people step beyond genital mechanics into the erotic: the meshing of body and spirit which happens when we give and take pleasure in the act of love. It ought to explain why, at times, this is so difficult.

Sex can be extraordinarily sensuous; it can also be funny, serious, light-hearted or sad. We have attempted to echo the changing moods in what we have written. The erotic pictures which accompany our text enrich the sensuous bits: Bruce's larger drawings illustrate our stories; the smaller, repeated through the commentaries, serve as guides to position and technique.

Although we offer plenty of advice, you will find much more than discussions of technique. Sex is not just mechanics or genital geography. It is a delicious part of the human condition with a history and a biology, a literature and some science.

We began our discussions a couple of years ago on how to set about such a book by asking each other how we learned about sex. Not just the facts, but what we might call the 'ways' of life: the reality of how people did it. Our sources were probably the same as yours: the discovery of our own sexual nature, whispers in the school playground, comparing notes with friends, a few sidelong glances at couples on park benches and the perusal of graffiti on lavatory walls. We owned the odd soft porn magazine.

But perhaps our best guess at how people went about doing it came from reading the 'juicy bits' in novels and films. Books and films, like life, emphasize that sex occurs within relationships. Our priority has been to treat sex not as an isolated event, but as part of human stories.

We start each chapter with a narrative of sexual experiences which are selected to illustrate points we later raise in the main text. We believe these characters are sufficiently real to bring our discussions to life.

Let us say something about how the encounters were written. The first and most important point is that while the originator of a story could be a man or a woman (it was in fact about 50/50), all the women's parts were written (or rewritten) by a woman, and all the men's parts by a man. If we have learned anything from the process it is that men's and women's experience of sex are not necessarily the same.

What were our sources? One was stories, based on life, specially written for us by friends, acquaintances and professional writers on both sides of the Atlantic. Another, which sometimes initiated a story, and at others simply embellished one, was reminiscences and written accounts of actual sexual experiences. We also talked to friends, acquaintances and strangers in bars and cafés, on planes and at dinner tables. Of course, names were changed, tell-tale characteristics were modified and sequences of events altered. But the basis of each story is factual. We thank everyone who contributed.

Last, but probably not least of the sources is our own contrasting experience. One of us grew up and lives in England, the other grew up and lives in New York. We have both been married and divorced at least once: a point which may be less relevant than the fact that one of us is a man and the other a woman.

C O N T E N T S

The first seven stories deal with mainstream sex – sex as we all experience it in growing up, in the high spots of a new love affair, in marriage and long-term relationships, and, indeed, when masturbating.

The next seven stories are about more complex sexual experience.

The final story brings you, in an important sense, back to the beginning. Andrew and Meredith, like Robert and Jenny, are particularly good examples (although not the only ones in the book) of people who make technique and emotion each other's servants.

Between them, the stories cover the whole world of heterosexual sex, a world in which pure physical technique has an important part to play, but not the only one. The different couples and individuals demonstrate, along the way, all the main positions, and variations on those positions, for lovemaking. To take in the full range, look at all 15 sections. In addition, the at-a-glance contents summaries below will guide you quickly to what is covered, and where, not just in terms of positions, but all the other important themes. The index, page 253, offers more detailed access.

Pages 14-29

Robert & Jenny, super-bonkers

Celebration sex

~

The chemistry of attraction.

•

Is it love, or lust?

•

Looking for the 'ideal' girl, or boy?

•

Big pricks: do they matter?

•

The smell of sex.

•

Positions: basic missionary and rear-entry.

Contents

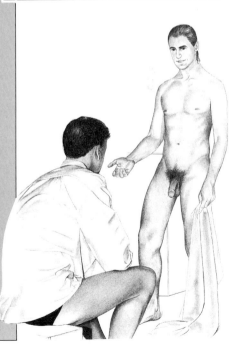

Contents

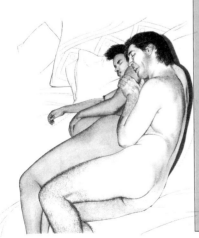

Contents

Contents

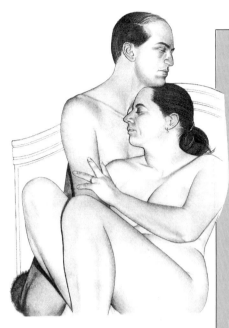

LUST
AT FIRST SIGHT?

Robert & Jenny

1 *Jenny*

He's talking to a red-head, and he has the smug look of someone at a party who knows they are at the centre of attention. I think 'I want you'.

I can tell he knows he's looking good. I move so he can see me better, then turn my back to get a drink. I know he has seen me, and I feel rising excitement.

2 *Robert*

Look at that woman in the black dress. The way she holds her head puts the other women to shame. Terrific legs, in those black stockings. Cute bum.

Can she really want to make it difficult?

I saw the way she looked at me before she turned round.

I'm going to have her.

3 *Jenny*

I'm always aware of his position in the room. Whenever I look in his direction, he looks up.

Now he's beside me.

4 *Robert*

"Excuse me, but I think there is something you ought to know."

"What's that?"

"I get real hard, I'm very gentle, and I never get tired."

She picks up an olive on a stick, looks straight at me, and slowly, deliberately, puts it in her mouth.

5 *Jenny*

We dance a little. He brushes the hair from my face, an opportunity to slide a finger across my cheek. I catch the finger in my mouth, and suck.

"Shall we go?"

As we go out into the night, he kisses me.

6 *Robert*

In the car, I say:

"First I will spread your legs with my hands. Then I will kiss your thighs. Then one or two light kisses you-know-where. Then I will gently take each part of it in my mouth and suck it."

7 *Jenny*

Home. He takes his time: the slow strip.

I am lying naked on the bed, my arms spread above my head, and he is just taking off his shoes. His idea of foreplay? – looking at me lying there as if I were fully clothed.

But I can see the rise and fall of his chest. One shoe. Two shoes. One sock. Two socks. Watching me. Making me wait.

8 *Jenny*

I can feel my breasts wanting to leap out to him. He moves towards me. I try to grab him with my legs, but he dodges. He stands just out of reach, laughing, in nothing but his T-shirt.

"You can hardly fool me."

He glances down and smiles. I try to grab him again, with my feet. This time I get him. I hold it between the soles of my feet, rolling.

I bend my knees and draw him quickly forward.

He topples, and we are rolling about, laughing and kissing. Down he goes, all tongue and lips. I am still laughing.

9 *Robert*

I feel her warm thighs against my face. I kiss up and down her pussy. I separate the labia with my fingers, and kiss them both.

Jenny says: "More, more."

I get her full female smell and taste. A few quick tongue flicks to the clitoris, then to the labia, then back. Then here and there, looking for the magic pleasure spot.

10 *Jenny*

What does it feel like?

A tickle, which you want stopped; but don't want stopped. A tingle, focused there, but then not. It moves in waves.

Where is the best bit focused? I don't know; it moves. But the feeling from the sides as he sucks me in is wonderful. So is the feeling from the top as he presses into me: press here to open. And so is the opening out and feeling myself drawing back, as if a balloon is slowly being blown up inside me. And so is the feeling of his tongue as it barely touches.

Mostly it feels soft. Sometimes it is directly on the clitoris, but usually it is further back. Directly on, and it feels too quick; I'm too busy trying to stop it.

But there are no rules for me; it's more a question of what not to do:

Like always on the clitoris; like taking notice when I say stop; like not taking notice when I say stop; like always assuming I want to come like this; that I don't want to go straight on; that just because I can come more than once, I always want to. Not realizing that sometimes I just want to build up to one glorious 'Catch-the-pieces-I'm-going-to-burst'.

Like now.

11 *Robert*

My tongue is beginning to tire, and her pubic hair is tickling my nose. She raises my head. Looking at her, over her belly, between her breasts, is wonderful. She says lovingly:

"Hullo. This is for me, isn't it? Just for me?"

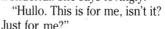

12 *Jenny*

He looks so loving and soft. I say, "Come into me." He slithers up. I catch my breath, melting. There is a sensation in the back of my throat: a feeling of opening up.

My hands move down his back until they rest on his bottom. I gently push him in, I feel myself sucking him in.

Who doesn't like this bit? Often, I want to go on like this, not wanting more, levelling off. Every inch of me is sensitized.

13 *Jenny*

Then suddenly I can't hold it. His mouth on mine; his tongue in and out in rhythm. Faster now; like this. Come on.

No stopping now. This is the fast call: I'm not waiting.

I find it quite sudden, that inevitable movement into 'No stopping me now'.

'I want' takes over, but there is something special about going it alone.

14 R*obert*

I roll and relax for a couple of minutes. Then she kneels on all fours. I'm back inside her, a full erection once more, pumping away, feeling fiercely masculine. I could fuck the world. She says:

"You feel as if you might come right up into my throat."

I pause again, pull the pillows under her pelvis, gently pushing her down on them: flattened dog position.

"I want you to be passive for me. Relax your muscles. Don't move. Let me have you."

I feel her softness ripple with each impact.

15 R*obert*

She starts to breathe hard and to moan. She can't help moving. I stop moving; withdraw. She eagerly pushes up to take me into her.

16 *Jenny*

"I'm about to come again."

He stops moving, to tease me. He says:

"You're not ready yet."
"Oh yes I am."
"No you're not."

I laugh. He says: "OK, you can have just a little," withdrawing so that only the tip is in. He moves it superficially. I moan, move up and try to grab more. He falls out. In again, and I can't help myself; the third time.

17 *Robert*

I reach forward, take her breasts in my hands, feeling the softness of her behind and back of her thighs with my pelvis and legs. I feel that my orgasm, long delayed, is now uncontrollably imminent.

My movements are automatic, driving me on. I feel the tingling all over my body as I come. I wonder what she feels.

18 *Jenny*

Robert says, "That was nice. Happy birthday sweetheart."

"Where did you get the idea of picking each other up at the party?"

"Some sex manual."

"Hey, don't go to sleep . . . I want to share it with you . . . "

"Good night, love."

Who hasn't looked across a room, as Jenny does, and felt: 'I want you'. Whether it is catching sight of a lover or a sudden desire for a complete stranger, we rarely analyse that first response. It takes the average man seven seconds to make up his mind, and we doubt that women are much different. (Although it may take a good deal longer to pluck up the courage to do something about it.)

Love, lust, or just simple attraction: at this stage of a relationship, it is mincing words to discriminate between them. We hear a voice, smell something exciting, catch the line of a silhouette. Perhaps there is a reminder of someone who was once loved, or perhaps she seems to say, 'I'll shed some of my veils for you'. Suddenly, the man could shed his skin too, invite her past some of the barriers.

Who hasn't felt pure lust? It happens, and, if mutually felt and enjoyed, it can be wonderful. Attraction without lust happens too. After all, we make friends as well as lovers. But we suspect that feelings, as potential partners eye each other across a room, are essentially mixed; there is more to it than just lust or attraction: if love is lusting after your best friend, it is not unlikely that you feel a little of that too.

Whatever it is we experience at these first encounters, it is notoriously difficult to express it with precision. Romantics say: 'My heart skipped a beat'. The less romantic call it a gut reaction: actually quite a good definition. Arousal affects heart, gut and all the senses. It also tunes us in, and once tuned in to sexual arousal, it is difficult to get the idea out of one's head, or anywhere else you feel it. This is not unique to sexual arousal, as anyone who has ever dieted will understand. The smells of cooking can be pretty compelling.

How does it happen?

Jenny and Robert are lovers playing a sexual game. It is a turn-on. Like planning a holiday, planning a sexual route and driving slowly along it is highly erotic. Watching yourselves playing the foregame is like having all the right mirrors in place. Catching sight of each other means the long delightful build-up can begin.

But what if they were just meeting? What causes this sudden rush between strangers?

Chemistry

The chemistry between people is difficult to define, except to say there *is* a real chemistry, both in the attraction itself and in the way we respond to it.

We know what we like; or we think we know what we like. Surveys have built up a standard description of the 'dishy man' of every woman's fantasy.

Order me a man

For most women, the dish of the day has slim legs and hips, a broadish chest, a flat belly and a trim, rounded behind. If asked to rate the favourite bit of their man's anatomy, the bum wins hands down. It has, after all, the obvious utility as a love handle, at least in the man-on-top positions.

The preference for small, rounded buttocks (like Robert's) is stronger in both men and women who were breast fed, so the roots of bum worship probably lie deep in our subconscious memories: in the warm sensuous pleasures of early feeding; in the hand placed on the mother's breast as one sucked.

Women like men who look at them with eyes (like Robert's) that sparkle with confidence and pleasure; and especially if those eyes are fringed in long lashes. Hide the eyes behind glasses, and most women see a man as less attractive but more intelligent.

A dishy man has regular (but not small) features, he is usually tall, confident, intelligent and has a sense of humour and fun. All in all, he has more than a passing resemblance to the stereotyped hero of the romantic novel.

Alas, most of them are snapped up in the first hour of the party, and as midnight approaches and we haven't got our man, most of us find that it isn't only the girls who get 'Prettier at closin' time'.

Ask her to rate the fellers as the prospect of going home alone approaches, and the broad-hipped, narrow-chested, pot-bellied, baby-faced man comes into his own.

But then, they often do. Women are a good deal less choosy about their men's looks than the other way round. Intelligence, charm, charisma, penis size, or simply fame and fortune play just as much a part as looks. Line up the world's most beautiful women, and alongside them their men. Well, what do they see in them?

Vulnerability? The feeling that no one else could love them? What we might call the Cabbage Patch Doll Syndrome – 'Only I could love something that ugly'.

Order me a woman

If the man of her dreams is utterly predictable, so research suggests is the woman of his choice.

He prefers a face that is regular and lacks extremes; eyes that are not too close together and sparkle with confidence; mouths that are red and 'pouty'. (The lips swell and redden during sexual arousal, so perhaps he thinks he sees a willingness here.) Often he likes a baby face; a look of vulnerability.

Ask about breasts as a turn-on, and most men say yes, any size and shape, but especially those that firmly fill a C cup bra. Curving hips and long, shapely legs topped by a small, rounded bottom complete the currently preferred body type. Jenny scores well on all of these. (But fashions do change: the beauties of yesterday were far more voluptuous than today's.) Even today, when women strive for model girl skinniness, many men claim to like 'a little bit to hold on to'.

But there are many variations on this basic theme. Some men are indeed 'leg men' or 'breast men', tolerating much variation as long as she has the necessary in the essential department.

Preferred dress is red (then black or white), open at the neck, but not too revealing. High-heeled shoes are appreciated because they make her legs seem more shapely, her body more voluptuous.

If the desired man comes straight from a romantic novel, the desired woman is predictably shapely enough for onlookers to guess at the details, demure enough to ensure only the chosen one sees the goods.

Take-home girls

And are these the women men take home to bed? You bet they are – if they can get them. Line up the world's rich and famous men. Then line up their women. No Cabbage Patch Doll Syndrome here. More a touch of the Barbie Dolls.

Indeed, line up rich and famous women, and what do you see? That sexual attraction is a much more important factor in a woman's sucess than in a man's.

It seems unfair. So why are women more tolerant than men? The standard explanation is that women need to keep a man around to help with the kids. (Girls, you are lucky to get one, just be grateful for what you have got.) Asking for all that, and looks too, is greedy. If he is going to do that for us, we need to give something in return: sexiness, beauty.

It all stems from the idea that it is in man's nature to wander, and in hers to tolerantly hang on. Man is polygamous. Woman monogamous.

The trouble with this theory is that in most species that pair for life, the male and female look alike (patently untrue of humans) and are neither showy (like humans) nor particularly sexy. Unlike men and women, who are the sexiest animals on earth, they mate to procreate. Full stop.

It makes sense. No need to keep each other interested if you are going to be around anyway. That some people look at marriage in this way does not prove that relationships are meant to be like this, as the escalating divorce rates only go to show.

But suppose that women were, like men, by nature mildly pro-

The missionary position gives him a sense of control and a good position for thrusting. It is the most conventional and may be good for starters, provided you already know each other's form, before going on to more exotic manoeuvers. A woman can find comfort in his weight on her. If he is too big and heavy, it can feel claustrophobic.

Going up on his arms like this lets him *move deeper into her; it also gives* her *more control. Pop a pillow under her bottom and thighs, and her pelvis tilts up to offer her clitoris to his pubic bone (always a good idea).*

With him elevated slightly above her, she can move and position herself to stimulate all the good places and/or put a hand down to help herself along. Women who masturbate with open legs will probably enjoy wrapping themselves around him like this. As she moves into the home straight she can grab his love handles and push him into the rhythm of her choice.

miscuous. It is, after all, partly to attract men that women have evolved features such as the big breasts and sexy smells that make sex sexier. Now, to this ability to keep men interested, add unreliable orgasm (to make her go out and look for more) and multiple orgasm (to remind her that it is worth searching out); and we have a couple (or couples) ready for sex.

It still leaves the problem of bringing up children. So how, if he thinks she might go out for a quick one when his back is turned, does she get him to bring home the bacon?

Answer: by hiding her fertile time. He cannot say, 'But I didn't do it then, it cannot possibly be my child'. Oh, clever Eve.

Unlikely? Well, if women are naturally monogamous, why have men throughout history placed cultural controls on women's sexuality? Why do Jewish women shave their heads, Muslim women cover their bodies in all-concealing robes, and why were the women of Europe universally covered in dull black clothing?

It is unlikely that women decided to do this in the interests of monogamy. Could any woman seriously have thought that the best way to hold on to her man, given the nature of her man, was to make herself unattractive to him? It is more plausible to think that the cultural controls were (and are) his idea.

Sex is as nature intended. Men and women were meant to enjoy it, have fun, turn each other on and keep each other guessing.

If there is a lesson here, it is to follow your instincts. Take courage; open up and enjoy yourselves together. The constraints on mutual enjoyment were imposed to restrict you as people as well as to control your sexuality.

Sexy men and women

All of us who have felt a strong sense of attraction are aware that whatever the surveys say the average man or woman thinks they want, we can often be knocked for six by someone who takes us completely by surprise: that a woman with irregular features and an AA bra can be stunningly sexy. And that plenty of snake-hipped men and C-cupped women turn no one on.

What hits us as we look across the room is often something essentially personal; they have got what it takes. Often, what it takes is no more than an indication that: 'I am interested in you, I'd like you to be interested in me'.

Sexy looks

In **2**, Robert says, 'I saw the way she looked at me'. He isn't fooled. All over the world, women flirt with their eyes. The sequence is simple and universal. She looks at him provocatively and smiles, then lowers her eyes and turns away.

She may look again through her lashes, or sometimes look around the room slowly ('I'm checking out the competition, I'm waiting for something to happen') before looking back. Sometimes she gives him a sidelong glance not meeting his eye, shy and demure. Some women look much more confidently and directly: bedroom eyes that say it all. Some will watch long and carefully, then turn away as Jenny did in **1**. But they always look back, meeting his gaze directly, and holding it in a a way that most men describe as very sexy.

Then there is the frank 'looking him over' gaze which blatantly undresses him with her eyes. Get closer, and there is more to the gaze than eye contact.

If she is interested, he will see it in the dilation of her pupils. The black spot in the middle of her eyes will grow. Eyes that dart away as she talks and come back to meet his gaze say more than her voice.

Flirting is fun, even if you take it no further. It is an enormous confidence booster if you can feel it working. Even if you don't want it now, it is good to know you could get it.

Knowing he is there

Have you noticed how buying a new car positively litters the streets with your new model? Or that the world is full of pregnant women when your period is a few days late? Ethologists call the phenomenon search image. You look out for those things which are in the forefront of your mind. Jenny describes the experience in **3**, together with the related phenomenon of tuning-in. Tuning-in occurs when in a noisy party, you switch into an interesting conversation that is going on behind you. For all of us, there is a foreground and a background. Robert and Jenny see each other much as they might 'hear' more interesting conversations going on behind them; Robert picks her out as his foreground; the rest of the women (**2**) fade into the background.

Arousal plays a role here. Jenny and Robert have sex in mind, and elsewhere. The rising excitement is wonderful. In so many different ways, there is pleasure in becoming aroused, especially when having to keep it under control. Robert and Jenny's delicious game is one all couples can play.

What did you say?

In **6**, Robert talks dirty, but it does not have to be especially blatant. Egging on, saying you like it, suggesting in veiled terms what you might do appears, from a recent survey, to be a common preference among women who rate their sex lives as excellent. Most of the men said they found it a way of showing that inhibitions are being shed, that they are willing to be adventurous. Sharing fantasies is another variant. Gentle lovemaking while you each build up an elaborate fantasy tale of sex with a third party is a strangely exciting experience.

Of course, not all women would be turned on by Robert's opening remark in **6**, even from a lover, in fact the reverse. Even if a woman does like a 'bit of rough', or an occasional sexual outrage, she won't always go for it. If, however, she is feeling in the mood, it could lead to a delicious few minutes, even if you never make it to the bathroom.

What did you do?

Sometimes our sexual displays are unconscious. Some of them are plain suggestive. Popping celery in the mouth, or sucking on his fingers (**5**) gives an obvious message. Know what I'd rather suck?

What about the unconscious ones? When she toys with her key-ring, strokes and squeezes her wine glass, is she saying: 'Do this with my nipples, I'll do this with your penis?' Sometimes she is, because both activities increase as you court her.

Then there are the body touches: hands behind the head, stroking the thighs, touching around the breasts, or playing with the beads which hang in this position, or licking her fingers. They are all effective, even if she is not fully aware of their turn-on value.

Crossing and uncrossing his legs says: 'I'm open, available'. So does running a finger (or her tongue) around her lips. One of the most effective signs is probably the shoulder shrug, or turning and looking back over the shoulder: a real, 'What the hell, come on' gesture.

Smells

The sweet musky smell of a woman: familiar, individual, hard to define, and exceedingly potent. It comes from scent glands in the armpit, in the cleavage and the areolas of the breasts; from the face, hands and feet; from around the vagina and from the hood of the clitoris. There is a different tone to the smell depending on hair colour and skin type and on the stage of the menstrual cycle. But above all other smells come the potent, musky vaginal odours.

Some women literally reek of sex. The odour is caused by a group of volatile fatty acids found in the vagina. These secretions change throughout the menstrual cycle, and are most concentrated at ovulation. Although men have lost the keen sense of smell of other animals, they find a woman's smell most pleasant as she ovulates; and they find the smell more pleasant then women.

Just as some women sweat more than others, some produce more of these acids. Perhaps it is the secret of some women's extraordinary sex appeal. But even if you are not a great producer, you can learn to spread it around. Don't mask it by washing your genitalia with scented soap, and certainly avoid vaginal deodorants.

If you have ever worried about the smell as he delivers genital kisses, forget it. It really is part of the pleasure. Liking how you smell is part of liking how you are. Which does not mean that you should never wash.

Women, in turn, are attracted to the smell of androsterone, a steroid secreted from a gland in the male armpit and around the genitalia. In Greece and the Balkans, they rub handkerchiefs under their armpits and push the strong odour towards women as they dance.

Many women love to bury their noses in the male armpit and in the folds of the genitalia. It can feel safe and secure as well as sexy.

Other women enjoy the slight urine taste as they start to suck their man, perhaps because androstenediol, a chemical similar to testosterone, is found in male urine and sweat. This is the chemical that makes the sow stand immobilized for the boar, and makes men and women call the people in photographs sprayed with it especially attractive.

Personal perfume contains all these smells together with miscellaneous traces of your daily life. It will etch itself deeply into your lover's memory, and can have a highly emotive power. Sometimes body scent can make it painful to get too close to a former lover. Sometimes it can trigger arousal at the most inappropriate times.

For him, the rear entry position reads: fuck her brains out: max control, deep penetration, fine view. *He can handle and position her easily or put his arms down and just admire his cock opening her up. If you want to feel besotted with each other, if she needs his loving looks or his mouth on her breast, this is not the one. But in certain moods, nothing else will do.*

For her, it reads: take it like a woman. *If she wants him to love her, but fears he is merely fucking her, give this a miss: it will reinforce all her doubts. If she is secure on the loving front, it is a grand opportunity for some fierce fucking. She can move around, changing the angle at which she presents herself or remain passive. Her hand, slipped between her legs, will gain her clitoris without opposition. If she wants to take control, nothing could be easier. He holds still, offering his hard cock for her to come up on, maybe circling it tightly at the base with thumb and forefinger to swell it still further. She works herself around, up and down, into a frenzy. Some women don't like doggie because it is too animal, others like it for that very reason.*

Penis size

Which brings us to penis size. It is a fallacy that it does not matter at all. The fascination with penis size is universal, from small boys comparing theirs with friends, to adult males looking at others' penises; with envy or despair. It matters just as much as breast size. Penis envy is not only a female characteristic. Call it irrational; maintain that women only have nerve endings in the first three to four inches of the vagina; but don't pretend that anything over three-and-a-half inches is just a waste of time.

Women like the look of a big one, even if once inside it is all the same to them. But even on that we are not entirely convinced. Women have been told for years that it simply does not matter what size their breasts are; but they still know that men prefer big ones. We are sorry to say that so do women. A little bulk is a very nice thing, all things being equal. But of course, they never are. If asked to list the most important aspects of a man's lovemaking, we doubt whether many women would place penis size anywhere near the top of their list.

Disembodied bits

Leaving aside the question of how size affects a woman's enjoyment, one of the most striking features of the obsession with penis size is the

A softer version of the doggie, with a pillow or two under her belly, suited to more gentle loving. The clitoris is not so accessible, but she could cross her legs to compensate. It is easier to turn to look at him. He can reach under to fondle her breast. Useful in the middle months of pregnancy, and for conception. If she relaxes on to the pillows, he gets to feel the softness of her bottom and thighs as he thrusts and can watch her flesh ripple with each impact. He can thrust harder because she offers no resistance.

way the penis is treated as if it were independent of its owner. Lovers often talk as if it were 'me, you and him'.

One of the things distinguishing men from women is their greater interest in the disembodied organ, unrelated to the owner of that organ. Erotic fantasies such as interacting through a screen with isolated genitalia are a particularly male enterprise.

Men of different cultures find one or more aspect of female anatomy particularly arousing. Among bushmen it is large buttocks. In the West it is breasts.

There are currently many magazines whose titles indicate their specific obsession with breasts. As with penises, the larger they are, the better. Breast size is the concern of men and the despair of women, the majority of whom think that their breasts are too small, and the remainder that they are too large. The strength of this concern is indicated by the fact that the single most common form of plastic surgery in the United States is breast augmentation. In 1984, for example, 95,000 such operations were performed.

It is interesting that among male homosexuals the organ of erotic interest changes, but the preoccupation with size remains. In male homosexual fantasy, pornography and life, the larger the penis, the greater its erotic quality. Men are indeed fascinated by big organs.

Big can be beautiful

There is a striking parallel between this obsession with size and something which scientists who study animal behaviour call the super-normal phenomenon.

Most animals respond instinctively to certain things within their environment. A goose, for example, will retrieve any egg she sees just outside her nest. The bigger the egg, the stronger her preference. In some instances it has been found that artificial stimuli very much larger than their natural counterparts are preferred. In one classic example, a goose tried to hatch an artificial egg even when it was too large for to sit on.

Perhaps men's fascination with large organs is a hold-over of the same phenomenon. The difference between man and other animals is the greater flexibility in what becomes the arousing object. Super-normal bottoms, breasts or penises all figure in male sexual fantasies.

But what of his own penis? Here we need to look at the role the penis plays in primate societies. Monkeys often use the erect penis in display, as you may have noticed on visits to the zoo. Its message is something like: 'Look at me, I'm the big dominant animal'. Perhaps we have some of this too.

But does it really matter?

It should be clear from all this that whatever importance men and women place on the size of the male member, it has little to do with the physical enjoyment of sex.

All things being equal, some women do get more pleasure from a large penis. But we suspect the enjoyment is in the eye rather than the in vagina. Sexual pleasure and orgasmic frequency rise as she gets older. So does vaginal slackness. Childbirth stretches. If a tight fit was important to women, the sex of their youth should be the high spot. It is not. Nine out of ten women report themselves content with the size of their man. And amongst women who enjoy sex, virtually no one has any complaints. By the law of averages, contented women must include the partners of some men with small penises.

Most of the vagina is quite insensitive to penetration, even by a large penis. Nor is it essential to stimulate the three or four inches which are actually responsive. Robert is fortunate enough to have a penis long enough to tease Jenny with, by inserting it only an inch or so; the same effect can be achieved with any size of organ.

'Holiday' romance

Planning and thinking about lovemaking is like planning a holiday. No one would want to do it every time they take a trip, nor stick rigidly to the plan. But Robert and Jenny demonstrate that sometimes it is worth taking this much trouble before you get each other into bed. Fantasy is not a substitute for bread-and-butter loving (see **William & Francesca**, pages 74-93); it is not superior, or inferior; just different. There is nothing wrong with bread and butter; only it gets a bit dull if you have it at every meal.

DISCOVERING LISE

Lise

June 5th, 1984

It was black. Long and slinky with a scooped neck. I borrowed Jessy's crimper, and made my hair very curly. "What a cracker," Dad said. But he's been saying that since I was a baby.

There was an old man on the bus carrying a bunch of roses. He picked out a red one and said:

"A red rose for a beautiful lady."

I had never thought of myself as attractive until then.

January 7th, 1985

If I squeeze the folds together I can feel a little hard tube. Then I rub it. I was trying to work out how to do this, and squeeze my breasts and put my fingers inside, when I caught sight of the red clip on some ear-rings. I messed about with these so they don't hurt when I attach them to the nipples. Then I can use two hands.

January 10th, 1985

You can't see them through the big sweater. I clipped one ear-ring on to each nipple, then I walked all the way down to the shop, smiling at everyone on the way.

May 10th, 1985

We saw the bluebells as we came over
the hill: like a blue haze, falling through
the trees. I just stood there. The birds
were singing, and the sun was dappling
the leaves.

I just did it: I took off all my clothes
and ran and ran down the hill. I don't
think Stuart knew what to do. But after
a while, he took his clothes off too and
ran down after me. We ran through the
bluebells, shouting and laughing. When
I got back to my clothes, I just sat
there.

We didn't say anything until we got
out of the woods. We just smiled.

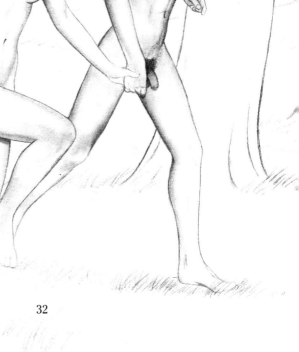

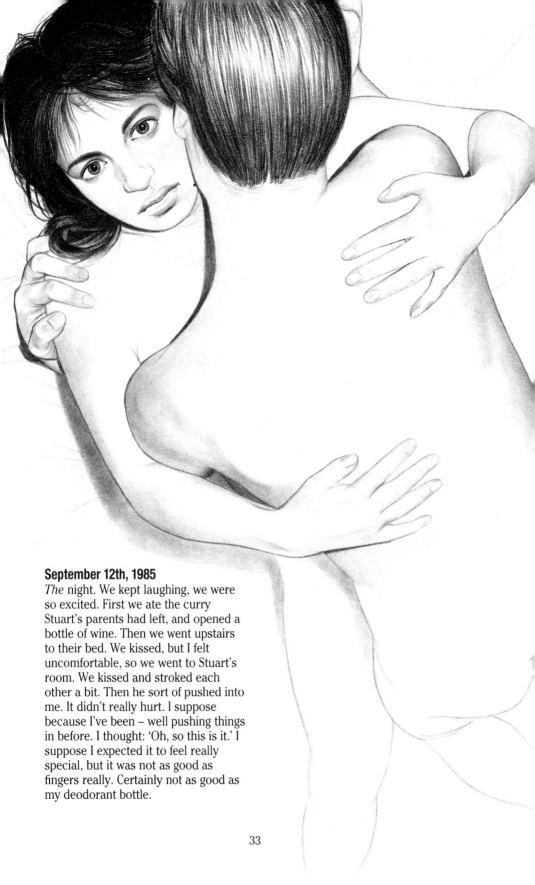

September 12th, 1985

The night. We kept laughing, we were so excited. First we ate the curry Stuart's parents had left, and opened a bottle of wine. Then we went upstairs to their bed. We kissed, but I felt uncomfortable, so we went to Stuart's room. We kissed and stroked each other a bit. Then he sort of pushed into me. It didn't really hurt. I suppose because I've been – well pushing things in before. I thought: 'Oh, so this is it.' I suppose I expected it to feel really special, but it was not as good as fingers really. Certainly not as good as my deodorant bottle.

33

March 6th, 1986
I'm in love. Birds sing, daffodils dance.

August 13th, 1986
Selling my soul, and loving it, I'm afraid. I have a job as a waitress. Flirting. I flirt with my customers, outrageously with the old men, sweetly with the women and families, and aloofly with the young men. I make a fortune in tips.

February 21st, 1987

We were sitting facing each other, both cross-legged, just smiling and smiling. Then he leaned over very slowly and kissed me. Just balancing, not holding. He put out a hand and stroked my hair, arms, breasts. We lay side by side, facing each other.

I touched him gently all over: just light feather touches. Then I sat up, caressed him with my hair, just wanting to please. I sat astride him and slowly lowered myself on to him. I'd done it before. It always felt good. He fondled my ears, my breasts, stroking the inside of my elbow. The excitement mounted. Like it does. I could feel it in the muscles. Then it happened. That something: a feeling of bursting and a tingling that went all down my legs.

I thought I had had orgasms before. I had had excitement. It had felt good. Afterwards, I had felt satisfied. But it wasn't this.

August 17th, 1988

I love John, John loves Michelle, Michelle only has eyes for Dave and nobody loves me. Boo hoo! Anyway, I've discovered my electric toothbrush is more reliable than any man. I hold the back of the brush to my clitoris and it's 'Three steps to heaven' – even before I've finished running the bath.

ise's diary traces her teenage years: her passage from puberty to womanhood; from feeling and acting like a child to being an adult.

Like all children, Lise was not born knowing how to share her own world. She loves, she feels, but she does not necessarily understand her emotions and feelings. She has to learn how to relieve tension and frustration in ways that are acceptable to others. She has no internal accountant to balance her love and her possessiveness, or to tell her how much to give, and take from others. She learns about love by loving, and how to express love by experience. There is no single, dramatic step which takes her across the line from child to woman, or from asexual to sexual.

She is fortunate to have this impulse to express her sexuality: not all of us do. Sex therapists often ask: 'Do you realize why sex feels so good to you, or why it is so difficult?' Does reading through Lise's diary prompt you to pin-point your own strengths and weaknesses in expressing sexuality?

Lise, in common with most children, was shielded from the realities of sex. She has been told the 'facts of life', but not the 'joy of sex'. At seven, she was told sex was for making babies. Since she never saw her parents doing it, she naturally assumed that it did not happen often. Even as a teenager, she considers 'real sex' to be about making babies, and it takes time for her to learn that baby-making has less to do with the expression of sexuality than the hugs, the kisses, the tears and the ready laughter of her childhood.

For sexuality is about expressing and sharing ourselves physically – something people do naturally as babies. Later upbringing often suppresses that natural expression, making it hard for children to think of the various aspects of sex as a whole.

Eventually, Lise manages. The diary extracts put together a few, but not all, of the strands which bring it together.

Lise's world

It has been said that men walk around with their hormones on their sleeves: girl watching. Forget all the songs which say he only has eyes for you: they are wrong. For men, sexual appraisal is like breathing. Love may tone it down for a week or two, but it soon pops up again. At its crudest, it is the catcalling of building workers, but even the liberated man responds, if only internally, to an attractive woman. It is just – so women are told – the way men are.

This catcalling world, which peeps up her skirt and mentally undresses her 20 times a day, is the world in which Lise blossoms into womanhood. The calls, and the eyes fixed firmly on her breasts, are both an irritation and an appreciation of her womanhood. The old man's gallantry on the bus gives Lise legitimate pride and makes her aware of herself as a woman. A coarser appreciation might easily have awakened shame.

Like it or not, the way most women feel about themselves is tied up with the way they feel about their bodies. Look good, feel good. Lise is typical in this respect and much adolescent behaviour is governed by this impulse. Everyone wants approval, and for a girl, as often as not, approval is a comment about her looks. How unfair. A plain girl's lot is not easy. Sure, he will love her for her goodness and intelligence, but how will he discover it when his eyes are tuned to the play of the light on her hair and the intriguing curve of her blouse? Beauty oppresses – if you don't have it, and also if you do.

Magazine blues

At nine, Lise wanted to look like everyone else. Come puberty, she would willingly shed that anonymity for the sort of looks that turn men on. The 1990s conformity is 'attractive', 'sexy', 'eye-catching': so she is told in every magazine she opens. The images on which she models herself are impossibly perfect: all imperfections eliminated by make-up, lighting and camera angle. The real girl is not like that. The nose that was O.K. through childhood becomes at 13 – well does 'yuck' sum it up? It is not just that the nose has changed, which it has, but that her perception of its importance has changed. She sees how it could be, and it could always be better. Glossy magazines make this reality harder than it need be for hundreds of thousands of girls such as Lise.

Is it this need to look good that makes Lise sexy? Or is it the dawning of her sexuality?

Hormonal blues

The inevitable discontent with her body is fuelled by many sources. There is her increased brain power: now, at 15, Lise is able to picture the noses of her classmates, and measure her deficiencies against them all. Her nose matters, and will probably go on mattering, until Lise learns that she can be loved for herself alone.

Up and down like yoyos go the moods of Lise and her teenage girl-friends, driven by the fluctuating hormones which are reshaping their bodies, their faces, their priorities and their lives. We catch in her diary entry for 1984 a glimpse of Lise in sunny mood. Her parents will tell you that her moods were changeable at best.

Oestrogen in girls, testosterone in boys, are the sex hormones which at puberty have such a dramatic effect on growth rate and body shape. 'The wee lift' they say in Scotland; 'Get his growth' they say in the American south. It is not always so wee. At the peak of the growth spurt, Lise could gain 3+ inches in a year, a boy even more. Most of that growth is in the limbs. They spurt ahead, the trunk catching up more slowly.

Her body reshapes too. Her hips widen, her waist stays narrow and her breasts develop. At the start of puberty her body is 20 per cent fat; at the end, 30 per cent. She feels soft, she looks shapely, and as she enters the room, her sexy, female smell precedes her (see **Robert & Jenny**, pages 25-26).

Meanwhile, his hormones keep his hips narrow, broaden his shoulders and chest, and increase his muscle mass to 40 per cent of body weight. His fat level drops, making him hard and firm. As he begins to sweat, he emits the sexual odour of a man. He looks and smells like a man.

It is the way our children look and smell and feel that, as much as anything, makes us begin to treat them like adults. When Lise's father does this, it helps her to begin to see herself in this way.

'Look at me'

"Not a blonde, but mighty fair." He was leaning on his shovel, un-deniably Irish, calling after a friend as she slipped her school hat into her satchel and hoisted her skirt to reveal an inch or two more thigh. At 14, she needed confirmation that she had the power. Coming out of that self-conscious stage, when rounded shoulders disguised de-veloping breasts, we walked best breasts forward, flaunting them for all to see. We had become sexual. And, like Lise, we knew. Today, you can see girls' breasts bouncing freely beneath a thin T-shirt. The 1950s generation had to make do with a Playtex and a few paper tissues.

Girls learn how to put up the signs 'Please look'. Boys have the leisure to appreciate this fact, but often don't click until much older that because she puts out signs *some* of the time does not mean she *always* wants male attention. When trying to have intelligent conver-sation, it is insulting to find his eyes wandering down to your chest.

F.S.H. and L.H.

The hormones that have changed her body at puberty continue to do their work in adulthood. The master hormone gland in the brain, the pituitary, releases F.S.H. and L.H., which control fertility in men and women. Each month, these hormones will prepare her for pregnancy by making her ripe to conceive about 14 days before her period.

Does Lise feel especially sexy at mid-cycle? The answer seems to be no. Like other girls, Lise masturbated before her hormones began to circulate, and, in common with most women, shows little evidence of an increased need to masturbate at mid-cycle. If there is a peak in solo sex, in women it occurs just prior to menstruation. Only when she is older, will Lise show an increased need for intercourse mid-cycle.

Couples have long been advised to tie their sexual activity in to the woman's menstrual cycle: an intense bout of activity at mid-cycle, and another prior to menstruation, is considered ideal. We would rather suggest that both men and women should feel free to initiate and veto sex. There are many ways of giving pleasure when we feel no need to take any for ourselves. The mutual willingness to do this is surely the hallmark of a good relationship.

Some reports say that women feel sexually more aggressive prior to menstruation; others, that she prefers non-penetrative sex at this time. Neither F.S.H. nor L.H. seems much related to orgasm. In fact, if there is a hormonal trigger to orgasm in men and women, it is testosterone. See **William & Francesca**, pages 87-88.

Masturbation

Some girls, of whom Lise is one, masturbate as teenagers; some begin as mature women, others claim never to do so at all. For boys, sexual excitement centres on the penis from the start (see **Marcus & Alex**, pages 44-49). For Lise, by contrast, sexual excitement is a whole-body response. She is drawn in by breasts, ears and lips, perhaps because girls expect boys to initiate sex, and this is the exploratory route boys travel in our culture. It is only after touching the breasts, that a boy's hand is allowed to travel down to her gentialia. So it is natural for a girl to include her breasts in solo sex.

In some cultures, the breasts have no erotic significance at all for men, or women. Which tells us that the ways of enjoyment are not naturally built in to us. The erotic power of different areas of the body are things we learn to love and need. And unless a girl masturbates, what she learns to love and need are those things boys do to her in her early sexual encounters.

Turning on

Most people are potentially sexual most of the time. Being young, Lise knows this; as they grow older, they sometimes forget. Freud said that it was the suppression of sexuality which makes humanity civilized. This may not be the whole truth, but it is partly true. The trouble is that sometimes people get over-civilized, passing each day in sexual numbness, afraid of turning on to their bodies. They fail to recognize the surge of sexual feeling aroused by the beauty of a wood full of bluebells; Lise, by contrast, is only too well aware of it.

As Lise will eventually learn, good sex is often a mutual way of re-

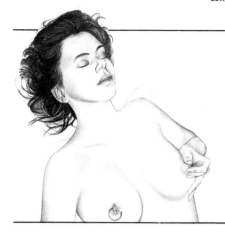

Just because it is a one-woman show is no excuse for not decorating the stage. Take your time, teasing your nipples and revelling in the slow build-up of your excitement. Or maybe tonight you can make an attempt on the land speed record: see if you can do it in one minute flat. Take what feels best. It is nobody's business but your own. See also Gwen & Jack.

sponding to beauty, sadness or indeed, any human emotion. A combination of sexuality and sex.

For many, the ability to express sexuality in physical acts is the key to heightened pleasure. But it takes time to re-open oneself if the childish tendency to act in this way has been stifled.

The body calls

Lise, like most women, learns only slowly to listen to her body calling. She lacks the obvious male sexual barometer: a penis which stands up to tell a boy or a man that he feels sexy.

As Lise walks to the shops in her big sweater, her sexual feelings may be secret from the world, but she has clipped her own barometer firmly to her breasts. 'Look,' she says, 'I'm feeling sexy.' Nobody hears, but that does not matter: it is a private lesson, well learned by Lise alone. As Freud pointed out, if things disturb us, we tend to hide them from our conscious selves. By walking out as Lise does, she is saying: 'I am not afraid of this feeling. So forget those innuendoes which teach women to fear sex, or that it is dirty and bad.'

The generation gap

Lise's mother was raised for love and marriage: love was kisses, cuddles and body worship. Sex was a duty, even if in time she found it was more than this. The sexual revolution of the last 20 years has changed her daughter's expectations. Many girls of Lise's age expect sexual pleasure, even without love. But the old standards take time to change, and the idea of love remains for many girls. Fuelled by a literature which places it firmly in the forefront of relationships, a teenage girl's idea of sex is usually more romantic than a boy's. More likely to be tied up with a candle-lit dinner than a frantic bonk over dust-bins in a back alley (a common homosexual fantasy).

First time

Although many women, like Lise, lose their virginity with a friend, a sizeable minority get it over with a stranger. Most expect something special: less than ten per cent reach orgasm.

We expect 'real thing' sex to be special. After all, it has all the big guns on its side; parents, church, state – even the odd psychologist says this is what it is all about.

But wait. Exactly what are we doing? After months, even years, of teenage kissing, stroking and petting, should we suddenly be engaging in 'Mum and Dad' sex? Did we ever think of them enjoying it?

As we indulge in the 'real thing', we are forced to contemplate the talisman of serious 'abiding' love. Is that what we feel as we race into the sex act and straight on to the big 'I' and 'O' (intercourse and orgasm)? Like most direct routes, it is quick, and that is about all. Of course, he has a sense of achievement; she is left uneasy that this was indeed the 'right thing'; and disappointed.

Advice for beginners

Lise, like most women, first experiences 'Mum and Dad' sex in the traditional matrimonial position. It would be hard to find a worse way for her to begin. She needs a position which provides stimulation where she needs it: see **William & Francesca**, pages 84-86.

Remember, you have hands. Use them. Don't choose a position which blocks their access to the genital area unless you are sure you can manage without their help.

You have mouths. Begin, end, or break off and use them. Find a position where you can suck each other's ears and mouths and nipples, and where you can kiss if mouth work has played an important role in your pre-intercourse sexuality.

You have time. Don't rush in. Men are often so near orgasm, and control takes time to learn. He should try to wait before entering until she is so close to the edge that she is almost jumping.

You can move. Choose a position which gives you both freedom.

You don't have a script. Sex is not about coming together, it is about taking turns. If she likes it on top, that is her turn. If he likes it on top, that is his. If he wants to thrust into her and she wants to come in his mouth, well that is fine too. And if they both want to come together, that is all very good, but the choirs who manage these harmonies have usually had years of practice. No one should expect to fill the Albert Hall the week after they form the Glee Club.

Everyday sexuality

Lise will discover that she does not always need orgasm. Just to feel

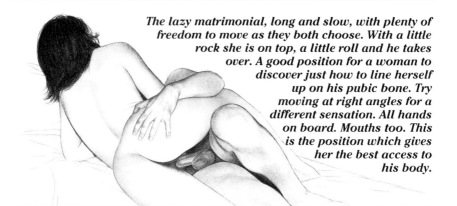

The lazy matrimonial, long and slow, with plenty of freedom to move as they both choose. With a little rock she is on top, a little roll and he takes over. A good position for a woman to discover just how to line herself up on his pubic bone. Try moving at right angles for a different sensation. All hands on board. Mouths too. This is the position which gives her the best access to his body.

him inside is pleasure enough. There need be no race to see how fast (or how often) we can make it. Sometimes, sex is just comfort, or a low-key celebration that a day is ending, a dawn breaking. It need not be overwhelming. Sex would be dull indeed if every time was predictably earth shattering; a bit of a pain if it always had to be deeply moving. Even passion can sit on the back burner. It does not have to be great love; just good to feel mutual care.

Frustration

That most women, in their early years of sex, fail to reach orgasm regularly does not mean they don't enjoy it. Nor that they necessarily feel frustrated. If she knows he will bring her to orgasm before the night is out, she can enjoy his coming, and later her own.

Stuart comes too soon for Lise, but it was not what he intended. Like Lise, he is inexperienced. But some men never learn; some don't even want to learn. They want, as Germaine Greer puts it, to masturbate into vaginas. If he is masturbating in yours, refer him to **Gwen & Jack**, pages 94-109.

Some women, it must be said, want nothing more than to offer their vaginas for masturbation. If this is what she does for you, see **Eric & Judy**, pages 60-73. Vaginal masturbation, even for him, is but a shadow of the 'real thing'.

First orgasm

Lise is typical in needing about two years of practice to achieve orgasm during intercourse. Only about a quarter of all women make it before they reach 20. The next five years doubles that figure, but even at 30, over 25 per cent have yet to come. Happily, most of them have made it before their 40th birthday; 6 per cent never learn. Within the latter group, a high percentage have been abused either as children or as adults.

Easy come

Eventually, a substantial minority of women learn to come very easily and quickly. But even those with such enormous 'O' potential rarely even reach the foothills first time. If you have not made it yet, do not despair.

Love

Love glows. Remember that just washed look of a world when love (and sex) were new? It is not the time or the place, but the mood which changes perception. Remember this. It is one of the keys to pleasure.

Tables turned

In childhood, Lise separated herself from boys who were rough and a nuisance. In a world where men catcall and chat her up, it often comes as a surprise to learn she has power over these former pests. In a world which warns her to beware of sexual harassment, it surprises her to find that she can sometimes make them eat their hearts out. Like all power, it gives a heady feeling of pleasure.

Vibrators

When fingers stimulate the genitalia, they rub and stroke and press and massage. This is what vibrators do, unfailingly, faster, more rhythmically and more steadily than any hand or penis could possibly achieve. So it feels good. Does it feel better? Well, sometimes it feels like a gourmet meal, which, at the right time or in the right company, is wonderful. And sometimes it feels like one of those fancy cakes with false cream and cherries that cannot fail to disappoint. And even when it is good, who wants seven courses at breakfast? What beats bread and coffee in the right company?

The moral

The point of Lise's tale is that a woman learns to enjoy sex and that learning extends beyond mere technique. Indeed, it is probably influenced far more by feelings and attitudes towards sex, than by her manual dexterity or the fit of his penis. It helps if she is raised in a home in which feelings of warmth can be expressed physically, and if she has a loving and considerate partner. Like Lise, a woman needs to feel good about her body as it is, not as she wishes it to be. But even if all factors at play are benevolent, it may still take time. It is no coincidence that Lise's story is incomplete, and ends on an uncertain note.

LEX'S DVICE

— Marcus & Alex —

Marcus, aged 13, is sitting on a bench in the rowing club locker room. Alex, a handsome, well-developed 15-year-old, comes in from the shower and ostentatiously drops his towel. He is, in his considered opinion, well hung. Marcus looks long enough to discover that Alex is circumcized, then averts his gaze.

"How's the cox?" asks Alex with a sly smile, glancing towards Marcus' crotch. Marcus' heart sinks. During practice he steered too close to the bridge, and, worse, he has no idea how big he is supposed to be. At one time, he inserted one of his sister's hair clips into his urethra to see how it felt. It was not particularly pleasurable, and now he worries that he has stunted his growth.

Alex persists: "Rather a cock-up, today. Do much of that, do you?" For his part, Alex experiences erections so hard that they are painful. It happens whenever he thinks of anything remotely connected to sex. Does he ever think of anything else? Certainly not in school.

"Ever seen your sister naked?" Alex suddenly asks with deliberate rudeness. Marcus, who is too shy to buy girlie magazines and clipped nudes out of magazine adverts until he found a sex book of his mother's showing girls' secret parts, hastily mutters, "Er, no."

He recalls handling and being excited by a bra that his sister had left in the bathroom. Extremely conscious of her growing breasts, Marcus teased her; she screamed and hit him.

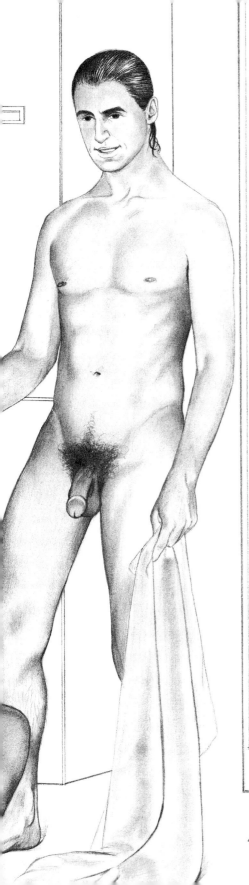

"You should," says Alex, thinking of the frantic years between 11 and 13 that he spent lurking about under the stairs trying to look up girls' dresses.

Now Alex teases: "Gone off with Madame Five Fingers yet? Had a bit of wank?" Oh dear, worse and worse. After a year of wet dreams, when he was worried about stains on the sheets, Marcus has just completed his first manual masturbation. Things got totally out of hand, so to speak, with his heart racing madly, an inexplicable feeling of heat in his groin, and evidence all over the shower curtain. Marcus was not sure he liked it, but he half wanted to do it again. How could this lout tell?

Marcus concentrates on the one shoe still untied. "This one time . . ." began Alex. He was going to tell how in the woods around Burlycliff he unzipped and dared James to stick his out. The stroked each other to creaming, then laughed at the idea of being discovered by the old couple tramping through the woods nearby. But Alex decides against recommending the buddy system; he isn't queer, after all.

Later, a group of his friends stood around in a basement to see, with great shouting and excitement, who could come first and who could spurt furthest.

Alex would rather die, however, than admit to his attempts at auto-fellatio. Bent double with effort, he could just get his glans into his mouth, but no more.

Reversing his usual order of dressing, Alex puts on his shirt, then his socks, and finally, having extracted the maximum dangling time, his trousers. "Have you been laid yet?" he asks Marcus, who says nothing.

Alex looks at him speculatively. "You know how to grab a feel, right? Pull the bra up, the goodies will pop out. Get a nice handful." "Sure," replies Marcus. The closest Marcus had been was

trying to work out exactly where Betty's nipples were when she wore the blue jumper.

As objectionable as the older boy was, he seemed to know things, so Marcus throws caution to the winds. "I never know how to talk to a girl. What do you say?"

Satisfied with his control over the situation, Alex relaxes a little. "You see, kid, girls are confused, they don't know what they want. You have to show them."

Alex figured Gloria was hot after her friend called her a boy chaser. She was cute, but a little too near-sighted, a little too plump, and a little too interested in Alex. But he recognized his chance to get laid. A few beers with her, then into his car; having her breasts touched made her dizzy, she said. Emboldened despite his anxiety, he tugged at her skirt. She struggled and said no. Grabbing her wrists with one hand, he pulled down her knickers with the other. He pushed into her hard and fast: the whole car rocked with his thrusts; it was over in less than two minutes.

"They like it right enough when you give it to them hard." She came back for more, didn't she? "You've got to warn 'em though, if they get knocked up, it's their own lookout. And I told her she'd better wash her thing."

He told the boys about it. Gloria still wanted to hang about with Alex and his band. One night at Mack's house, Alex explained to her that the band shared everything. She refused intercourse with them, but they took turns going into the bedroom where she had each of them off with her hand.

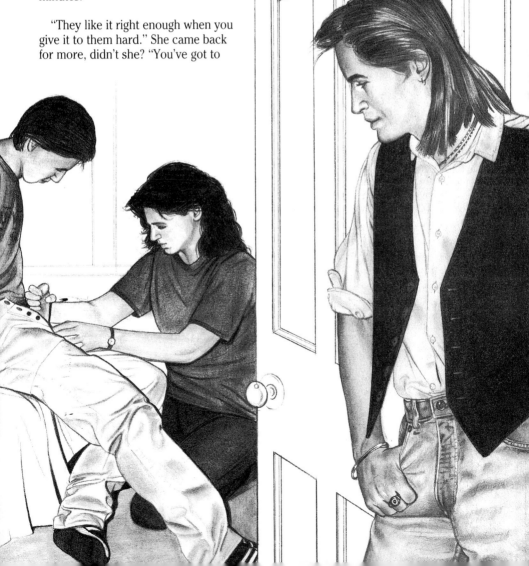

A four-year-old boy we know can always be found running around in a Batman costume, except when he is dressed as a Ghostbuster. When he is a Ghostbuster, any ghosts hanging around the house stand no chance of escaping his 'zapper', unless they happen to be loitering in the darkened passage upstairs. On no account will the Ghostbuster approach this passage. It is hard to grow up to be a 'real man' when you are small and frightened of the dark.

Boys, among whom Alex and Marcus are typical, but different, must struggle to develop the feeling that they are 'real men'; to have a secure sense of their gender identity. Owning a penis is a help, but not always enough. Four times as many boys as girls sense that nature has played a cruel joke on them; that they have been trapped in a body belonging to the opposite sex.

They voyage to manhood is hazardous, full of blatant competition and challenge which girls don't have to face. If some of Marcus' and Alex's teenage antics make you wince, that is as it should be. Alex's immature boasting, the vulgar competition in the basement, the patronising attitude of the older boy, are all give-away signs of the gnawing insecurity which underlies male sexual development. Perhaps it is no coincidence that boys and men are afflicted exclusively by mischances of sexual development such as fetishism.

Mummy dearest

As part of the process of gender identity development, the little boy must sooner or later differentiate himself form his mother because he is a male and she is a female. He may not be a sissy girl. He must climb trees, have a pocket-knife, get dirty with the other boys. But for all his 'super hero-ness', he is well aware that the woman raising him exercises complete power over him. She weans him, toilet trains him (always a greater problem with boys than with girls), sends him to bed when he does not want to go. In struggling to break free of this power and develop his own autonomy, he, like Alex, may acquire negative feelings towards women that surface during and after puberty.

At least part of the training he receives from his mother is aimed at restraining his sexual expression. The small boy's hands will be pushed away from her breast; he may be told not to masturbate; if she catches him playing doctor with the little girl next door he is in serious trouble. Early on, he can form the impression that women don't like sex.

Pride and prejudice

Every wizard needs a magic wand. Many little boys go through a phase when they talk enthusiastically about their willy, run around shouting about it or showing it off, playing games focused on it. Symbolically, the penis (when erect, the 'phallus') defines the boy as a male. This gender distinction must matter deeply to men because all cultures are as one in laying such stress on it; the struggle to break free from female domination in childhood is at least part of the drive which makes men, well, behave as men do. Later in life, Marcus will be called a 'dick' by other boys, challenged to 'whip it out', sarcastically asked if he pees sitting down, and mocked about 'getting it up'. Direct competitiveness and aggression are the stuff of male life. The not inconsiderable aggression of girls usually takes more indirect and manipulative forms (My mother has nicer rugs than yours').

The penis looms large in the adult male mentality, too. The early Greeks, for example, had 'penis on the brain': they were a phallocentric culture. Their writings contained innumerable obscene jokes and references to the penis. Freud explained this emphasis as a reaction to castration anxiety: the little boy fears castration by his powerful father with whom he is competing for the sexual attentions of his mother (and he threw in penis envy to bedevil women).

There certainly are things that seem to invite such explanations. *Koro*, for example, is a name for the delusional belief among the southern Chinese that the penis is shrinking back into the abdomen. The sufferers are panicky about impending death, imagining they are turning into ghosts since it is well known that ghosts have no genitalia. *Koro* is blamed upon excessive sexual activity, particularly masturbation, and the concomitant loss of semen. Fortunately, there is a culturally prescribed remedy: place a clamp on the penis. This has never failed to work. Epidemics of *Koro*-like symptoms have occurred in other parts of south-east Asia and the Malay peninsula; a few cases have turned up in Britain and North America. *Koro*, by the way, is a Chinese word meaning head of the turtle.

But, important as the penis is in the minds of boys and men, fear of castration is far from an inevitable part of male sexual development: think of all the boys raised in households without a father figure. The ever-present nature of phallic symbolism, may, too, have been oversold. It is now difficult to imagine guns as anything other than phallic; but some have suggested that dinosaurs, lorries or construction kits are phallic, too. Little boys love them all, but they don't have to be symbols.

Mine is bigger than yours

Marcus secretly compares his penis with Alex's, but boys will sometimes compare lengths in open competition. In urinals and locker rooms, men find it hard not to look. Where there is anxiety, there is

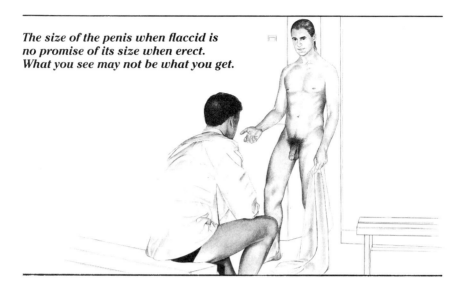

The size of the penis when flaccid is no promise of its size when erect. What you see may not be what you get.

usually an attempt to resolve it. *The Perfumed Garden*, a famous six-teenth-century Arab guide to the sexually perplexed, had a whole chapter devoted to 'prescriptions for increasing the dimensions of small members and for making them splendid'. The ones which re-quire rubbing in warm water followed by honey and ginger would surely work, at least temporarily. The hot pitch treatment should be ignored. In contrast to these stratagems, modern penile implants for organic failure do work. (See **Martin & Giselle**, pages 222-239.)

Circumcision, the ritual

Circumcision rituals in some cultures seem to confirm the strength of men's unconscious childhood memories of female domination. This painful procedure, a rite of passage from boyhood to manhood, was also a propitiation to the magical powers of women, a feeling with which Marcus might have had more than a little sympathy. Among the western Arunta of Australia, the foreskin, dried and smeared with red ochre, is presented to the boy's sister, who wears it around her neck. In other tribes, the boy's mother drinks some of the blood which has been collected in a shield. Mummy dearest, indeed. The starkest example can be found in the Murngin sub-incision ceremony. Four men hold the boy down while a long slit is cut in the underside of his penis to make it resemble a vulva.

Only 20 per cent of British men are circumcized. In America the figure is 80 per cent. When queried, circumcized men announce that theirs is more beautiful, but then uncircumcized fellows feel that theirs is the beauty. Circumcision horrified the ancient Greeks who considered it a barbarian practice. In turn, those who advocate it shudder at the mere thought of smegma, the secretion that collects under the intact foreskin.

In modern practice, the cutting is done soon after birth. This follows the ancient Jewish ceremony of the *bris* which, like many religious practices, was originally designed to set the Hebrews apart from surrounding groups. When confronted by their foreskinned neighbours, boys bearing the mark of the tribe (as it is called in the ceremony) were forced to recognize their tribal identities. Anthropologists have also suggested that circumcision affects the adults of primitive groups, too. Infant and child mortality made children, particularly male children, highly valued. Thus, submitting a son to the stone knife, with the very real risk of an accident causing emasculation or infection and death, may have functioned to test and intensify the loyalty of the father to his group.

Circumcision, the medical dilemma

In the nineteenth century, patients in mental asylums were circumcized to reduce their penile sensitivity and to forestall 'masturbatory insanity'. This notion of the learned doctors got it the wrong way round, of course, since public masturbation was the result, not the cause, of their insanity. In any event, even though the foreskin is continuous with the most sensitive area of the penis, there is no evidence of an appreciable loss of sensation after its removal.

Although earlier evidence linking the foreskin with cancer is now under serious question, the latest data suggest that circumcision does reduce the frequency of genital ulceration. If circumcision becomes necessary when the boy is older, recovery is slow and painful. Very recent evidence suggests that circumcision also reduces the risk of AIDS infection. On the other hand, as British physicians argue, the risks of an accident during circumcision are about the same as the risks of later diseases of the penis in the uncircumcized.

Marcus and Betty

Some four years after the locker room encounter with Alex, Marcus has another key experience, this time with his new girlfriend, Betty. She allows him to *look*; sprawled on the bed, having inserted her diaphragm, she spreads her legs and lets him examine the mystery of the folds and wrinkles edged with red. He touches it gingerly, then kisses her all over in gratitude. He knows he is lucky to get this essential basic education, but not *how* lucky. His wife, Linda, still undresses in the dark when they are 40. The story continues at **Marcus, aged 28**.

Would that all teenage girls had the foresight to carry contraception with them. Teenagers are the most at risk in the sense that, even with the AIDS crisis upon us, this age group is the least likely to use protection. In the United States, well over a million teenage girls become pregnant every year. The most rapid increase in pregnancy rates is occurring in girls under fifteen.

What if you don't have the opportunity to insert your diaphragm beforehand? Some women say that stopping to put it in interrupts the flow of lovemaking. This objection can sometimes be an excuse: if sex must be only and always spontaneous, then a woman can escape the sense of guilt she would have if she deliberately chose to 'do it'. She reassures herself, in effect, that she was swept away. One solution is to let her partner insert the diaphragm, making it part of the loving.

The birds and the bees

Once, when Alex returned from a date, his father asked him if "he'd had any". This constituted the entire sex instruction Alex received from his parents. Marcus did little better: his father eventually gave him a dissertation on sperm and ova which explained little. His father had said that if he had any further questions he should ask his mother; Marcus ignored this offer, knowing that her advice would be restricted to: "Don't get anybody pregnant". The book Marcus' father handed to him was a little more informative.

Most boys receive little or no instruction at home, certainly nothing dealing with foreplay, orgasm, or the emotions involved. Most information, and misinformation, is acquired from their mates. Yet boys

Naked bodies may be the official uniform of sex – but we do not always have the time or inclination to change. A half-naked woman is better than none (this goes for men, too).

expect themselves to be knowledgeable, and girls expect them to be, too. It is little wonder that boys approach their first time with intense curiosity and equally intense trepidation.

The first time

One thing Marcus and Alex had in common was the burning need to 'do it', to find out what it was like, to get past the barrier of virginity, to prove themselves real men. We know, from comparing their stories, that the luckiest men are those who find themselves with an older, experienced woman who gently guides them. For other boys, the first experience is awkward and, often enough, a let-down. But at least they have done it. The idea that women should be for sale is awful, yet there may be something to be said for the traditional practice of an older male relative taking a young man to a sympathetic prostitute for his first experience of sex.

Kiss and tell

For Alex, one of the best parts of the episode with Gloria in the car happened long after she was gone. Lounging back comfortably with beer in hand, he slipped the details to the lads in the band: how she looked and acted, what he said and did. This is the second stage in male sexual competition. At 13, it is what you have; when you are 17, it is what you do with it. If Alex had not 'scored' he would have lied about it. When he was less experienced, Alex simply made up the details, some of them quite extraordinary. He quickly found that his friends would nod and applaud the story, as Marcus did, rather than reveal their ignorance.

At the same time as it is a move in a competitive game, Alex's recital of his conquest to the boys is also an example of male bonding. They are sharing a triumph. Those boys who have Alex's predatory attitude will consider Gloria fair game.

The dominant phallus

Some may suspect that Alex's display advertises homosexual intent, but his little show was about aggression, not sex. As a symbol, the penis is *the* representation of male virility and, as Alex demonstrated to Marcus, male power. Male squirrel monkeys, only slightly less subtle than Alex, display their dominance by spreading their thighs, erecting their penises, and urinating in the direction of the monkey (or human) they wish to threaten. This display is inborn, and is expressed by one-day-old males. If a baby squirrel monkey makes the mistake of displaying to a dominant adult male, it learns a quick and rough lesson in who is the boss.

In exactly the same spirit, totems consisting of an aggressive face above and an erect penis below, guarded houses, gardens and fields, and warded off evil in ancient Greece, Bali, Japan and many other cultures around the world. On the Greek island of Delos, phalli can still be seen perched atop walls, looking like small cannons. Not surprisingly, the same theme turns up in mythology. Priapus, the phallic demigod of the Greek pantheon, is described as the son of Aphrodite and Dionysus. He actually started life as a rude, crude and nasty local deity of certain Greek towns. His statue, complete with erection, was placed as a scarecrow in gardens to keep out thieves. The statue was inscribed with threats: if the thief were a young woman or a young man, she or he would be punished by being forced to have vaginal or anal intercourse, respectively, with the garden's owner. If the thief were an older man, he would be irrumated (forced to perform fellatio).

The Roman god Fascinius was represented simply as a penis. A fertility symbol showing a penis standing on dog's legs with a set of smaller genitalia tucked between the legs was worn by matrons of ancient Rome. In modern times, at certain veterinary schools, the *os penis* of dogs (the bone in the animal's penis) has been spotted dangling around students' necks as a decoration, particularly the women.

Why men are angry at women

Men may feel anger towards women for reasons that are deeply rooted in childhood struggles, but there are also more immediate reasons. 'If she wears a miniskirt up to her crotch, wiggles her bum as she walks down the street, presses her nipples up against her blouse, surely she wants it? Then why won't she give it to me? Because women, cold and snobbish from their long red fingernails to their high heels, don't really want sex. And because they don't, they have the power to use it to tease and manipulate men.'

Women get themselves pregnant, and then they marry a meal ticket. She gets economic security, he has to work all day at a job he doesn't like in order to support her and the kids. And she'll live longer, too. At this early stage in their lives, both Marcus and Alex have suspicions of this sort. Marcus will grow up to feel differently, but Alex will continue to think this way for the rest of his life.

Marcus, aged 28

Even after marrying Linda, Marcus keeps asking himself 'What *do* girls want?' As far as he could see, girls had sex because their boyfriends, or husbands, asked; because of 'love'; not because they liked it. He is still not sure where he should rub Linda. Once he asked her for a guided tour. Her reply: "You have hands. Use them."

It would be wrong to say that this cursory reply made Linda responsible for what happened three years later; but she was in part to blame. Although she made him feel grounded, secure, and although they could talk about most things, she would not discuss sex. They could lie in bed talking and cuddling, but if sex was to happen, it had, for her, to be spontaneous. He could never say, "Let's screw"; he did not dare ask if he might insert her diaphragm. If he slid a hand between her thighs, sometimes the ambush worked, sometimes not. She was capricious; he learned not to ask questions.

What happened three years later was what ought to have happened to Marcus at 17. Yvonne, a self-confident blonde of 40-plus, arrived in his office and blatantly set about seducing him. Dropping her back after the office party, he had accepted her invitation to go in for coffee. They made love in the shower. Even afterwards, she continued touching, licking and sucking him all over. He was bewildered, asking himself the usual question: 'What *did* she want?'

Gradually it dawned on him that Yvonne not only liked him; but that she really liked sex. And that she was giving him the same loving attention he had given Betty; and which he would give Linda if she would allow it.

Alex at 28

In his bachelor days, Alex grew tired of the endless negotiation just to get some pussy. He married, partly to ensure himself a steady supply. Once married, he began to feel that his wife was tying him down with her endless domestic fussing, her cattiness, her empty chatter, her refusal to join him in doing anything exciting, her incessant nagging about money. He quickly began to see her as weak, and dependent upon him for everything. As her interest in sex declined, he started to visit prostitutes and to have affairs, feeling entitled to do this in order to keep his marriage going. (See also **Joe & Sue**, pages 151-154.)

Alex's sexual misery may be largely of his own making, but his view of his economic situation has a grain of truth. See also **Paul & Rosie**, pages 122-123.

For Alex, frequent sex without great finesse had become standard operating procedure, and this was one reason why his wife grew steadily less interested. As with Gloria, a lack of finesse sometimes spilled over to coercion.

In the extreme, the anger of men at women becomes rape, an act which is at least as much an expression of hostility as lust. Like Alex on Gloria, rapes of women by acquaintances – date rapes – are a more frequent occurrence than rape by a stranger in a dark alley which will make the morning tabloid.

Alex represents the dark side of male sexuality; Marcus represents the potential for a happier outlook. In **Paul & Rosie** there is an exploration of the dark side of female sexuality.

Male views of women

Is it any wonder that many men have to struggle towards positive relationships with women? Yet when men are asked to choose, most say that they prefer a love relationship with a woman more than a friendship with a man. On the other hand, many men think it would be difficult to maintain a friendship with a woman without having sex raise its beautiful head. A number of men say that they consider their wives as their best friends. In general, men view women as a humanizing influence.

When asked for their happiest moments, men say that they were when they were in a love relationship. Men, well known to be hopeless romantics, enjoy being in love, on cloud nine, having their heart soar when *she* comes into view. They report that they can talk more honestly about personal topics with a woman. (Presumably they do not do not feel the competitiveness they would do with a man.) But talking about emotional topics is still a problem for men. Some, like Marcus with Linda, think that sexual interchange is a substitute for verbal intercourse, that they can say with their bodies what they cannot find words to express. And some, women must recognize, just cannot express emotions in words.

What is it about women that men especially like? Men uniformly report liking women who are sweet, gentle, sensitive, supportive, compassionate. Marcus cuddles Linda in bed, his arm around her. Her smallness and softness makes him feel protective. He likes that feeling. It expands him, makes him feel masculine. A man's support of his wife and family is a sign of manhood in some places around the world (and the number of children is taken as evidence of his virility). In some Latin American cultures, it is thought that the fatter the wife, the better the husband must be at looking after her.

As much as men complain about marriage, most say they need and want the security and permanence, the look of a familiar face across the table. Men say that they are willing to pay the price of restriction of freedom and, in some cases, sexual dissatisfaction for the rewards of sharing common interests, children and companionship.

In short, men like the company of women. The statement 'I like women' coming from a Casanova (see **Claire & Tony**, pages 137-138) can mask the most ferocious misogyny, but most men really do enjoy the society of women. *Vive la difference* – it really is one of the spices of life.

Men's views of the inner woman

They range from Alex's 'It's pink and it stinks' to Marcus' unabashed pussy worship. Some talk about 'working all night just to touch it'. And what is 'it'? That sweet slit, the muffin, the crumpet, the cunt; in America, the beaver, the box, the muff, the poontang, the snatch. The synonyms are endless. The fascination of the vagina is not just a matter of deprivation and horniness. Polynesian boys, for whom sex was more available than their western counterparts, still carved female genitalia on to tree trunks. Although Polynesian girls participated enthusiastically in the culturally appproved adolescent sexuality, they did not return the compliment in their handicrafts. In *Citizen Kane*, Orson Welles' movie about the American newspaper publisher William Randolph Hearst, Hearst's last word as he dies is "Rosebud". The movie shows us a sledge emblazoned with the name *Rosebud* that Kane had as a boy, but the *cognoscenti* knew that this was actually an insider's reference to the pet name that Hearst had for the private parts of his mistress, Marion Davies.

Several women investigators have remarked that it is a challenge to get past men's use of street words such as 'pussy' to recognize the affection for women and their parts that lies beneath their rough language. In America, certainly, 'cunt' is heard much less frequently as a derogatory term than 'prick'. While 'pussy' can be a sexist term, it is also used by men as a celebration of female genitalia in the abstract. Note the gender difference: women are not known for celebrating 'dick' in the abstract.

Alex, unlike Marcus, has negative attitudes towards women and these spill over to his feelings about their genitalia. Such feelings are echoes of a distant past when the vagina was taboo. In Greek cities under seige, the women would turn around on the wall and show their genitalia to attacking troops, warding them off by this forbidden sight. In Celtic mythology, the hero Cuchalainn is treated to a similarly threatening spectacle by the Queen's women upon his arrival in Ulster. Even today, a gypsy woman can have a man ostracized from the tribe by flipping up her skirt at him (husbands excepted, of course). His only recourse is to take his case to a gypsy court. If, after hearing his plea, they eat with him, he is being welcomed back into the group.

Alex's ambivalence expresses itself as loathing rather than fear. From the Old Testament onwards, writers have impugned the vagina, the organ itself or as a symbol of womankind, as smelly and dirty. The unfortunate aphorism that 'Woman is a temple built over a sewer' is quoted too often. Did Alex's feelings arise from a quick childhood peek at a female orifice? Freud would say that a glimpse is sufficient to provide a horrified little boy with living proof that the vagina is a wound. But this is just not the response of the majority of little boys who get to see one. When these little boys grow up, they are more likely to feel like Marcus than Alex. Asked to describe the clitoris, one man in the Hite survey called it 'a pearl in a velvet pouch'. Misogynist maledictions notwithstanding, the simple fact is that the recent surveys of male attitudes show that the vast majority of men's responses to women and their organs are at heart enthusiastic, affectionate and warm.

Male complaints

To say that men like sex is, to most, a cliché of record proportions. They are *supposed* to; it is part of the macho image. For some, the Scout motto, *Be prepared*, becomes *Always ready*. One woman, having had perhaps one drink too many, announced: "I want the best lay in town". A man took her home, despite a lack of real interest and against his better judgement. He just could not refuse the challenge. She was disappointed. So was he. Roll the dice, slide your token into the next box, if you land on the woman pick up an orgasm card, collect more points than the other men playing. When sex is a board game, everyone can lose.

Men are in a bind. If he does not think about her pleasure, he is a selfish, insensitive sod. Yet he had better not ask her if she has come because:

  (a) that is pushing her (why must he always make sex into some kind of performance?).
  (b) what is wrong with him anyway, can't he tell? It is not surprising that men think they have to work too hard at sex.

Men are tired of being told it is all the fault of their pricks. Given the nature of the penis, both as an instrument of auto-erotic pleasure and as a symbol of manhood, is it little wonder that men tend to be phallicly oriented? What is the use of a vagina if it is not for penetrating? At the end of the day, here is this chap and he just wants a little friendly in-and-out; but if does not get on the radar and find her clitoris, the sisterhood will have him up on charges.

A proposal

Here is one way to deal with who gets what when both of you are tired. How about a policy of mutually agreed upon, alternating selfishness? Tonight is my night: we do everything for me, I will be the focus. Next time will be yours and we will do it the way you like it. But of course, this applies only to to a steady relationship.

Male pleasures, male passions

Many men can recall, and recount, passionate erotic interludes with women who turned them on because of their seductive style, beautiful body, or intense sexual responsiveness. But, the men say, the times that really count are those when desire, trust, and a strong emotional bond with their woman were all blended together. These men find that sex gets better as the relationship deepens and they are able to communicate specific desires. These factors all intensify the feelings of loving and being loved. As someone once said, "Love is the best aphrodisiac".

Men also talk about the importance of sharing a sense of fun and freedom in bed. They want a woman who is uninhibited, who can take pleasure and give it. Men like older women for this reason; they are less inhibited, as Marcus finally finds with Yvonne.

For Alex, dominance is the invariable theme of sexual activity. There can indeed be an aggressive component to male sexuality. In men like Marcus, it depends on time, place, circumstance, and partner. Aggressive feelings may emerge with hard thrusting. To be sure, fierce fucking is appreciated by many women when they are fully aroused. Some of the advanced lovemaking techniques involving pinching, biting, or hitting would be painful and a turn off if one were not sexually excited. At other times, there is a fusion of the sexual and aggressive feelings with a little roughness being appreciated by both partners.

The fusion of feelings can be experienced by men as a sense of control, the sense of 'doing' a woman. Yes, men most often choose the time, place, and positions for lovemaking. Is this, of itself, an authoritarian, phallic evil as some feminist extremists would have it? He is making love *to* her, but it is love that is being made. Many men experience feelings of power, even godlikeness when making love. A woman can feed into her partner's feelings by encouraging him verbally: "Do it to me"; or even: "Fuck me".

For most women some of the time and for some women all of the time being 'done' is just fine. But as Yvonne persuaded Marcus, there are other possibilities. Many men say that there are numerous occasions on which they enjoy relaxing their control and letting the woman take over.

Sometimes the strongest emotional tone for a man is one of tenderness and protectiveness. The feeling is of pleasure given and taken, communication and sharing. At these times, entering a woman is experienced as a giving of himself: here is my cock, feast on it. Men feel the hardness of their erection not as a weapon of domination, but as a bridge of shared pleasure.

IT *T*AKES TWO

— *Eric* & *Judy* —

*E**ric*

The world out there still seems to say you measure your manhood by how much sex you can get. You know, how much you make her cry out for it. How much you squirt as you come. Judy and I have sex once a week. But I would say, and I think she would agree, that although we are reasonably happy sexually, the strength of our relationship lies elsewhere. She is not a particularly sexual woman. But she is intelligent, warm, good company. She is my friend, a good mother to my children. I would like to think that I turn her on. Not my body, I mean, although I work out sometimes, run, and play racquet ball, try to keep in shape. But I want it to be *me* that gets her excited.

*J**udy*

And he does. I can imagine more exciting lovers. Never a better friend.

*E**ric*

We still do things much the same as we always have, I guess. Sometimes she gives me a hand job. Especially if she has a really heavy period. It's too messy, then. I can occasionally persuade her to do oral sex, but then she never takes it in that far or holds it very long. What we lack is enthusiasm. Sometimes I wish she would act as if she were enjoying it more. I suppose it's the kids. The walls of this place are plasterboard. I get us started with baby talk; Judy just loves that. Then we smooch and hug for a while.

Judy

It is perfectly possible to enjoy sex without orgasms. In fact, it can be wonderful without. As long as you aren't aiming for one. It's frustrating if you aim and don't make it. If you do it again and again and never get there, the only way to keep sane is to forget it. Quite honestly, that's what I've done. I've given up all hope of reaching orgasm with Eric. That way it is not a strain on our relationship. It would be better if it wasn't this way.

Eric

Since we had the children we've calmed down. You have to be a bit inhibited, you know, keep the muzzle on. No loud moans and groans these days. Judy was quite noisy when we first married.

Judy

Don't get me wrong. He isn't a selfish, arrogant bastard. Far from it. He's a gentle, loving husband, a good father. But sensitive and insecure. Other than saying "Look, you've had it all wrong for the last six years," what can I do? I suppose I didn't help the problem by faking orgasm in the first years. Not always. In those days I didn't have to fake enjoyment, or excitement. I still don't. I do enjoy it.

The way we usually start is by caressing each other. I say, "Grandma, what a big mouth you've got," and he says, "All the better to munchy wunchy," and sucks my breasts, which is nice. Then I fondle him until he is hard. Then he tries to do the same for me. And that's when things begin to go wrong. It just doesn't work.

E*ric*

I have tried to excite her. I read a book on it. But she isn't much into, you know, clito-whatsit stimulation. She often pushes me away. Sometimes I know she needs it, because she pushes my hand down. But quite honestly I can't tell if it does anything for her.

I wish she would move. I wish she wouldn't leave it all to me. I wish just once she would make love to me from start to finish. Sometimes I feel like saying "Move damn you.". Of course I don't, but maybe I should. When it's really boring, I think about another woman. In my mind I imagine a woman who is really hot for me, who rips open my pants because she can't wait to get to me. I imagine putting it in her mouth because she really wants me to orgasm that way.

J*udy*

I've tried to give him instructions in the nicest possible way. You know, exaggerated moans when he hits the right spot, and getting out from under his fingers when he doesn't. I've even tried putting my hands on top of his and guiding him, but he just pushes them away. He presses too hard. He acts like my clitoris just needs a poke or two. I start getting irritated and decide the sooner we get this over the better. So I tell him to come in. And once he is inside, he feels good. He really does. If only he would let me move, or I felt I could put my hand down to help. But I know he would feel insulted.

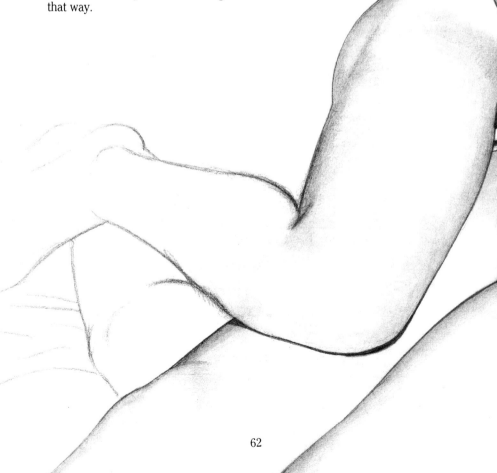

E*ric*

Now I have to admit it. The missionary
position is my favourite. I like to thrust,
and I think she likes it too. What I like
best is to raise myself up on my arms.
Make a really powerful thrust, you
know, bang her into the bedstead. I
know she likes the woman on top – and
sometimes we do it – but I can't really
get enough movement that way.

Judy

I've tried pushing him over on to his side so I can rub myself up against him, but he always pops back on top, pinning me down. I've tried putting his hands down, but he always pushes me away. I'm trapped.

Eric

What I really think is, it's important that you try to please women. In my experience it is often quite difficult. I have known really sexual women. Judy just isn't one of them. Sometimes it's like making love to the mattress. Sometimes she does ask me to stimulate her and I am happy to help. I wish she would ask me more often.

Judy

Oh yes, I can if I say, "Please, just a little bit." He'd do it for maybe five seconds. But then he likes to get up on his hands – like he's doing push-ups – and that's that. The way he pushes my hands inhibits me. I couldn't masturbate in front of him. I sometimes think if I did he would begin to understand how to please me. I think he thinks I never masturbate. I do. After he has rolled over and gone to sleep.

Eric

I'll tell you one thing, though. When it's all done I get the old itchy tickles and I have to come out, I'm always careful to pull out slowly and kind of hold her between the legs to prevent sudden loneliness.

Has the Western world ever experienced as much good sex as it does now? Maybe long ago, certainly not in recent times. Eric's and Judy's difficulties were so commonplace fifty years ago that everyone assumed they were normal. Women were supposed to 'lie back and think of England', while their husbands 'took their pleasure'. Certainly they were not supposed to masturbate on the side as Judy does, or, like Eric, to complain that a wife showed little enthusiasm. Nice women were never enthusiastic, and men just got on with what they had to do. He, we must assume, was happy with vaginal masturbation, bolstered in this joyless activity by a mythology that told him there were two sorts of women, the Madonna and the Whore. The good and the sexual. Men who recognized the fragility of their own Madonna did not pester her for sex – or that was the theory. In practice, things were never so black and white. Sometimes she needed to have a 'headache', and if he could afford it he may have visited a prostitute, or seduced the maid. The myth in Victorian times was that prostitutes and common women could enjoy sex.

The double standard goes deeper than the behaviour of the couple. It includes their sexual expectations. Sex outside marriage was wrong, but given men's appetites it was inevitable. Her appetite did not come into the reckoning. We know that some Victorian women enjoyed sex. A small scale survey of well educated females conducted at the time found that most had orgasms, enjoyed intercourse and thought sex a normal part of everyday life.

Changing expectations

Once sex was bad, now it is good. And most of us follow the common view. But just as some women probably rebelled against Victorian ideals, so some today have difficulty in shaking off the burden of history. Even in the 1960s, women like Judy were told that although sex was good, it was still primarily for men. Gone was the innocence of lying back and thinking of England. Now she was advised by her gynaecologist that she should try some 'simulation of sexual responsiveness'. In other words, it will more exciting for him if you fake it. Therein lies Judy's, and many women's, most common problem.

Your choice

As attitudes to sex changed, women like Judy moved from being the passive partner to making it better for him. But where was her pleasure? When asked what men think about her orgasms, she usually replies: 'Sometimes they ask, sometimes they assume, and often they just don't care'. There is only one excuse for regularly servicing a man who does not care, and that is, you don't either.

Of course, we know that it is not that simple. Men can be bullies, and women may not want to disrupt the power base of the relationship. If he would hate you to become assertive, and you are happy to concur, that is your choice. But having decided, like Judy, to aquiesce, it is pointless grumbling about how Eric gets it all wrong.

If the *status quo* is not of your choice, the questions you must ask yourself are: 'Why do I let it happen?' and 'When am I going to do something about it?'

Don't keep it to yourself

Shere Hite's survey on women's sexuality demonstrated clearly that women find it easier to have orgasms alone than with a man. (It is also the case, of course, that men find it easier alone.) Orgasm is within every woman's grasp – she just has to reach out and take it. But making sex reciprocal requires a major transformation of the traditional ways of going about it. Most women know what is wrong and how to put it right. Surveys suggest that many feel, in theory, that they should explain what is needed, right down to the clitoral caress; all that is missing is the will to put this into practice.

Faking it

Almost all women follow Judy's course of faking orgasm at one time or another, just as men fake things they think women care about, such as her choice of bathroom wallpaper. They do it with the best of intentions. The occasional white lie *is* a kindness, but the habitual lie helps no one. If he has an aversion to pink roses, but says "That's nice" when she shows him the fabric, he can hardly complain when he wakes to find himself beneath a rosy quilt.

Moreover, man is not born with an understanding of female sexuality. He knows what pleases him; pleasing her he learns by trial and error. Given that the tool of his trade, is, many women would contend, less than ideal for the purpose of pleasuring her, and that his natural inclination is to work in the wrong area, saying "That's great" when it was merely OK, is to condemn him to working in the dark.

Female passivity

Women have a long history as passive partners. When in 1971 Judith Bardwick asked college women why they had sex, few mentioned their own pleasure. Sex was the price they paid for romance. Have things changed? For some the answer is surely yes; but in a recent British survey, many women complained men did not bother to *make sure* that they reached a climax.

Deep down, most women *expect men to make love to them.* They take it for granted that a man should be sensitive to their needs, in-itiate the things they like and take both the time and care to help her reach orgasm. And when men do not share this view, women complain.

But this is an expectation easily turned on its head. For if it is to be expected of men, then women must also acknowledge the responsibility of seeing that a man has a good time; reaches the heights of pleasure, how and when he wants. Do they make love to men when love is needed, and have sex with them when sex is the order of the day? Do they take full responsibility for pleasing their men, or do they expect men to do it for themselves?

Women do not expect men to need their help. Their input is the icing on the cake. The point is that men have learned the necessary skills to bring themselves to orgasm. Her active participation is not essential.

Too many women are innocent of the skills to bring themselves to orgasm, or fail to realize that they must acquire these skills if they are to teach men to pleasure them. Maybe she was lucky enough to find a man who had undergone instruction; the rest of us have to be prepared to become instructors. Passive hints, like Judy's pushing him over on his side, get you nowhere. Women often act as if bolstering his ego (by not criticizing his technique) is more important than pleasure.

He is not a mind reader

Sometimes, of course, her frustration gets out of hand, and she lets fly. Or maybe she tries to get the message to him some other way: sulking, turning over, saying she has a headache – again. One thing she does make clear: that she has had enough. The essential, underlying message of exactly what she needs for sexual satisfaction, remains obscured by ill-feeling.

But, be fair

Men are romantic, too. Most surveys suggest that they are the more romantic sex. They like to make love, and when they do, they traditionally initiate lovemaking by doing what comes naturally. He can look lovingly at her, stroke her, pet her. He can kiss and fondle her breasts. He knows – unless he has had his eyes and ears closed for the last ten years – that women want clitoral stimulation. So he offers it. If she is like Judy, she fails to communicate exactly *how* to stimulate her clitoris, or for how long. So, he does the best he can do – in Eric's case, a useless five seconds' worth of fumbling.

Supposing, on the other hand, we ask her to do the best *she* can – to make love to him? What does she do?

Most women would probably start by saying 'What would you like?', even if not in so many words. And unless she has done what he likes many times before, her insecurity would make her check at intervals that she is indeed getting it right. She would expect, and need, guidance; just as men need it.

Communicate

If we want to share our bodies we need to take *equal responsibility* for pleasuring them. No moaning or complaining, shouting, sulking or dropping hints like Judy. You have to *say* what you want, and *keep* saying it. You don't have to be aggressive; but you do have to be assertive, positive, clear. Your partner should never need to say as Eric does, "quite honestly, I can't tell if it does anything for her".

The messages might go like this:

'Mm, that's nice; no, down a bit, that's the spot. Could you suck my left breast just a little bit harder? Put another pillow under my bum.'

And like this:

'Is that good? Is that the spot? Would you like me to suck you a bit more?'

And this:

'Not yet, I'm not ready for you. I'm sorry, but I'm just not in the mood to make love. Not the missionary, let me turn over.' And this:

'Sometime could we try making love without penetration? Let me make you come, I don't need to just now. Let me massage you.'

Sexual difficulties

It is estimated that in Britain and the U.S.A. over half of all marriages run into sexual difficulties at some stage. Difficulties are different, and not so serious, in the sex therapist's terminology, from 'problems' which are discussed fully in **Martin & Giselle**, pages 228-239. Typical male difficulties are with erection or ejaculation; female difficulties include vaginal dryness, lack of sexual interest, infrequent orgasm or pain on intercourse. Minor difficulties include an imbalance in the desire for sex, or for certain practices like oral sex. Half the men in one survey had some difficulties, 40 per cent some problems, while more than 60 per cent of their wives said they had problems, and almost 80 per cent had difficulties. Thirty-six per cent of men ejaculated too quickly, and almost half the women had difficulties getting excited, or reaching orgasm. Few asked for help.

Imbalance in desire

The monthly cycle of a woman's body often gives a natural rhythm to her sexual desire. Most experience peaks just before and just after menstruation, and again at ovulation, midway through the cycle. At these times, women may need little to arouse their sexuality. The heaviness of breast and body can be felt as a constant background desire; just one kiss is all it takes. At other times, her libido may sink so low it feels impossible to raise the smallest desire. Understanding the baseline from which your arousal springs makes it easier to respond. Men do not have these obvious patterns of desire, although desire itself probably fluctuates as much.

How often should couples expect to make love? There is no answer. It is not a competition. For some, it has to be twice daily, for others monthly is about right. We all know that within a lifetime, and within a relationship, our needs fluctuate enormously. It is inevitable that at some time or another, most couples find themselves mismatched.

This does not have to be a difficulty – if we recognize that sex extends beyond intercourse and mutual orgasm. "You look in need sweetheart – want to come in my mouth?" is one of the most delightful things he can say to you. Or you to him. If he doesn't want the compliment returned, he can always say, "Thank you, but no." Masturbation is not something people do when they have nothing better. It is an alternative, and a delightful one if you feel happy to take it. Many people feel embarrassed to discuss it. The embarrassment is purely conditioning. Self-reliance is not weakness, but strength.

Why won't she suck me?

Although complaints of insufficient oral sex are voiced by both men and women, a number of investigators have suggested that this feeling is most common in men. Eric is spokesman for millions when he admits that he fantasizes about a woman who will take his cock in her mouth. Certainly, many men complain that although they bring their women to orgasm this way, the treat is not reciprocated. Understandably, men think this unfair. Some investigators have even wondered whether modern surveys are correct in suggesting that large numbers of women enjoy fellatio. Do women taking part in these surveys feel compelled to adopt more liberal attitudes than they actually possess?

For a small percentage of men, the significance of cock-sucking lies in the perceived submission and humiliation of their partner; for women who have been the recipients of this humiliation (and oral sex is a common form of sexual abuse in the rape of women and children) difficulties surely persist. It is hard to see pleasure in something which has in the past been associated with humiliation and fear. Men who value oral sex because they think it humiliates may well visit prostitutes for the purpose, or save it for when they wish to humiliate.

When asked why they do not like to suck their man, however, most women say that it is because he never reciprocates. The pleasures of oral sex for the giver are, after all, almost entirely in the pleasure of the receiver. Other difficulties experienced by women are that sucking a large penis can be tiring work, especially if she has to control the degree of entry with her tongue. Just keeping the mouth wide enough and the tongue pushed up to guard the throat entrance needs effort. Only if she is excited can the muscle strain be tolerated for long periods of time. Some men like oral love play in the missionary position. We feel this misses the point. She is making love to him. He may like to be free to thrust, but for most women a penis thrusting into the mouth and throat is no pleasure: the desire to gag is too great.

"The heavy hand on the back of the neck" as one friend put it, may also discourage future voluntary and enthusiastic participation, especially if that hand pushes her down before she has taken her own pleasure. For many men, sex lasts until he comes, and if this is in her mouth, that is it. Knowing this, who would greet the prospect with enthusiasm, especially if she feels a strong sexual need of her own.

The fact also remains that there are probably women who for no obvious reason simply do not enjoy oral sex; as indeed there are those who dislike rear entry positions, anal sex or masturbation.

Finally, it must be said that some men unconsciously underestimate the extent to which women like it: to acknowledge her delight is to psychologically transform their 'good wife' into a 'bad girl'.

Learning to like it

Oral sex, if mutually enjoyed, can enhance the sexual bond. There is no reason why anyone should have to do it, but if you would like to try, here is some advice. The first thing to remember is that this is not a battleground. By taking one step towards his position, you are not compromising your own. You must only go as far as you feel comfortable, and even then you must know that you still have a line of retreat.

The second step is to ask yourself why you dislike it, and to confront these fears together. Do you think he might be dirty? If so, let him take a bath, washing the genital area thoroughly. A clean man smells clean.

Are you afraid of choking? If so, discuss this with him. It is not necessary to take more than the tip of his penis into your mouth. And there are ways of ensuring that choking does not happen.

Are you afraid of him ejaculating in your mouth? Again, this need not be a problem if you discuss it together.

Step by step

Step one is for him to lie on his back while you move down so that you are close to his penis. Stroke it, look at it, even rub some butter on it.

71

Making love means taking pleasure in his body by sight, smell and touch.

Step two is to taste him. Start at his mouth. Kiss and lick his lips, face, ears and neck. Move down to the body. Gradually make forays from familiar to new ground. Fingers, toes, knees, armpits.

Step three Once you are comfortable with this, you can approach his penis. Only when you can lick should you consider sucking. Start by licking the base and then move towards the tip. Lick it like a lolly.

Step four If you are happy licking and kissing, try sucking. Take the tip gently into the mouth. Always approach this from above or from the side. So that it is possible to withdraw. Do not panic if he seems big. Even those who suck confidently rarely take in the whole penis. You will not gag unless it touches the back of your throat. (Or you panic.) The penis is a very blunt and insensitive instrument: it cannot tell the difference between your mouth and the wet tunnel you make with your hands. For further discussion and refinements of fellatio, see **Larry & Wanda**, pages 206-221.

For many, this is progress enough. The point of compromise. Taking a man's ejaculation is not something all women enjoy. The obvious way around this difficulty is for him to withdraw and for you to bring him to orgasm in your hand; or alternatively some prefer to suck him to orgasm while he wears a condom. For more about this difficulty, see also **Larry & Wanda**.

Getting her share

Women are slightly less enthusiastic about cunnilingus than men are about fellatio: 90 per cent of men and 75 per cent of women say they like doing it and receiving it. Women's inhibitions may be due in part to their belief that men don't *really* like doing it (see below). Perhaps also because this is really just for them. Deep down they may feel it is unfair to demand all this pleasure while giving nothing in return. Another factor is women's ambivalent feelings about their own genitalia. (Tidying up surgery is nowadays surprisingly sought-after.) Not all women are easily convinced that they look, smell and taste good, even when their men tell them they do. A girl's genitalia are secret – even from her; viewed, often guiltily, with the aid of a mirror. There is nothing to show the world or talk about, and most names for her sexual apparatus are derogatory. In fact, most girls, as children, are provided with no specific name for it: they make do with euphemisms such as the 'bit between your legs'. Such euphemisms tend to emphasize the primary use for urination. Some English girls call it their 'Fanny', a name Americans use for female buttocks.

It is not surprising that a number of women should suspect that men feel about cunnilingus the same way as they might about licking the anus. (And the other way round.) Also, for most women, sex is private, not a performance art. Being exclusively pleasured puts her on stage. With mutual caressing or intercourse, excitement mounts in tandem: you share the stage.

Finding the way

For men who find it difficult giving their women pleasure in this way, we suggest much the same cure as we did for her. Ask yourself why it is so hard. Confront this first, because it is usually here that the problem lies. After that confrontation – and if you truly want to proceed, we suggest that you take the first steps outlined above. Look. Touch as you look. Kiss, then lick and finally suck lovingly.

Don't be smug

If, reading Eric and Judy's story, you think you have nothing to learn from it, stop and think again. Don't be misled by the fact that they are a couple into their twelfth year of marriage. At some stage of our sex lives, there is something of Eric and Judy in almost all of us: there is bound to be, especially early in life, when we experiment with partners, testing our ability to communicate sexually and inevitably failing with some.

It must also be said that to communicate your way out of Eric and Judy's predicament, you have first to know yourself; to thoroughly understand your own sexual needs before even attempting to explain them to others. You can explore these fundamentals in **Gwen & Jack**, pages 100-109, or if, having been depressed by Eric and Judy, you want to read about a couple have it right despite two children and ten years of marriage, simply turn the page to **William & Francesca**.

The moral

If there is a moral to Eric and Judy's tale, it is that we do not get the sexual pleasure we deserve, but that which we, in our heart of hearts think we deserve. That which we feel truly free to take from each other. We can take it by right, as men have done. We can take it because it is freely given, as surely some women have always taken from men who wanted to share their pleasure – even at times in our history when society as a whole felt that to have such 'animal cravings' demeaned women.

Or it can be mutual: each partner takes, because each gives.

Our bodies have all the switches and the dials to tune us into pleasure. We can learn the tricks of the trade, but without a central belief in our right to enjoyment, they are but tricks and switches and dials.

TUESDAY NIGHT
William & Francesca

Francesca

Sometimes it only just works, and sometimes it's special, and sometimes, for no reason, it's William and Francesca on a Tuesday night. No fancy techniques, no great excitement, just the old faithful missionary or maybe me on top. Face to face with an old friend.

How does it begin? Something like this:

William

"Your cold seems better." I put my book down.

Francesca

"Mmm. But Matt seems to be catching one. Is it tomorrow you're late, William?"

William

"I shouldn't be too late. I'm glad of my bed."

I turn to you, rising on one elbow and running my hand across your face. "Tired?" You smile at me. You feel like it too. We don't need to say anything. I move over to kiss you, your lips rise to meet mine.

Francesca

Predictable, well practised. An old routine. I rise on my knees above you. It's slow, familiar. Bread and butter.

William

I lie back and say to you with my
hands, "Want to come on top? Want to
be on top and come with me inside
you?" We kiss again, your hair falling
around my face. But now you slide
backwards, wrapping yourself around
my leg, rubbing yourself against my
thigh with liquid pelvic movements. I
love the way you lean forward to kiss
my nipples, lick the skin under my arm.

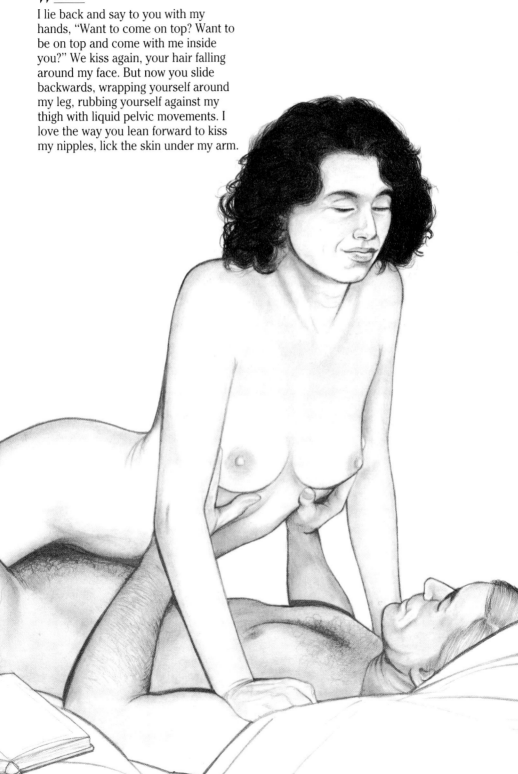

Francesca

I slide further back over your knee until
I can take you into my mouth. Not
serious. Just a friendly little suck
because I know you like it. I know
you. My hand slips down. Stroking
that spot you like me to touch as I
suck. Then you are inside me.
Slipped in easy. Soft and
sloshy. You kiss my
breast. I squeeze you
with my thighs.

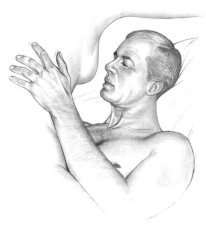

William

"Stop, let's feel us." Pausing with me only partially inside you, two hands, yours and mine, ten fingertips, touch us where we are together, where I disappear into you. Then, without warning, I've flopped out.

Another old routine: I press myself against your belly. I reach almost to your navel. "Look, see how far into you I go."

Francesca

I smile and put him back where he belongs. "You fit better like this." It builds. Not just down there. All over my body. This feeling of riding just above an explosion. Hovering there. I flow like candle wax to you. You mould me. There is nothing except this now.

William

I squeeze the base of my penis to make it harder as you lower yourself on to me. Oh, that delicious sensation of heat and enclosedness, of being engulfed in a warm haven. So much for technique. Now your weight is on me, your bottom rubbing my pelvic bone. Mmmm, your movements are rocking the bed beneath me. Pleasant, comforting.

Francesca

Occasional kissing of breast, ears, mouths. Smiling. Watching. Me and you. Your fingers trace the outlines of my lips and squeeze the tips of my ear. Yours, you know.

William

I move my hands to your hips as if to guide your slow rhythmic movements, to show you that you are doing just what I want you to be doing. Ride me, up and down. It's delicious when I'm passive this way. But activity is good too. My hands bring you to a halt; I tilt my pelvis and thrust into you with short, quick strokes. I lick up your moans of pleasure. Years of practice have made this perfect.

Francesca

Everything now from me to you. "Take me."

William

"Come on. Come on." I watch your face as you approach climax, your expression twisting with pleasure and concentration. When I hear that hungry moan, it's my signal to take one nipple gently between my teeth and rub the other between thumb and forefinger. Take it, Mary, take your climax. I am the man who satisfies you.

Francesca

Ooooh. My arms, spread high above my head, fall back and encircle you. There is a blankness. For a moment, the world stops. Then you are coming. I hold you to me.

William

Soon, yes, now . . .

Francesca

"Mmm. Good."

William

"Only good?"

Francesca

"What do you think?" No, not just good. Not on Tuesday night with William.

"Thank you."

William

Mind the wet spot.

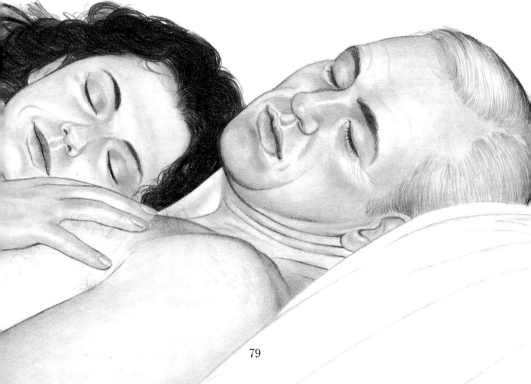

William and Francesca: long-term successful lovers. No fancy techniques needed to make things special – they are, were and probably always will be able to 'make the earth move'. It is not the equipment: William is just averagely endowed, and Francesca, after a couple of children, is probably slack. Nor do they succeed because either one or both of them is a 'good lay'. Swop Francesca for **Judy** (pages 60-73), and sex would probably become a disaster area for William as it is for Eric; swop William for **Robert** (pages 14-29), and no one would receive any medals. Will and Fanny work as a pair, in a special way. What exactly makes it special?

Self and others

Why not start with something other than sex? Maturity, for example.

Are you more mature than your partner? Of course. Most people are – or so they say. In fact, most of us choose a partner who is equally immature. Someone as uncertain about balancing the needs of a relationship as they are about retaining their own sense of identity.

What are those needs? Ask William about Francesca, and he will begin by saying, "She is her own person". Ask about their strengths as a couple, and he may pause but eventually say, "We are secure in ourselves, both separately and together". It is this security which makes their relationship work.

Francesca and William don't have to perform a balancing act between being part of a pair and being themselves. Their needs are integrated. Strength comes from feeling that being close and being separate are equally safe. In practice, this means there are few hidden 'agendas' between them. When William says, "I'm off to bed," he means just that. Francesca does not feel she has to put down her book and trot after him, nor does William feel rejected when she simply blows him a kiss. She can add, "I'll seduce you if you are still awake," and he can say, "I'd rather you woke me early," and nobody feels manipulated or used. That is maturity.

Most of us are but children: trying to balance the need for a close, emotional relationship with the need to hang on to ourselves as separate individuals. Or, as some therapists put it, to be part of a 'we' without losing the 'I'.

Groupies

If someone is very insecure about the 'I' and the 'we', there tends to be borrowing and trading within a relationship. Sometimes, one partner will borrow the 'I' of the other, becoming something of a groupie. Unconsciously, he hives off his fears on to her. Or, if beneath his stolid appearance there is a hidden craziness, perhaps she expresses it for them both in her dress and lunatic beliefs. Or, he might reveal her hidden anger in the way he shouts at waiters. There can be so many of these hidden 'agendas' that problems are almost inevitable.

People with the groupie mentality are faced with a paradox of contradictory feelings: they both need and fear separation. They are afraid of the lone 'I', yet cling to it. The 'we' sustains them, but it also frightens them. Their sense of themselves as separate people is so weak that they are afraid of losing it in the 'we'. So they fear closeness, too. They cannot live alone because their sense of themselves is so fragile; but nor can they live together.

Their relationship is a tangled web of put-offs and come-ons, and so, often, is their sex life, because at bottom they feel that being separate and being close are equally dangerous.

A partial solution

How can one get from being a groupie to being Francesca or William? Most people don't. Along the way, some find partial solutions: they choose either to maintain themselves as separate, or to form a relationship. They deal with one problem, but not the other. She expresses her need for warmth and closeness, and solves the problem of separateness by unconsciously choosing someone who has jumped the other way. He is the 'I', she is the 'we'. Often, neither he nor she is conscious of this division.

The problem such couples face is how to be distinct and yet remain attached. These are the couples who, years into a relationship, find they have little in common. Or who, after children are born and the patterns of their relationship inevitably change, find it impossible to renegotiate the contract.

Most people's solution

Between this partial solution and William and Francesca's maturity are numerous couples doing their best to keep it all together. Most of us, in fact, are here, consciously juggling the need for a separate identity with the need for a close, supportive relationship. Sometimes we are close, sometimes separate. It tends to depend on what we are doing at the time.

These are the couples who have, to a greater or lesser extent, developed a degree of tolerance for each other's needs for intimacy and autonomy. There is not always, or even usually, a battle royal between them. Maybe, in time, they can reach the peaks that William and Francesca inhabit. Or maybe they are content to scale them occasionally, content with a system that works nine days out of ten.

So here is the first, perhaps the main, reason why William and Fran-

cesca are so good together: sex is an expression of their whole relationship, integrated into lives which have nothing to prove to each
other, and nothing to fear.

The fit

And now for something altogether different: the fit of his penis in her
vagina. There may not be much variation in the size of a penis: an inch
or two in length and rather less in circumference, but there are differences in shape and positioning. Some hang high, some low, some are
straight, some curved. In the long run, it seems they are all viable.
Women may state a preference for something of average length and
above average girth (too long, and it is often painful), but in the long
term, few complain about the way their men are hung.

In the short term, it has to be said that most women need stimulation of the area *around* the vagina: the shaft and glans, the clitoris,
the labia, the urethral opening, vestibular gland and bulb. Page 89 carries a detailed illustration of all these. It is difficult for a man to provide
ideal stimulation to a passive woman. She needs to position herself
properly to get the best she can. At the start of any relationship it takes
time to get the angles right. William fits Francesca because they have
had years of practice.

Visualization for him

If William reflects on what excites him, how it feels to be touched and
rubbed in certain places, and the way he likes to be stimulated, he can
also understand what she needs.

Let him consider where those special places are in Francesca. If he
thinks where the tip of *her* penis lies, and where *her* shaft is, it
becomes clearer why excitement and orgasm in most women takes
time and practice. And perhaps why so many women do not climax
during intercourse.

We all know the first bit: that the tip of the penis corresponds to the
clitoris. In fact, the clitoris has as many nerve endings as the tip of the
penis, or more, but it is, of course, very much smaller. This has two
effects. First, it is harder to find, and can, in some positions, go completely unstimulated. Second, its sensations can be very intense. Few
women stimulate it directly during masturbation, (see **Gwen,** pages
94-97), and many find direct stimulation painful or distracting. (Some
men report similar sensations when the glans is touched.)

When aroused, Francesca's sensitive structures fill with blood, as
do William's. Rubbing them when thus engorged leads to orgasm.
Simple, and not so simple. How best to rub?

William simply stuffs it into an orifice and moves it up and down.

82

Nothing could be easier, as long as it stays stiff. And Francesca?

She has several options. First, she can stimulate the clitoris directly using her (or his) fingers. If this is too intense, she can rub by pushing herself hard against his pubic bone. This will stimulate the area between the vagina and the tip of the clitoris directly and the clitoris indirectly. This is much like direct stimulation of the area just below the ridge of his crown which, if he is uncircumcized, will stimulate the crown indirectly. Third, she can squeeze and rub by means of circular movements which pull the hood back and forth over her clitoris. The hood is attached to the labia which are inevitably moved when he pushes into the vagina. This last always happens, but may not provide enough intense stimulation for most women. The first three only happen if she makes them happen.

Active or passive, tough or tender, man or woman in control, this position allows her to cross her legs to heighten the clitoral stimulation and to squeeze and suck with her vagina to heighten it for him. Men like it because it is the only time when they can fuck up and be appreciated. Men who like watching their woman get off appreciate the view. Easy to rub her nipples to enhance her orgasm. Like all woman-on-top positions, it will not work well when his erection is a bit 'iffy'.

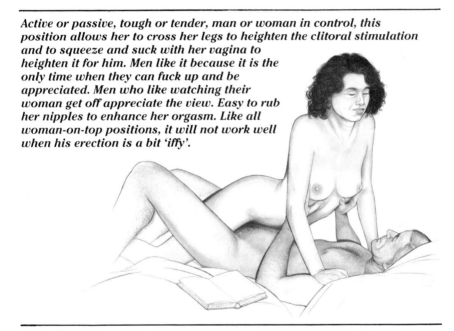

William's best move

When William was a young man, he read somewhere that to gratify a woman he should imagine he had a long piece of chalk jammed in his anus. Drawing a figure-of-eight with it on the ceiling would provide pretty good stimulation; it is not bad advice, for it does not go far wrong for her whatever position she adopts. There is a well-known exercise programme which suggests you practise this movement along with using your pelvis something like a scoop, especially when on top or in rear entry.

Give it time

Sexual know-how is knowing what your partner wants by reading the signals and giving it before he or she asks. Mutual know-how is when he or she knows what to give you in return. Long before we send, or answer, signals, we have to learn the codes. No two people are exactly alike in needs or bodies. If it were literally true that a woman was just like a man, sex would be a matter simply of finding the right buttons and pressing them. It is not.

Nothing substitutes for learning. True, there is some transfer of training from one partner to the next, but there is still much to learn with each new partner. William is not a great lover; great lovers do not exist. He is Francesca's lover: and wonderful at that.

At the beginning of a relationship, much time is taken up learning the basics; when we know each other in intimate detail, we can start to perfect technique – as William and Francesca have.

William meets needs Francesca was unaware she had, as she does for him. It is like that when we love each other well.

Choosing positions

It has to be said that the in-out of his penis in her vagina provides excellent stimulation for the bottom section of her Mary Ellen (for an explanation of this term, see **Gwen & Jack**, pages 101-103). But by itself, it is rather like William masturbating only the bottom third of his shaft. (Nothing else allowed but the occasional touch of the glans on the bedcovers.)

For this reason, the missionary position is not ideal for beginners. If he manages to stimulate her Mary Ellen as he ins and outs, it will be by chance. (Unless the vaginal entrance is slackened by childbirth, it is almost impossible to get the position right.) Luckily, in-ing and out-ing is not everything a man wants – if it were, sex would be very dull indeed. Sometimes he wants her to take charge; sometimes he wants to watch, sometimes to be frantic and at other times to be gentle; as she does, too.

For beginners

The easiest way for her to get the best stimulation is to grind. In a grind she can rub her Mary Ellen on his pubic bone – and if she is free to move, she can arrange herself so that she receives the right amount of stimulation to the best places. Good grinding positions are the 'X' position (see **Joe & Sue**, pages 160-161) and woman-on-top, as adopted by Francesca, front- or back-facing. Try them both front- and back-facing in the same session or on subsequent nights. There is nothing like systematic research.

It is simple to control the degree and point of stimulation by adjusting whether you sit upright, lean forwards or lean backwards. Adjusting leg positions also helps. You can sit astride, squat or lie. Once you get to know how to 'line up' you will discover many ways to do it. The disadvantages of these 'primary grind' positions are that they do not give him much opportunity to thrust, or, it must be said, to move.

However, she can alternate the grind with a little 'thrusting': squat over him and move up and down on his shaft. If he wants to come this way, he can experience totally passive orgasm: it can be mind blowing (see below).

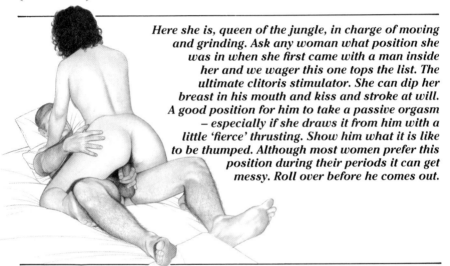

Here she is, queen of the jungle, in charge of moving and grinding. Ask any woman what position she was in when she first came with a man inside her and we wager this one tops the list. The ultimate clitoris stimulator. She can dip her breast in his mouth and kiss and stroke at will. A good position for him to take a passive orgasm – especially if she draws it from him with a little 'fierce' thrusting. Show him what it is like to be thumped. Although most women prefer this position during their periods it can get messy. Roll over before he comes out.

Of the facing positions, side-by-side is probably the best compromise between a grind and a thrusting position, since it gives much more leeway for both partners to move. He can satisfy his need for thrusting while she satisfies hers for grinding. By moving the upper halves of their bodies apart, they can both watch him entering. He has access to her clitoris, and she to his balls. And she can either open her legs so that the stimulation comes from his pubis or, once he has entered, she can cross her ankles and squeeze.

In her major survey of female sexual behaviour, Shere Hite found that women are pretty much divided between rubbers and squeezers. Which are you? It probably depends on how you masturbate.

Once you have mastered the side-by-side position, you can move on to the more advanced missionary. She has little room for adjustment unless she raises her bum on two or three pillows, and he lifts himself up on extended arms. She needs to know the measure of her man before she can easily succeed, and again, leg positions, and moving between them, can help her with fine tuning. Try legs crossed, both together, or apart. Put them around his back or up over the shoulders and around his head; have one up and the other down; then sample the stimulation produced by moving slowly between positions.

And when he is fully excited, tell him to stop, holding himself just above you. With a cushion or two under your bum, you should be able to move up and down on him.

Passive orgasm

Totally passive orgasm is more difficult, and quite different from one achieved actively. The key word here is totally. One partner to be active, the other to lie absolutely still, and as orgasm builds, to become even more relaxed, preferably limp.

To reach total relaxation, tense each muscle in turn, then let it go. Work all around your body; as you relax, think about the heaviness of your limbs.

Reaching this state, and staying in it while orgasm floods over you takes practice, but it is worth it.

The obvious position for the recipient of passive pleasuring is on the bottom. Try it for hand and mouth work too.

Rear entry

Rear entry positions have further possibilities. Clearly, rubbing on the pubic bone is out, but a cross-legged squeeze is perhaps most enjoyable like this. Try it in a spoons position, or a flat doggy. Both are good thrusting positions for him.

A great advantage of rear entry is that it gives clear access for the hands: his or hers. Let the fingers do the walking while his penis does the rest. But tread lightly: no stamping on the clitoris.

Another easy 'finger' position is for him to stoop or stand while she lies flat on her back or stomach. He can watch himself thrusting if the fancy takes him.

Don't forget the 'No Entry' position. She simply makes a tight tunnel by crossing her legs. Gild the lily with a little butter or body oil. Her Mary Ellen is stimulated by the in-out of his penis and if she squeezes him tightly as he comes forward he does quite nicely, too.

The scientific view

In the 1950s, William Masters and Virginia Johnson began their long, objective stare at people having sex. They watched, at a conservative estimate, 10,000 'completed responses' of all kinds. The participants were wired up, monitored, observed and filmed. At the end, Masters and Johnson had a description of sexual behaviour which was as scientific and objective as a description of urination or the functioning of the heart. But of course, it lacked heart, and soul . . . the truths it tells are only part of the truth about how Francesca, William, and anyone else, feels.

Part one

Within seconds of initiating a sexual encounter, both partners experience a heightened blood flow: blood rushes down to the genitalia faster than it can be cleared away. The net result is that William starts to become erect, the three cavernosa of his penis (see **Martin & Giselle**, page 229) fill with blood; the valves in the veins of the penis close, trapping the blood. So he stays erect.

Meanwhile, the increased blood flow to Francesca's genital area also fails to clear, so her blood vessels are engorged. A watery, viscous substance (actually blood plasma) sweats and oozes from blood vessels on to the walls of her vagina.

Next comes an increase in muscle tension. Voluntary muscles tighten, involuntary ones in the breast and elsewhere tighten and untighten; the nipples become erect. At this stage her genitalia, engorged with blood, open like a flower, spreading to expose the vaginal entrance. Her clitoris doubles in size. Inside the vagina, she expands like a balloon slowly filling with air, and her womb, full of blood, rises, rotates and moves back. End of part one.

Part two: the orgasmic platform

Francesca has a cushion-like platform of moist, fluid-swollen tissue in the bottom third of her vagina. Its swelling cuts the size of the vaginal opening by up to 50 per cent, thus conveniently tightening her grip on his penis.

He, of course, has grown too: a small penis may almost double in size, a larger one grows, relatively speaking, less, but may still end up bigger. Breathing rate goes up, blood pressure is high, the pulse has quickened and the heart rate rises to about 160. Muscles become very tense, especially in the face.

Part three: orgasm approaches

Her clitoris suddenly disappears from the scene. It rises, turns 180x, and retracts into its hood. The scientific description says this is nothing more than a series of muscle contractions, and occasionally that is how it feels, but usually it is explosively pleasurable: 'God that was wonderful, how can you do that to me?' In women, the muscle contractions are best seen in the orgasmic platform. Sometimes orgasm is preceded by a mild shudder, then the whole platform goes into a series of contractions occurring at 0.8-second intervals. The uterus joins in. So do the pelvic floor muscles. All the muscle tension and constrictions of the blood vessels release.

For a few moments they all contract and expand and release together, then they slow down and squeeze and release more slowly. Then they stop.

Much the same happens for William. Part two leads to emission. Sperm and the various other liquids are gathered together in a little bulb at the base of the urethra ready for ejaculation. He feels impending orgasm, ejaculatory inevitability. Part three, ejaculation, comes within seconds and consists of vigorous rhythmical contractions (at precisely 0.8-second intervals) generated by the prostate gland, and the muscles at the base of the penis. After the first few contractions, the pace slows and the remaining semen is released in small, gentle spurts.

Part four: resolution

Muscle tension is relieved throughout both their bodies; blood rushes away, but does not entirely leave the penis, remaining in one of the three cavernosa for up to half an hour. Men now enter a refractory period – minutes in young men, days in older ones – when they cannot become sexually aroused.

Blood leaves her orgasmic platform, the ballooning shrinks, the uterus grows smaller and returns to its normal position. So does the clitoris, though, like the penis, it remains tumescent for up to half an hour.

For her, there is no refractory period. If stimulation continues, she can easily move on to another orgasm, going from part two to orgasm and back almost indefinitely. A hundred orgasms in a night are within the range of some women.

It is probably ejaculation that makes multiple orgasm impossible for him. There are reports that men can learn to become multi-orgasmic by suppressing ejaculation. They seem to be able to move from emission to orgasm and back a number of times without reaching a point where ejaculation is inevitable.

Not me

Women come when they get the right stimulation, yet told that orgasm occurs when the clitoris is stimulated, many women, like Francesca, say that this is not the whole truth.

Some women have a special fondness for rear entry positions because nothing else feels half as good. Noting this, Shere Hite suggested that during rear entry women rub themselves on the bed-clothes. This is hard to believe because the bedclothes are, after all, often absent, as when leaning on a tree, chair or up in full doggy. Others simply say it feels better, even essential, to have him inside as they come. Others that an orgasm from rear entry simply feels different.

Are women mistaken? Or have the researchers got it wrong?

G is for feeling good

And also for Grafenberg, who can claim to have 'discovered' the G spot. U is for unlikely and unicorns, but also for urethra. And M is for mons and also for missionary – and therein lies a tale, or two.

G is the spot

Francesca swears she has a spot, and will readily tell you that this spot, notwithstanding William, always feels better when she has a full bladder.

The Grafenberg spot lies (if indeed it lies) in the spongy tissue on the 12 o'clock side of the inner vagina. The way to find it is to put your fingers into the vagina and move under the pubis as if to lift her up. The bit you touch with the fingertips is the G spot. It feels quite dull at first, but with a little stimulation it will begin to swell, and once swollen, a good hard push feels divine. Or so some women say.

Believers insist all women have a G spot, others that a select 40 per cent do. Some insist it is a figment of the imagination. The 40 per cent with vivid imaginations are not complaining.

Believers explain that the G spot is only sensitive during arousal:

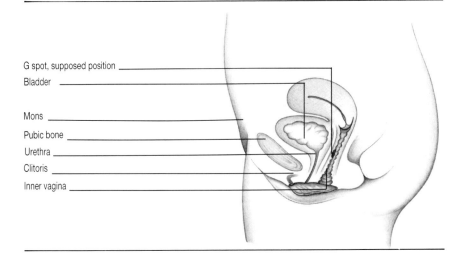

G spot, supposed position
Bladder
Mons
Pubic bone
Urethra
Clitoris
Inner vagina

that there is not much point in looking for it in unaroused women. Dissidents say that the women showing G spots in experiments are highly suggestible and would 'find' a sexy spot on the elbow if someone said they should. What is the truth?

First, we suspect that one cannot simply dismiss the experience of a substantial minority of women. What seems to be stimulated is an area around the urethra. Whether it is the whole length of the urethra, or just a small section, is open to dispute. That something in there feels good is not.

It is often said that the G spot is analogous to his prostate gland. (Also that some women squirt as they come.)

Don't believe it. The prostate gland, like all male internal sex organs, forms a part of the embryo called the Müllerian duct. The inner part of the vagina, like the rest of the female internal sex organs, arises from the Wolfian duct. If the G spot is a part of the inner vagina, it certainly has nothing to do with the prostate, no more than, say, the bladder or kidney has. Women do have a little Mllerian gland, but it is doubtful whether this has much effect on sexual feelings.

In fact the 'G' is a piece of spongy tissue that lies in front of the urethra. Is it pressure on the urethra, via the G spot, that feels good? Possibly. Many women report that sex feels good when the bladder is full, and find stimulation of the urethral opening pleasurable. What is more, some aphrodisiacs such as Spanish Fly act by irritating the bladder and urethra.

Whether or not the 'G' is a separate and special erotic spot is ultimately academic. Some women find breast stimulation wonderful, some find it essential, and some women can take it or leave it. There may be nothing special about the tissue: but there is something very special about the way some women feel about a penis inside them.

Female ejaculation

In spite of recent reports to the contrary, there is little reliable evidence that any women do. Some produce copious secretions, and others occasionally pee, but the evidence for anything else is suspect. After childbirth, many women find they sometimes urinate as they come. Childbirth plays havoc with the pelvic floor muscles. Kegel exercises will put it right, and, incidentally, improve your sex life a hundredfold.

Pelvic floor exercises

The pelvic floor muscles support the pelvic floor and are part of the musculature which vibrates at orgasm.

Before exercising, find them by stopping and starting a full flow of

Naming the parts – basic male and female anatomy

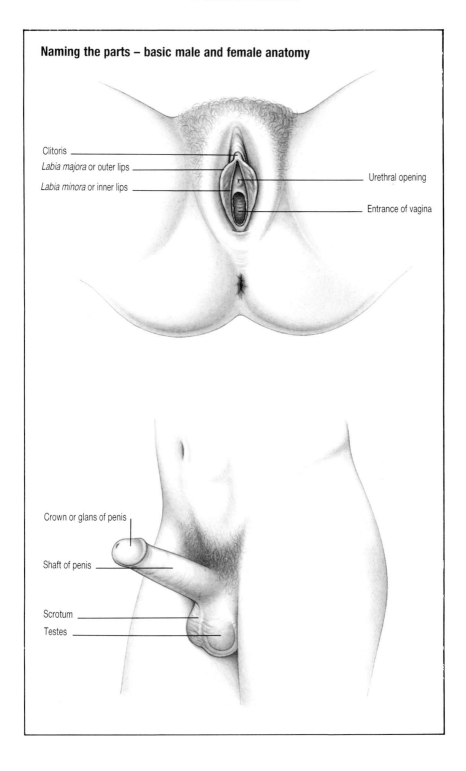

Clitoris

Labia majora or outer lips

Labia minora or inner lips

Urethral opening

Entrance of vagina

Crown or glans of penis

Shaft of penis

Scrotum

Testes

urine four or five times. This alone will improve pelvic floor muscle tone enormously.

Now try a vaginal kiss. Imagine the ring of muscle that becomes the orgasmic platform (see **Part two**, above). Tighten it, count to ten, and release. Practise this with a finger inside the vagina: you should be able to feel the finger, unless the muscles are very slack. Then practise with a penis inside, and/or practise kissing him like this. Anywhere. Everywhere.

We often exercise the pelvic floor muscles spontaneously when we make love. It is good to do it voluntarily, especially when he is being passive.

Now imagine you are sipping cider through a straw, or slurping up juice that has spilt. Use your vagina to suck. It will help if you suck with your mouth at the same time. If juice, why not a penis? Let him partially enter, and see if you can invite him further in.

Next, imagine you are lifting something up into your vagina. Start with a cherry. You are lifting it up from a chair. Manoeuvre until you have your vagina over it; then suck it in and chew. Suck and chew the flesh, then swallow it deep into your vagina. Don't forget to spit out the stone. It may help if you also chew with your mouth. This is a useful exercise to practise as you suck your man.

Now try using the vagina like a hand. Explore him with it. Let him turn over so that you can explore the curve of his bottom and thigh.

Finally, try crossing your legs and trying to pull your thighs apart, then putting a waste-paper basket between your thighs and squeezing. Extend the movement of the thighs to the pelvic floor, tightening and releasing the pelvic floor muscles as you hold the thighs steady. Having found the muscles, keep using them.

The mons

Most women who regularly reach orgasm know that even though the missionary is a rotten position for stimulating the clitoris, and pretty useless for the G spot, it can still work wondrously well. What does it stimulate besides our fancy? Most probably, the mons.

Masters and Johnson report that most women stimulate the mons during masturbation, and that women who have had clitorectomies can reach orgasm by stimulating the mons. They also say that women who have 'late' clitorectomies seem to carry on masturbating as if nothing much had changed.

Back to the breast

In many parts of the world, women are quite happy to leave the breasts entirely out of it (and most women in our culture manage to breast feed without a twinge of sexual stimulation). So, the way we feel is surely a result of conditioning: of expectations and past experience. If we have – for whatever reason – found pleasure in intercourse, some of that pleasure-producing potential will have 'rubbed off' on to other things. Maybe the clitoris once did it all for us. In time, other forms of arousal developed. We began to associate orgasm with those things that were happening to us at the time: like having our breasts nibbled, or his penis pushed hard into us, or even the heavy breathing and moans of his coming. There is no one place where we feel orgasm, and no one place where it is produced. It may well be that many women who answer surveys in the U.S.A. say that it has to include stimulation of the clitoris. We do not doubt that for them this is true. But elsewhere in the world, women reach orgasm without a clitoris. Some women claim that orgasm is difficult after their hysterectomy, others that it was never as good. Most of us would include kissing and having our breasts fondled as part of the orgasmic build-up. To others they are not essential.

Most of us know that we form certain expectations with our regular partner, that if we are good together, nobody actually has to do very much, as is the case with William and Francesca. On the other hand, if we have zero expectations of a particular person, no amount of twiddling the knobs will get us tuned in.

Is this all?

Is it just that William and Francesca know each other well? Is the secret in the head yet again? It may not be the whole truth, but we think it is probably most of the truth. If they had had a history of failure, this would surely colour their every coupling.

That does not mean there are not other factors at work in making them a near-perfect couple. They have had to pay attention to pure technique in the past, and still do. But these days the whole performance is usually so well tuned that she no longer thinks about it.

One thing Francesca knows for certain: that she likes having William inside her. She is sure that there is no single sensation of his being there: he feels different, for instance, when he comes in from the rear. She may describe her sensation as tickling her G spot, or rubbing her C spot; but what turns her on could also be stimulation of the mons, or the cervix, or even the look he gave her as he got into bed. Then again, it could be the pride he takes in her as a person, or the way he always knows when she feels a little down. Or all of these. A cocktail of physical and emotional responses, learned over a lifetime and mixed differently for every individual, in the head: the most erotic organ in the body.

GETTING TO KNOW GWEN

Gwen & Jack

Gwen

How to begin to tell you. Difficult for me. I was 42 before I even tried it. Nice girls didn't. Men could do it to you – but you mustn't do it to yourself.

Jim was often away at the time – still is – and I felt so much sexual need. Being menopausal, I suppose. Anyway, one night just before my period was due, I started to touch myself. Hesitant, I remember, until I discovered I didn't need to touch. That liberated me.

How? Well, take tonight.

I was watching TV when I began to feel I wanted to make love to myself. I say it like that, because that is what I feel it is. It makes me excited just thinking about it.

I gathered everything together: candles, matches, body oil, took them through to my bedroom. It wasn't very tidy, so I put away the clothes and took out the morning coffee cup, I never was into making love in messy places. I'm a romantic, I suppose. I closed the curtains, lit the candles and took the phone off the hook.

I don't undress at first – just take off my dress and stand in my slip in front of the mirror. I stroke my nipples, watching myself. I feel them hard under my fingers and begin to scratch them gently through the fabric using the nails of my forefingers. I watch my face.

Then I put on some music, undress and lie on the bed.

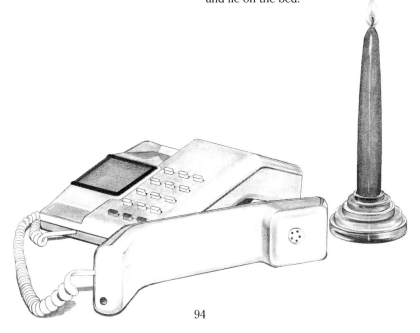

94

I like to oil my body, especially my breasts and down across my stomach and round to my bottom. I massage gently, breathing slowly and rhythmically as I do it. What's the point in speed? I could finish in minutes, but I like to slow it down a bit.

I lie on the bed, on my back at first, with my legs crossed. I squeeze, rhythmically, using my upper thighs, bottom and my pelvic floor.

I say to myself 'Gwen, this will be good.' A little chant sets up in my head. A rhythm I squeeze to.

As I get more excited, I roll over on my side, rocking back and forth and flicking my fingers across my nipples. Just before I reach orgasm, I cross my legs a second time at the ankles to make the squeeze really tight. I hold on to the squeeze, moving only the muscles of my pelvic floor.

I am stroking my breasts faster and squeezing my vagina. It feels empty, like an itch, a pain, a pleasure. I squeeze harder, my body is poised.

Then, a feeling of intense relief. Starting around the clitoris and in my pelvic muscles, and extending deep into my itching vagina. Then the contractions. I come down slowly.

I lie for maybe five minutes, feeling warm all over. Then I go and clear up the kitchen.

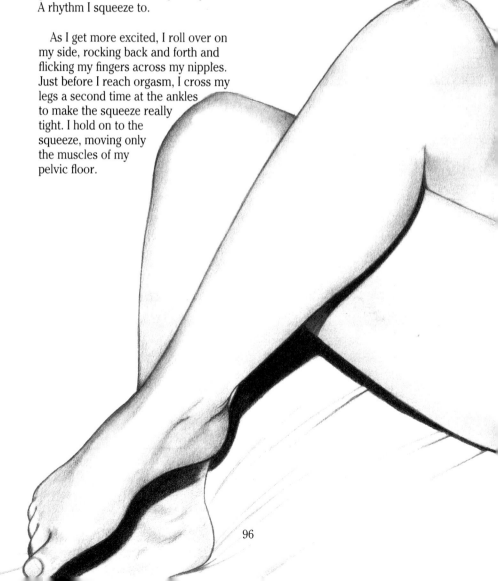

96

Meanwhile, across town . . .

As Gwen is tidying her room, across town Jack is bringing home a copy of *Wet*, a magazine for the labially inclined. The centrefold is a photograph of an open vagina taken at such close range that even her tonsils are visible. Sometimes he'll set the magazines up next to him in bed, lie on his back, and stroke himself to orgasm, spitting into his palm for lubrication. This evening, however, he sits down on the WC seat and unzips. His penis seems to him to jump out of his pants in anticipation. He rises to soap his hands and sees his erect member glowing redly in the mirror. He likes the look of it, standing out from his body at an upward angle, and runs his hand over its length. He puts the magazine down beside him and begins turning the pages with one hand. As he stares at the pictures and excites himself with his other hand, the pictures somehow become more three dimensional, more erotic.

On other occasions, Jack has dispensed with visual aids and concentrated on his fantasies. He has given up on his favourite actresses, thinking it fair only if they were offered royalties for appearing in his fantasies. He has thought instead of Darlene, the cute secretary who works in the office below his. She would smile at him as he slipped her knickers over her nice, shapely bum. And what if she were joined by the tall redhead who worked down the hall? Yes, the redhead could take off Darlene's knickers for him, bend her over, and spread her labia. The redhead would crouch down. He would withdraw from Darlene and unhurriedly enter the redhead's mouth. Ah, lovely.

Jack has a set of fantasies, and picks among them depending upon his mood. Mostly they are erotic, featuring women he knows and to whom he wants to make love. Occasionally, there are aggressive ones, as when he has seen a woman, or women, he cannot possibly ever have. These are about rape and even dismemberment. How would a detached breast look?

Jack has masturbated since he was ten, to ejaculation since he was 13, sometimes several times a day, never less than twice a week. He thinks his masturbatory habits immature and has never discussed them with male friends. Once he told a lover that he did it while thinking of her, supposing she would consider it a tribute to her sexual attractiveness. She was disgusted and didn't want to hear any more. Sometimes masturbation is an anodyne for loneliness, sometimes it's a soporific when he can't get to sleep. Occasionally he has masturbated from residual excitement after a night of sex with a lover. He has even masturbated in his office once or twice with the door closed.

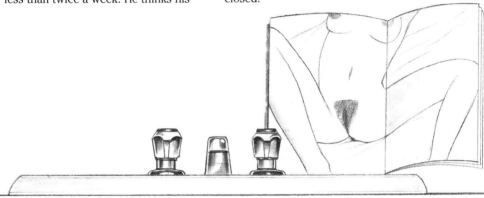

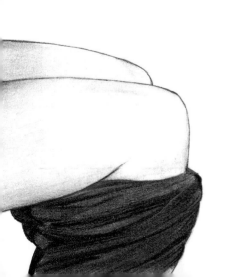

As an adolescent, Jack could come in under a minute, and almost always did so. Tonight, in the bathroom, he decides to draw it out. He stops stroking for a moment and just holds himself. Then he changes his mind and switches to very short, rapid strokes just behind the head of his cock. There is that feeling of warmth, of hardness, and then the sensation of imminence. Thoughts and images vanish as he closes his eyes and concentrates on the sensation. He throws back his head and grunts as he comes. Jack prefers sex with a woman, but this, this is so easy. He lets go and washes himself off, gingerly. He is always a little sensitive just afterwards.

Masturbation was once a temptation to which one gave way for want of character or control; now, as Gwen and Jack settle into their respective rhythms, we might ask where the guilt went. Apart from Gwen's 'hands-off' technique, it seems to have evaporated.

Party time

As you read this, somewhere out there a group of ordinary women – call them suburban wives and mothers – are gathering for a 'sales party': an evening of coffee, cake, and hard sell. Last week it was children's clothes; this week it is sexual aids. The number-one seller is a penis-sized vibrator. Sex aids can still be found in the small ads of soft porn magazines, but increasingly, the outlets of this multi-million pound industry are home parties; the customers, women. Thirty years ago, who could have predicted that ordinary women would be stretching their housekeeping to buy pulsating shower heads?

Vibrators are not just for personal use, nor, of course, are they just for plugging into the clitoris. Try giving yourself a whole body massage with one before zoning in on the genitalia. (The French make a remarkable spongy massager which is about four feet long and looks for all the world like an overgrown phallus – but they all do essentially the same job.)

Tuning into the same vibrations is incidentally, well worth a try. We have been told that a small vibrator in her anus, and a penis in her vagina, works wonders. The less adventurous, or more fastidious, may prefer the penis between the thighs and the vibrator on the clitoris. She will need to cross her legs to keep everything in place. Best not to thrust, but he can move around to suit, and she can of course squeeze him, and it, into position.

Into the bathroom

Masturbation may have come out of the closet to join Jack in the bathroom; but he is still glad of the lock on the door. It is a very private occupation, for which the bathroom is the most popular venue. But it is also a respectable subject for scientific research: over the years, the sexologists Masters and Johnson watched hundreds of men and women masturbating, most of them ordinary married folk.

Masturbation is private, and people are nosy; it is natural to wonder whether Gwen and Jack are typical. The answer: he is, she is not.

Among men, Masters and Johnson found a standard theme with few variations. Not so women. Gwen is not typical because no woman is: women are all variations and no theme. Almost every woman has her own unique style. Gwen's pleasuring is just one way to do it.

Is this difference because men lack imagination, or because women

There is no really wrong way to do this, but some men get in the habit of holding themselves so tightly that they later find a vagina does not give them sufficient stimulation. Loosen up, guys. And, for your information, the reason the head of the cock is bigger than the shaft is to prevent your hand from slipping off and poking you in the eye.

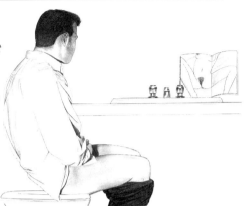

fail to see the obvious? We suspect neither. Once you look beneath the surface, what Jack and Gwen are doing is not that different. He just has a more obvious way of going about it. Because the bits Jack has to stimulate come more obviously to hand.

Gwen, like most women, does not find penetration essential or even necessary. Like Jack, she is pleasured by rubbing the parts which fill with blood: that means both labia and the area which lies between.

Male and female genitalia are sometimes depicted as his hand and her glove; a better analogy might be rubbing an itch by poking a finger in a hole, compared with rubbing a hand against the bark of a tree.

In order to see exactly why this is so, it is worth coming to grips with how male and female genitalia develop, from conception.

John Ellen

Imagine that Jack and Gwen are variations on a single theme, as indeed they are. Both male and female genitalia start off in the foetus as exactly the same structure: call it John Ellen. The key to understanding the similarities of Gwen's and Jack's sexual arousal is to realize that for each part of his sexual anatomy, she has a corresponding part. See the illustration.

For his foreskin, read her clitoral hood; for his scrotum, read her labia. When we ask each other, "How does that feel?", the best answer is, probably, "Much the same as it does to you".

What does John Ellen look like? It is, more or less, a mini penis together with a slit and some swellings of skin behind and on either side of it: half-man, half-woman.

At about six weeks after conception, everyone has a John Ellen, though the foetus destined to become a boy has also by now begun to develop testes. These testes are not in the scrotum as they are after birth, but in the body cavity. Nevertheless, they manufacture the hormone testosterone, which acts on John Ellen to make it develop into John Thomas, or male genitalia.

A foetus destined to become a girl waits a week or two, and then, having made sure there is no testosterone about, goes ahead to make Mary Ellen: female genitalia. At this stage, girls have working ovaries, but female hormones play no part in development: John Ellen listens only to one chemical 'messenger', testosterone.

So John Thomas and Mary Ellen share the same original structure; their difference is in the way they grow up.

John Thomas

John Ellen becomes John Thomas essentially by being 'zipped up'. First the slit is closed, making a column of spongy tissue which extends right up to the mini penis. The urethra passes through this tissue out to the mini penis, properly called the tubercle. This will be the front third and the head of the penis.

Next, the two inner folds fuse together and join the lower part of this column. Together, these three form the shaft of the penis. The little

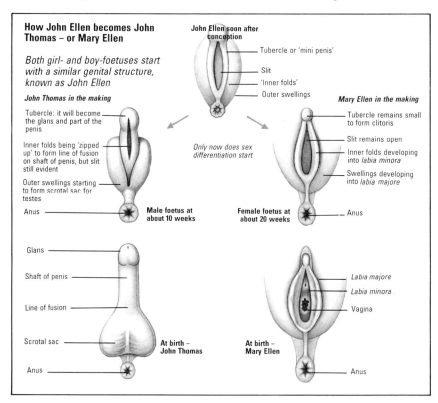

How John Ellen becomes John Thomas – or Mary Ellen

Both girl- and boy-foetuses start with a similar genital structure, known as John Ellen

John Ellen soon after conception
— Tubercle or 'mini penis'
— Slit
— 'Inner folds'
— Outer swellings

Only now does sex differentiation start

John Thomas in the making

Tubercle: it will become the glans and part of the penis

Inner folds being 'zipped up' to form line of fusion on shaft of penis, but slit still evident

Outer swellings starting to form scrotal sac for testes

Anus

Male foetus at about 10 weeks

Mary Ellen in the making

Tubercle remains small to form clitoris
Slit remains open
Inner folds developing into *labia minora*
Swellings developing into *labia majore*
Anus

Female foetus at about 20 weeks

Glans
Shaft of penis
Line of fusion
Scrotal sac
Anus

At birth – John Thomas

Labia majore
Labia minora
Vagina
Anus

At birth – Mary Ellen

tubercle at the top expands to become the glans or crown (the sensitive tip of the penis) and is covered by a little hood of skin, the foreskin. All three columns of the shaft are wrapped in skin and the whole thing hangs down from the body.

When 'zipped up', the shaft encloses three empty spaces; later, when the man is sexually excited, all three will fill with blood. It is the rubbing of this engorged tissue which feels good to Jack.

Meanwhile, the outer swellings have expanded to form a two-pouched bag into which the testes (balls) descend just before birth.

Boy and man, he will carry the 'stitch marks' of his making. The little seam along which it was all 'zipped up' can be seen on the underside of the penis shaft.

Mary Ellen

As you would expect, the slit remains open if a baby girl is to be the outcome, and the tissue around it forms the bottom third of the vagina. It is arranged in two bands between the labia. Where the two bands meet at the front is the clitoris, which began as the tubercle. So the bottom third of the vagina is the counterpart to the spongy tissue forming the shaft of the penis.

The swellings and folds remain separate. The outer ones (which form the scrotum) are now the *labia majora* – fleshy folds, hairy on one side, smooth on the other. The inner folds (the ones that come together to make a penis) become the *labia minora*. These come in all shapes and sizes, and are often much more prominent than the outer folds. Some women, and men, think them ugly, and go as far as to get them beautified by plastic surgery. (Could you imagine him shaving a slice off his penis in the name of neatness?)

The tubercle remains small, and forms the outer part of the clitoris. Sometimes it is difficult to see, because not only is it small, but it is enclosed in a hood, this being the counterpart of his foreskin. Another incomprehensible operation involves taking away this hood: its foolishness will be appreciated in reflecting on how Gwen and most other women masturbate. Indirect stimulation of the clitoris is what Gwen, and most women, find so good. (Much better than the heavy hand on the clit.) The hood is attached to the labia and tickles the clitoris delightfully each time they move. So why cut it free?

Befriend a pussy

Where better than a discussion on masturbation to urge everyone concerned to make friends with female genitalia?

Standard advice is for women to hold a mirror to the crotch. You can do this 'cold' or, better still, while feeling sexy, when you will see the colour and the swellings. You may feel brazen as you witness your own excitement. More power to your fantasies. If Jack can have a clear view, why not Gwen? The sight of Jack's ramrod cock adds to his excitement; why shouldn't Gwen benefit too?

The theory of the parts

If we suggest to Jack that he pushes his penis between his legs and squeezes rhythmically, there would be an exact parallel with Gwen. Her 'penis' is not only her clitoris, but her labia and the area between them as well. Forget that it is flat and spread out, and that quite a chunk of it is under the surface. Obviously, there is no question of wrapping a hand around it, but she can, and does, stimulate it from all sides as she squeezes. The movement of the thighs squeezes the labia at the front, and squirming and squeezing the mons pulls the labia against the clitoris. The internal movement of her pelvic floor muscles (see also **William & Francesca,** pages 84-85) provides some additional stimulation from behind. (Some women find penetration gives a similar effect.)

If nothing else, masturbation puts us in the picture about our genitalia: through it we learn, more precisely than anyone else, how we are to be pleasured. Understanding the other sex's genitalia, and how he or she gains pleasure through masturbation, is surely one of the keys to the treasure chest.

When did they start?

Jack has masturbated since he was a teenager, Gwen came to it much later: a not atypical pattern. As a teenager, Gwen knew touching herself 'down there' was dirty, so she did not do it. Jack felt guilty at first, but did. In the past, there was no uncertainty about masturbation: it was disgusting and positively dangerous. A man could go blind, be plagued by warts and acne, and eventually become insane. Masturbation drained him of his semen and used up his manhood.

As well as blindness and acne, she ran the risk of uterine disorders, bad breath, nymphomania, ugliness and a long, lingering death.

Since nymphomania and blindness were rare – at least in the leisured classes – the Victorians must have felt reassured that masturbation was uncommon except among the insane and 'low' men and women. This view continued until Kinsey published his research into the sexuality of the American male and female around 1950. By then, 92 per cent of men and 62 per cent of women owned up to masturbating at some time in their lives. Today, some surveys suggest that the figures for women are on a par with those for 1950s men, while men push up towards the 100 per cent mark. Although magazine surveys probably over-estimate the true levels, Jack and Gwen can rest assured they are not alone tonight. In our different ways, most of us have been here.

Effects of masturbation

Kinsey, and all the surveys that have followed, show that most women, like men, first reach orgasm while masturbating. It may be significant that for men this usually happens *before* they have had intercourse, but for women it is often afterwards. This pattern was certainly true for Jack, although Gwen had experienced occasional orgasms from intercourse before she began to masturbate. She would claim masturbating has made orgasm during intercourse more reliable; others would argue that she is simply more experienced.

Female masturbation has had a good press in recent years, partly for the advantage which Gwen believes it gives. Some people say that those who masturbate simply have more sex drive and more experience of sex than those who do not, but we think that this is an oversimplification. Gwen's masturbation has expanded her experience of orgasm and sexual pleasuring. She knows what feels good, and how to get herself into the right mental and physical 'position' to make it happen. In her teenage years she was inclined to ignore, even avoid, signs of arousal. In common with other women who do not masturbate, she probably developed a subtle pattern of withdrawal from sexual contact, and an unconscious way of suppressing her sexual feelings and tensions. She was probably not aware that she did this.

Some therapists believe that the responses men and women learn when they avoid 'giving in' to sexual desire may be hard to forget. This is one of the reasons that they recommend masturbation as a voyage of self-discovery.

Why do women masturbate less?

For Gwen, masturbation is an occasional activity, carried out when her husband is away on business. For Jack, even within a relationship, it is fairly regular. Since she began to masturbate, Gwen could point to long periods during which she never gave it a thought, but Jack would be hard pressed to find a single clear month. However we look at masturbation, whether it is the age of onset or the regularity of indulgence, we are faced with a difference between men and women. Men start earlier and do it more often and more regularly than women. By 20, most men have clocked up at least four figures' worth of orgasms. Most women have not yet crossed the starting line. Why?

Explanation number one is that women find it harder to discover their genitalia than men do. Not discounting the fact that women are more likely to get lost in a new place, this is surely bordering on the mythological. After all, a 13-year-old girl has wiped her genitalia front to back with toilet tissue four or more times a day from the age of two.

Explanation number two is that men wank more because the penis is so accessible. While erections announce themselves with greater force than vaginal lubrication, masturbation without hands is impossible for Jack, whereas Gwen can squeeze her legs together as she stands in the bus queue; she can sit on the arm of a chair, or the edge of the bath, and rub up and down; she can ride a bike, sit on a vibrating spin-drier or simply arch her back and push her pussy flat on to a hard-surfaced chair. She can do all these things without anyone noticing and, best of all, she can stop immediately if disturbed. There is no incriminating evidence, such as the erection in his hand. Only if vaginal insertion is essential for successful masturbation – and less than seven per cent of women say this is so – does this argument hold.

Explanation number three is that men have more intense or pervasive sex drives. It is certainly true that men have a more sexualized view of social encounters, and if we take gay men as a marker of 'pure' male rates of sexual activity, and gay women as a marker for women, then men are more sexually active. However, all of these differences and more may be due to different social conditioning.

Explanation number four has at least a few elements of truth: it is that men are naturally more aware of sexual arousal. Obviously, an erection is difficult to miss; and sexy is the way you feel when the penis is big. Once he has made this connection, he can recognize sexual arousal by the bulge in his trousers. Even if he wanted to suppress the feeling, the bulge tells him otherwise. (Which gives ample basis for feelings of guilt, and an easy association between guilt and arousal.)

Her sexual responsiveness is harder to learn, and easier to hide. Women do seem to be able to suppress the connection between vaginal lubrication and sexual arousal. Perhaps some women learn only

No two women do it the same way. Use your style as a guide to the intercourse positions which suit you. If you cross your legs like this you'll probably prefer intercourse positions where you can keep your legs together.

to recognize arousal in the 'right' context: when with a man. For her, there is little need for guilt: suppression will suffice.

The most likely explanation for women masturbating less than men, given recent changes in its popularity, is that society has told women that female sexuality is something to be awakened by a man: a passive pleasuring induced by love. In as far as society has changed its mind, so have many women.

Ways women masturbate

Gwen crosses her legs and squeezes. Most women place a hand over the mons and stimulate the entire genital area with hand or fingers. Some close their legs, others keep them open. A few women squeeze the little root of the clitoris from the side. Then there are those that insert something – fingers, deodorant bottles (see **Lise**, pages 30-33), hairbrush handles – into the vagina: men who worry about penis size may be pleased to note how small most of these objects are. Some direct sprays of water on to the genital area; some stimulate the breasts at the same time. Most, like men, stimulate quite directly. Whatever men and women want from intercourse, masturbation tends to be fairly and squarely centred on the genitalia. Jack, like many men, avoids stimulating the glans directly; in this he is in good company: very few women go directly for the clitoris. Both are ultra-sensitive.

Sexual release vs social sex

Masturbation is often considered to be something we do from sorry need. Which indeed we do. But the need filled by masturbation may be altogether different from the need filled by intercourse. For some, masturbation merely replaces sex with a partner, for others, it runs in parallel. The more they have of one, the more they want of the other.

After he has gone, or when he is away for a while, a woman can become especially aware of this. However often we come alone, it does not fulfil sexual need. The need is for a man.

That men pay prostitutes for straight sex bears this out, especially if you consider that many report their most intense orgasms during masturbation.

Fantasy

Jack knows that his mind is the most erogenous zone of his body. Fantasy heightens sexual arousal – to the limit. Both men and women can come on fantasy alone, although it is more common in women. It might be a day-dream or a night-dream, but more often than not it happens in that state somewhere between sleeping and waking.

Tonight, like most nights, it is visual images, and a simple story incorporating women he knows. In contrast to the female fantasies in which male figures are often masked, hidden or anonymous, Jack will save up a clear-cut image of a particular woman glimpsed earlier in the day, to be played back later on his mental screen.

Three in the bed

Jack's most treasured fantasy involves having two or more of these women successively, maybe even simultaneously. He imagines sampling the willing girls, blondes, brunettes and redheads, dipping into each like a bee buzzing greedily in a garden of beautiful open flowers. Very different from how multiple sex turns out in practice: the effort of arranging feasible positions, the feelings of jealousy, the unrelenting effort and, ultimately, rug burn (not enough room in the bed).

Day-dreams and realities

His elaborate, day-dream form of fantasies illustrate basic sexual themes of male life. Since he is always wondering, 'Will she, or won't she?', his fantasies dwell on female willingness in one way or another. His thoughts become enlarged and shiny as the unconscious secretes layer upon layer of pearly invention around the gritty little pebble of female reluctance. A common one is 'I am the hero': he bravely stops a run-away coach with a trembling maiden inside; which leads with almost no need for persuasion to a graceful coupling. In these rescue fantasies, his cleverness, strength and courage are sufficient to win her; no danger of rejection of sex or masculinity here. Similarly, the lascivious housewife who seduces him as soon as he opens her door is too horny to be critical of his technique.

Another, related fantasy, is 'Do women really *really* want me?' A lifetime spent trying to persuade reluctant ladies makes him ask this question every day. Fantasies in which women initiate sex provide the reassuring answer, hence the popularity of female masturbation and lesbian activity as soft porn subject matter. The same unconscious preoccupation emerges in a different perspective when he masturbates, or has sex with one woman while another woman looks on approvingly. (This is again seen in pornographic videos.) Gadgetry provides another way around the problem of her compliance: mirror arrangements, and trap doors with chutes leading into the bedroom provide further scenarios.

S. & M. fantasies

For some, these themes can be discovered in more unlikely fantasies. A careful reading of stories of sado-masochism shows that the woman either gives her permission ('I'm a bad girl, whip me'); or her punishment turns to pleasure ('I whipped her until she came'). More difficult to explain are the S. & M. fantasies in which men themselves are the objects of humiliation and torture. (There is a discussion of the role of guilt in male sexuality in **Marcus & Alex**, pages 44-59.)

At the extreme end of the erotic spectrum are the fantasies of rape. In most men, for whom rape is not a way of life, these fantasies can be traced to a preceding anger at a particular woman for a real insult or an imagined slight. 'All I wanted was a smile, a chat, some sign of respect while we conducted our business. She was uninterested, cold, unpleasant. I'll teach the bitch a lesson.' No negotiation with women needed here.

Women's fantasies

Do women's fantasies differ from men's? Their cultural heritage is different. Like men's fantasy, women's frequently depict them as stepping outside the controls on their behaviour. Fantasy woman has power and pleasure; is wanton and free.

• She has sex in forbidden places: churches, supermarkets, the dentist's chair – with forbidden people: the doctor, a neighbour, a friend's husband or a stranger.

• She grants favours, and witholds sex as punishment. Frequently, she fantasizes about holding this power over many men. Rampant with desire, she keeps them at bay: she is all-powerful, not powerless.

• She is watched, or watches others through keyholes. She blatantly exhibits her sexuality, having it in a busy hotel foyer in full view of an appreciative audience. Sex is not secret, it is open; she is admired for her sexuality, admired for enjoying it.

• She is a prostitute with men lining up to take her. She has pleasure and power without degradation.

• She meets him half-way up the stairs, enjoys him, and then carries on up to the next floor: she is free, sex has no consequences. Fantasy lets her shout against controls; as it does him.

Fantasy is a way of coming to terms with your inhibitions, a way of playing with your sexual worries as well as with your wildest dreams. Mostly though, it is just a way to turn you on, to up the pace, and to hold you delightfully on the edge before you jump.

PAUL, ROSIE

AND THE LUMPKIN

Paul & Rosie

Afternoon

Rosie

"Would you like another cup of coffee? No, I don't mind making it. You know, I feel like a ship in full sail. I go ploughing along regardless. Nothing fazes me. I feel so good. I think I'm beginning to understand sexuality. I suppose this is how men feel; and the girls I knew at school who chased boys constantly. I wake up sexy, I'm even tempted to lock my office door and masturbate at lunchtime. Can you imagine? It's never happened before. It's hard not to jump on Paul the minute he gets home."

Paul

"Want another beer? It's on me."

"August was the worst. As soon as I come into kitchen she puts her arms around me. I'm hot and sticky, all I have on my mind is a cold beer and the next thing you know, there's a lot of rubbing and bumping and squirming. Maybe she'll hit me with "You haven't got a headache, have you?" At least then I could dodge with stuff about the pollen count. I hate to tell you, there hasn't been any action in months. At first, back in May, June she looked

good. You know me, I'm not really a tit man in any major way, but . . . she has this white blouse with this, uh, frilly thing, this fringe in front. She would put it on, it looked full, like promising. You could really see the difference when she stood sideways. She would be getting undressed, take off her bra, and her breasts would knock me out. Her nipples are darker, the skin is tight and smooth. It was a real turn on, but then I'd look at her face. She looked so tired, like she was sleep walking. It just killed it for me. And she wasn't interested herself."

"Yes, I've got to go too. So like I was saying, by last month she was hot all the time. I can't figure it. Here she is all bloated, with that big belly, and she wants to get it on. It wasn't like that before she got pregnant. I used to have to coax her. The thing is, now I really can't get it up for her, the way she looks. Oh, hell, it's probably not good for her, or for the kid, either, for that matter. She should be thinking about being a mother. See you."

* * * *

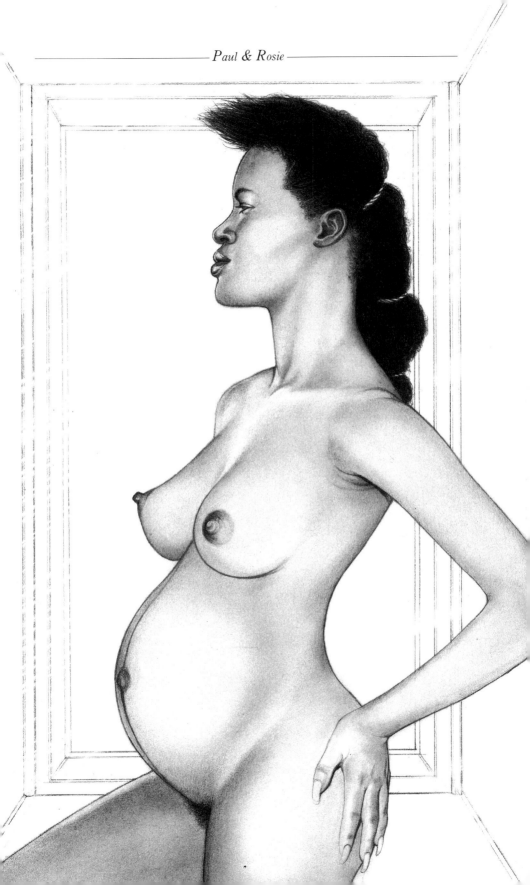

That evening

Paul

The kitchen smells nice. I can tell that she's been out in the sun. The freckles make her look young and cute, like a teenager. And she has those streaks in hair, really pretty. Mostly, though, it's her face, it sort of glows. She looks very happy. And here I am, bitching and moaning, wanting to hug her because of the kid but not wanting her. Before, when things clicked, it used to be great. I'd put her on top of me and we'd go for a long ride. Sometimes she would play that she was the trucker. She would horse around with my pecker like it was a CB, talk into it, stuff like that. We had a good time. We will again, but not now.

She wants me to love her and what can I say? I put my hand on her belly. "What will the Lumpkin think?" It's a delaying tactic. Before she can answer, I'm down on my knees, my face against her belly. "Hey, you in there, I'm talking to you. Listen, are you ready for a little fun, a little excitement in your life. You ready for the old white snake attack?" I turn my head, pressing my ear against her belly. "Ol' Lumpkin, he lay low. Wait, wait a minute. Ol' Lumpkin don't want no snakes, he says 'Keep them snakes out.'."

Rosie laughs. "I know what Lumpkin really says. That I love you."

Paul

"I love you too, baby. I don't need to cross my fingers. I do."

Rosie likes it when I clown around. I pick her up because she likes that, too, it shows her that she is still my girl. But clowning around only holds things for a while. I'm leaving earlier in the morning, coming home later at night. At the beginning I thought, OK, I'll hang around, I'll just hire my truck out for local jobs. Now I'm making longer runs. The doc says everything is fine, maybe I'll go for a transcontinental run, stay out for a week or two. The money wouldn't hurt.

Rosie

I have never felt so close to him as I have these last months. Paul is a big man. I like it when he holds me, it makes me feel *petite* and feminine. I like his big arms, too. I wasn't too wild about the hair all over him, but now I don't mind. It's kind of sexy. I have never been so excited by the thought of him inside me. I'm going to kiss him.

Paul

That's my kid in there. When we first found out that she was carrying, I felt great. I was superman, I could impregnate the living room sofa if I wanted to. I come from a big family, I want kids, lots of kids. Lumpkin, Mr or Miss, is only going to be the first. I feel such warmth for Rosie. Being in bed with the mother of my kid was great at the beginning, even if she wasn't too interested. Once she began to show, it was different, it was like being in bed with a real mother'. Rosie always kisses good, her mouth is real soft. It always turned me on, but now, how about a good night kiss and that's about it.

* * * *

Night

Paul

She is hauling her great bulk around, like me behind the wheel of my truck. I say: "What, no preliminaries?"

Rosie

I laugh. "I thought you could sort of stuff it in. Then we'll see what happens."

Paul

"Just for that I'll make you suck me." She laughs and says, "Make me," and I say, "No sucky, no fucky, house rules."

I love her, that's for sure. Her skin, her breasts, are so beautiful, but her belly just gets to me. I guess you can't help it, what you feel and what you don't. I miss her old shape, but it's more than that. There's something creepy about the thought of the Lumpkin in there. There's one too many people in this bed. I bury my face in her hair. It's not house rules, but necessity.

Rosie

I know he isn't excited. I continue, regardless, laughing like a schoolgirl. It's still all floppy so I say, "We'll have to see what we can do with this." I'm bouncing along, knowing I can get my way.

Paul

She goes burrowing down under the blankets. Sucks me right up. I close my eyes. I want to tell her I love her. I feel . . .

"Rosie." She lifts her head, grinning. I look down at her head peeping up, all surrounded by the sheet.

"Hello, trucker," she says. I feel so protective towards her. I want her. This time, I'm ready for her when she lies on her side, pushing her back into me.

Rosie

I want to prolong it. "I'm feeling really greedy."

Paul

"Happy to be of service." I say it, not really meaning it all the way. "You can always come in my hand." Even though my heat is up, it still doesn't seem right that she should want it now. She is a mother, and looks it.

Rosie

It takes so little. Wham bam and I'm there, wham bam and I've done it again. He is pumping faster now. Caressing my clitoris with one hand. I can feel myself ready to crescendo. Staying there, still ready to leap. Then I can't help it any more. I'm gone.

Paul

Yesterday I held Maggie's baby. It sucked against my cheek. It's ridiculous, but I keep thinking of Lumpkin in there getting ready to suck me.

"I can't come."

Rosie

"Here, let me hold you. It's alright, don't worry. You can't hurt him. He's in his bag, all safe."

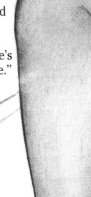

114

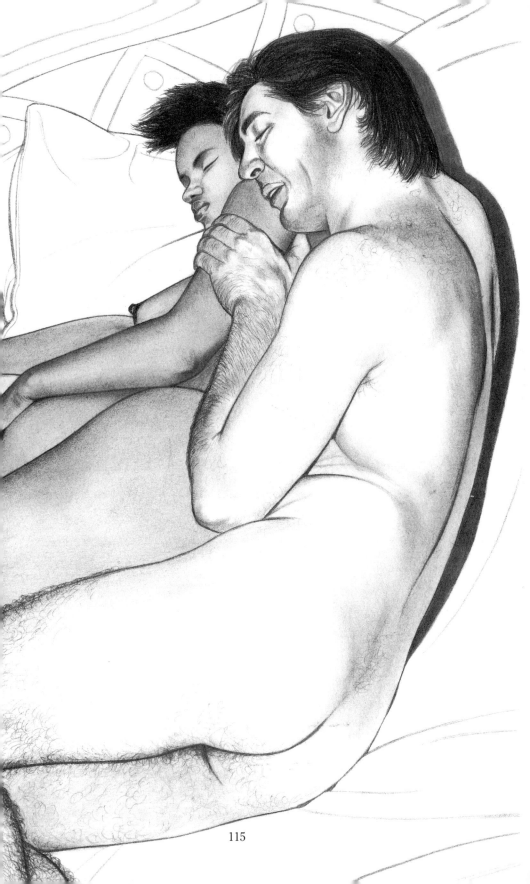

Paul cannot think of the pregnant Rosie in the way he used; and nor, come to that, does the rest of the world. Quite apart from her swollen belly being a turn-off, Paul suspects that from now on sex will be dull and infrequent. What is at the root of his anxiety?

At least part of it is surely the conviction that mothers should be asexual: a hang-over from the adolescent view of procreation, in which parents come on heat, like dogs, for a brief but serviceable coupling; sex was not something they did for fun. As Paul watches Rosie becoming more motherly every day, he feels he should become more like a parent, too. But that is not all.

Like all boys, Paul grew up knowing that mothers were taboo. The love of a son for his mother cannot be otherwise. The strength of the taboo shows in the incest statistics: mother-son sexual liasons are extremely rare, even though the bond can be very close.

Paul is uneasy about the mother in his bed, but has no one in whom to confide his feelings. So, like many men, he lets his body provide the escape mechanism. Temporary impotence is not uncommon when men are insecure about sex. Women who have shared a man's first steps into adultery know that his conscience, all of sudden, can reside in his penis. (They often say, in their own defence, that the mind was strong, but the body weak; in truth, it is probably the other way round.)

Confusions

Not only Paul, but society at large, has a confused attitude to motherhood. Rosie will hear from one quarter that this is fulfilment; from another that it is a denial of her potential as an individual. This contradiction does not help Paul's feeling of being on the outside. He sees Rosie in full bloom, carrying the Lumpkin, strong, happy and sure. Yet as he drives his truck on a spring morning, radio playing, glad to be alive and happy in his work, he knows that if he were Rosie, he would not want to give up his male world of work for a baby. He agrees with the contemporary propaganda emphasizing her sacrifice. And after all, the baby was his idea.

And now that it is on the way, he realizes he has lined himself up for the greatest sacrifice of all: to have, to love, and then to lose his child. What would Rosie say if he told her this worried him?

It is a difficult balancing act. At one moment he is expected to be the strong back that supports Rosie and the coming child; the next, he must be sensitive and caring, a second mother. It is true that women take on both roles – of provider and of carer – but if a mother has a partner, she is not *expected* to work outside the home when the offspring are small; many do, but we are talking here of expectations.

Men, on the other hand, are expected to perform the traditional role of supporting the family, *and* to share childcare and housework. Some, of course, don't do either, but many, these days, try to do both. There is, nonetheless, more criticism of men for not helping enough at home than there are suggestions that she should meet him half way with the financial burden of supporting the family.

Blooming

Is it hormones that make Rosie feel so good in the middle months of pregnancy? Or just the excitement of the developing baby? One thing is certain, that although the majority of women find the early months of a first pregnancy a sexual turn-off, the middle months can be a time of high sexual excitment. Never so consistently good is the most common verdict. Orgasm comes easily, reliably and multiply.

Why this is so may have less to do with hormonal balance than with her general feeling of well being. The increased blood supply to the breasts, womb and pelvic floor mimic sexual arousal. Womb and breasts are bigger, the increased blood supply to her vagina produces slight but constant lubrication. Vaginal lubricating fluid is blood without the bigger cells, including the red corpuscles. It is pushed out of the arteries under pressure during sexual excitement (the artery walls acting something like sieves) because during arousal so much blood is trapped in the pelvic region. If Rosie feels as if she is half way there, she is right, if only in terms of the blood supply to her pelvic region and breasts.

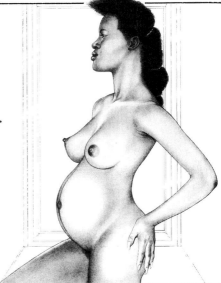

Somehow, the whole world has begun to look pregnant to Rosie. The middle months of pregnancy, with their heightened libido and sense of well-being, often bring a new sense of closeness, especially with close female friends, sisters, mothers. They are somehow part of the act; whereas Paul feels outside it. With all that emotional support, Rosie feels strong. No coincidence that she is pictured here standing alone, revelling in her sense of independence and fulfilment.

Sex during pregnancy: practicalities

From the medical point of view, there are rarely any reasons why a couple should not make love throughout pregnancy. Her womb will exercise itself with a few contractions each time she reaches orgasm, but they happen anyway during pregnancy, sex or not. Muscles need exercising. Except where there is a danger of miscarriage, sex probably does more good than harm and women who have reliable orgasms are thought to have easier births.

It must be said, however, that during the first three months the breasts are usually tender, and that the extra blood flow of sexual arousal can make excitement painful; but often enough this does not arise because anyway she is too tired and sickly to be interested.

In the middle three months this stops being a problem, but in the final three months there may be new difficulties. Many women feel short of breath and physically uncomfortable until the baby drops into the birth channel. Once this happens, there are renewed (but generally unnecessary) fears of harming the baby. Some women also find that the contractions which usually follow orgasm are now quite painful.

Sex during pregnancy: the fun

If we think about sex at all before pregnancy, we probably assume that love-making during these months should be a sedate, predictable business. But sex during pregnancy can be highly charged and passionate, not to say loving and warm. The best positions are probably side by side, woman on top, spoons or doggie.

Your sexual preferences may well change. Perhaps because of the vaginal discharge, many couples report a reduction in oral sex, and some women say that they are less interested in vaginal sex. There is a time towards the end of pregnancy when intercourse may be difficult, and a time after the birth when it will be impossible. If mutual masturbation is not yet in your sexual repertoire, now is the time to introduce it.

In love, but out of tune

As Paul amd Rosie show, it is possible to love your partner, but not to want sex. Paul was turned on by her initial blossoming; now it is different. Rosie will probably feel less sexy as labour day approaches; that, at least, will get him off the hook.

You can't have a baby without losing your figure, and although, ideally, Paul should accept the heavier thighs and protruding belly, he is conditioned to the pin-ups he has plastered in his cab. After all, women have conditioned preferences, too.

After the birth

Sexual excitment will develop slowly, if at all. To begin with, vaginal lubrication will be sparse. The vagina stays pinkish, as do the labia. The orgasmic platform (the swelling at the entrance to the vagina) develops, but is relatively small. Orgasm, if it occurs at all, is often less intense then previously.

If Rosie has no stitches, she can expect to get back to normal by about three months, maybe longer.

Out of 71 husbands interviewed after the birth of a child, 31 had withdrawn from intercourse in the last three months, some because they feared hurting her, others for no obvious reason. Only five found their partners' bodies a turn-off. Twelve began affairs; six others had affairs immediately after the babies were born.

In a survey of women three months after delivery, almost half reported little or no sexual interest. Breast feeding seemed to increase sexual desire. Some women reported sexual feelings while suckling; even orgasm sometimes occured.

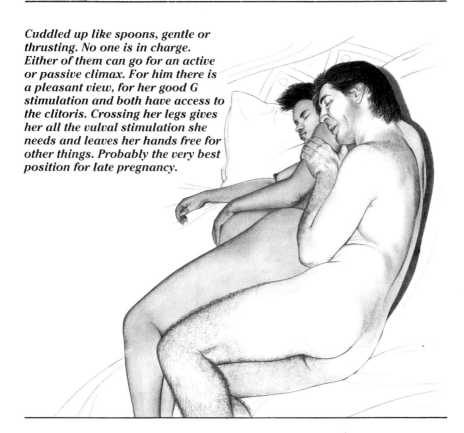

Cuddled up like spoons, gentle or thrusting. No one is in charge. Either of them can go for an active or passive climax. For him there is a pleasant view, for her good G stimulation and both have access to the clitoris. Crossing her legs gives her all the vulval stimulation she needs and leaves her hands free for other things. Probably the very best position for late pregnancy.

The breasts

Normally, the breasts enlarge during sexual arousal. The nipples become erect and increase in length. As she enters the plateau phase of sexual excitment, the areola becomes engorged. All in all, the breasts often grow by a quarter.

When she is breast feeding (and often afterwards) the suckled breast rarely grows by anything like this amount. The more children she suckles, the less her breast size changes with excitment. After a few children, Rosie's breasts will have lost some of their supporting fibrous tissue. Nursing women often spurt breast milk as they come. Others find they let down milk when they think lovingly of their man.

Not in front of the children?

Spontaneity goes out of the window when babies come in through the door, and more or less stays out until the children leave home. Parents feel that it is right to protect children from theirsexuality – even when children are old enough to expose us to theirs. Is this a reliable instinct? There is probably no way of telling, except perhaps to judge for yourself how children of one-parent families turn out. They are probably exposed, more than children of conventional families, to the sexual nature, but not usually the sexual activity, of a parent.

Power

Men are powerful. Over the past two decades, the feminist movement has made us all ultra-aware of that power, and how it can be abused in relationships with women. Rape is but an extreme version of something which is within the experience of most women (and men). Sex can hurt, whether it is a man pushing a woman beyond her stopping point, or a husband who fucks everything that moves, then comes home for more. Which does not mean that she cannot hurt him. She can and she does.

Men have feelings. And when they show these feelings, women think them good and beautiful. Men make commitments to women and when children come along they are there at the birth and ready to change the nappies. When men show love and sadness, women feel their vulnerability is special. Many men have answered the calls of feminists; show the feminine side of their nature.

Sometimes women appreciate the changes; and sometimes they expect more. Often, they give little in return. They cling to their instinctive belief (or did they learn it from their mothers?) that the way to change a man, or simply to get things done they way they want them, is to nag him until he gives in out of desperation. Such women don't believe in meeting their partners half way.

Too many women seem to be unaware that nagging is the ultimate-deadener of sexual desire; yet complain that their sex life is dull.

Women are powerful. No man who has a mother can doubt this. To say that some women abuse this power in their emotional relationships with their sons is taken as given. The archetypal Jewish mother is an exaggeration of someone we have all met. She is the ambitious, emotional blackmailer who demands love and success from her men; she nags father, son or both to achieve what she cannot herself.

Women can also abuse their power by cynically bedding the boss. It is remarkable that in these liberated times this is regarded as generally O.K., rather than potentially suspect. Marrying him seems to be accepted even more readily.

For the millions of women who read romantic fiction, the dream is to find love in the arms of a rich and powerful man. They have no thought of working themselves. That the heroine has nothing but prettiness to offer in exchange for his hard-won earnings is not thought demeaning.

Allure

A woman's beauty allures, and most women learn to use beauty and sex as a promise which is not always fulfilled. Conventional wisdom says that that is the core of a woman's power. Anyone who has opened a glossy magazine knows that our culture accepts this conventional wisdom wholeheartedly: teaching women to use that power is big business.

Men are accustomed to fall prey to female allure, knowing she can be his only if he fulfills her dreams.

Those dreams usually include a pleasant home, a car, two kids; and they can include much more. She does not love him for his bank balance and success alone, any more than he loves her just for her beauty. But it helps. As she stops working towards the end of her first pregnancy, he often faces this for the first time.

Masculinity

It used to be said that if women ruled the world, there would be fewer wars and that society would be more caring. Now that some countries have had women as leaders, we know that this is untrue. In the worst sorts of dictatorships, there is often a woman just behind the scenes. Whether it is famine in the Third World, saving the rain forests or fighting poverty, the activists are still most likely to be men. When it comes to the good – and the bad – neither sex holds the monopoly.

Feminism demands that men show their more feminine side and also to accept women's masculine side. They call it meeting them half-

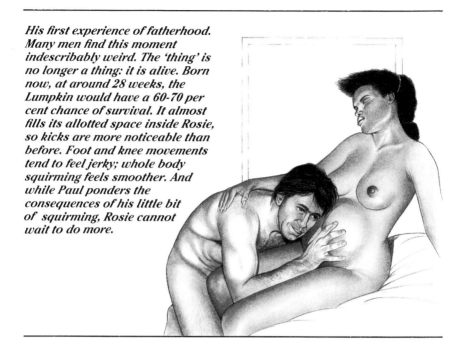

His first experience of fatherhood. Many men find this moment indescribably weird. The 'thing' is no longer a thing: it is alive. Born now, at around 28 weeks, the Lumpkin would have a 60-70 per cent chance of survival. It almost fills its allotted space inside Rosie, so kicks are more noticeable than before. Foot and knee movements tend to feel jerky; whole body squirming feels smoother. And while Paul ponders the consequences of his little bit of squirming, Rosie cannot wait to do more.

way. It may be. But half-way is also agreeing to value that side of men which is sexy, powerful, masculine and protective. And to accept that he may want to love women for their femininity. To accept that men, like women, are a product of their culture, and that society does not change because we move one set of goal posts. To be honestly and truly liberated, women need to change their attitudes to men as much as men have towards women.

Penis envy

The psychologist Melanie Kleinn placed a woman's power firmly in her breasts. Nowadays, when the majority of relationships are broken by women, and few courts award custody of the children to the father (however badly she behaves) many men must feel that Klein had it about right. Not only is the the average breast rather larger than the average penis, there are two of them. On the home front, at least, this reflects the power struggle rather well.

Is Paul aware of the symbolism? As Rosie's belly swells, so do her breasts. As she gets ready for motherhood, her power within the relationship grows.

Modern marriage

As Rosie sails forth, sexy and fulfilled, Paul stands on the sidelines wondering if family life will lower his standard of loving; as it will his standard of living.

It is not that he is unwilling to take on the life-time support of Rosie and the children. He is a nice guy. And nice guys like Paul look after their families even if they no longer share the home or see their children.

It is easy to say that in the past men made use of women, but that use was not one-sided, nor is it. Generations of men kept their side of the bargain, handing over unopened pay packets to wives who disliked and avoided sex. Her distaste may not have been her fault, but neither is his need.

Today, between a third and a half of all marriages fail, yet regardless of her earnings or the comparatively light pressures of her work, parting couples divide the spoils. Her gender, not her lack of ambition, is accepted as the excuse for her small pay packet.

Even after the last child starts school, his alimony and child support will arrive unmodified whether she works or not. And if he finds another woman and starts another family (after all, he had children because he wanted to raise them), he is still expected to support both families. If overtime means he rarely sees daylight in the winter months, he is only doing what hundreds of other men do every day.

Because we see male power as the reason for women's powerlessness, we have tended, in recent times, to turn a blind eye to men's problems.

The stakes

Paul sips his beer, lingering before going home to Rosie. He cannot say what makes him uneasy; only that he is. We have chosen him, the gentle, inarticulate trucker, as hero if this story because we felt his anxieties deserved to be broadcast. The stakes are high in modern relationships, but so are the rewards. If you doubt that the rewards are high, or indeed that they exist, see **Robert & Jenny** or **William & Francesca**. It would be unnatural for Paul not to have doubts as Rosie's belly swells. To express these worries in his sexual performance is normal. The blunt instrument, like its owner, can be a sensitive soul. Rosie, in her happiness and enthusiasm, does not always see the problems facing Paul. Add a third person, who will absorb the rest of her attention, and Rosie is even less likely to recognize his cry for help.

Facing all these problems in pregnancy gives no guarantee of success. But it is easier than facing them after birth. Not facing them at all is potentially a disaster, not just for your sex life, but for the relationship itself.

NIGHT AT THE PLAZA

Claire & Tony

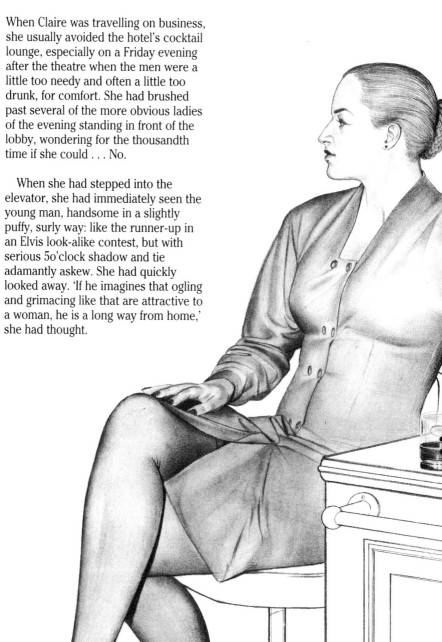

When Claire was travelling on business, she usually avoided the hotel's cocktail lounge, especially on a Friday evening after the theatre when the men were a little too needy and often a little too drunk, for comfort. She had brushed past several of the more obvious ladies of the evening standing in front of the lobby, wondering for the thousandth time if she could . . . No.

When she had stepped into the elevator, she had immediately seen the young man, handsome in a slightly puffy, surly way: like the runner-up in an Elvis look-alike contest, but with serious 5o'clock shadow and tie adamantly askew. She had quickly looked away. 'If he imagines that ogling and grimacing like that are attractive to a woman, he is a long way from home,' she had thought.

Tony had been looking forward to the poker game in Abe's room. It would be the usual happy evening.

Well, look at who just got on. Older, but not too old, her fine, somewhat angular features carefully made up, her long hair pulled up tight and elaborately plaited. Her long, high-necked dress, expensive and fashionable, had been cut to de-emphasize a full bosom. What the hell, give her the old smile and wink. Come on lady, you can look, a little smile won't cost you anything.

* * * *

She hadn't given him a tumble, but that was OK. The same lucky feeling that won him the hundred last night said Plaza Lounge, one more time. He could tell about women. After all, it had been like a neon sign. And there she was.

Claire thought 'Oh, no, not him,' when the young man sat down next to her, but there was the feel of his biceps under his jacket when he leaned against her and there was his shiny grin. His teeth had shone. Another uncertain affair? Might she be oversexed? She quenched the once familiar doubt. She was alone, not busy, wanted to talk about yesterday's triumph at the agency, and her life was her own. And she had always liked tall men.

* * * *

Dinner had not been ideal. Claire talked confidently and knowledgeably about theatre, million-dollar advertising campaigns, and agency politics. Tony, trying to remain unimpressed, responded only with some weak jokes. Well, now they were in her room, and at last now   it was up to him.

"Would you like a drink?" asks Claire, standing close to him and making absolutely no move towards the liquor cabinet. Tony, knowing that women like men who take charge, reaches round to undo a few buttons on her dress, picks her up, then deposits her on the bed, none too gently. He undoes a few more buttons, fumbles with her brassière, gives up and pushes up her dress. He has her panties down, his leg between her knees. Give the box a rub and get in before she can change her mind. He says, "I'm going to fuck your brains out."

The coarseness, but not the speed, suits Claire's mood. "Wait, just stop," she says urgently. Tony, freezing, knows he's lost it, but then she reaches up and pulls him strongly down towards her. He lowers himself reluctantly. "Where's the fire, Tony?"

What was that promise in the strong, womanly voice in his ear? Claire tugs his pants down, pushes him on to his side. Tony's cock is long and curves up and slightly to one side. Kind of cute, Claire decides, as she takes it in her hand and begins stroking up and down. Tony, sighing with pleasure at the silken strokes, relaxes.

* * * *

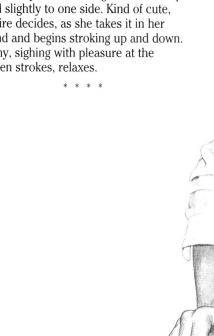

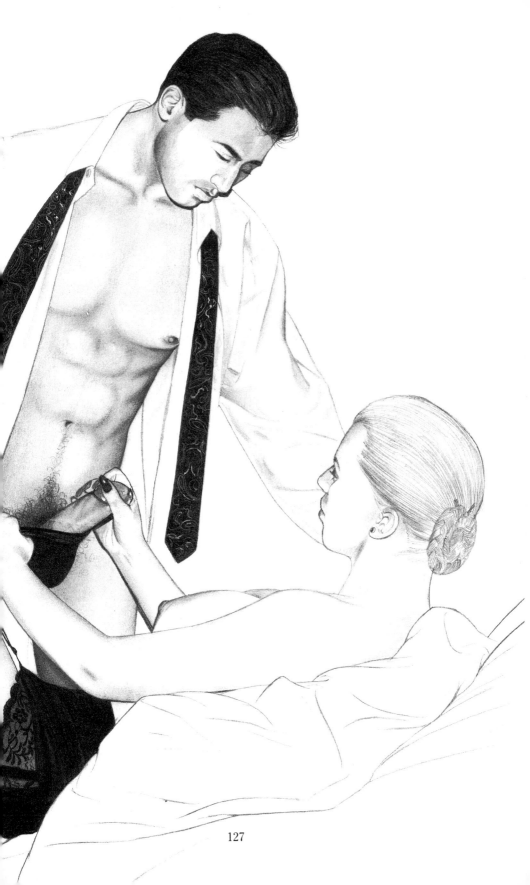

Claire's breasts are round and full, stretch marks are clearly visible, but her brown nipples have not lost their upward tilt. Poised above him she looks like a goddess. "You like my tits, don't you?" With the tightness in his throat, he can hardly speak. Claire pushes her breasts up and forward with her hands, her spread fingers only partially covering them, emphasizing their size. "Fuck me here." She moves down and turns so she is lying on her side, looking up at this beautiful boy. Claire manoeuvres his rigid cock between her breasts, folding and holding herself around him with her hands, her nipples peeping between her fingers. As soon as he feels the warmth and smoothness

of those sweet mounds, sees himself surrounded by her soft flesh and the top of his cock emerging from the cleavage under her throat, his passion is irresistible. Two thrusts and he is pulsing, spurting, gasping; coming and coming between her breasts, on to her chest, her neck, her hair.

Claire feels the friction in her chest, her nipples pulled between her fingers. His cum is warm and sticky, but less so than she remembers. (Isn't it always?) She laughs, wipes some off a liberally coated breast with her forefinger, and puts it in her mouth. "Yum. Want some?" He recoils slightly, then "Yes. OK. Why not?" He grins. "So that's what I taste like. Now what shall we do?"

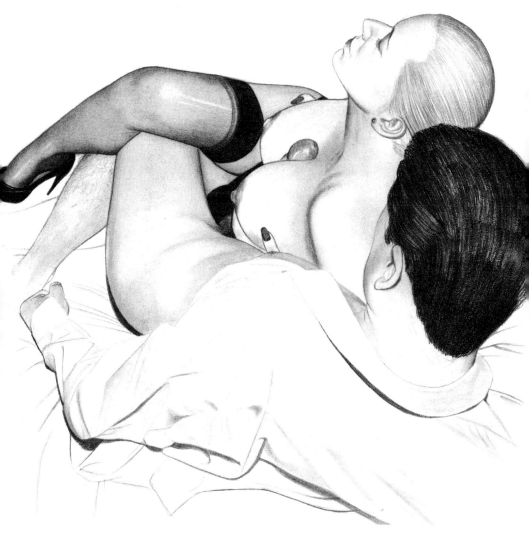

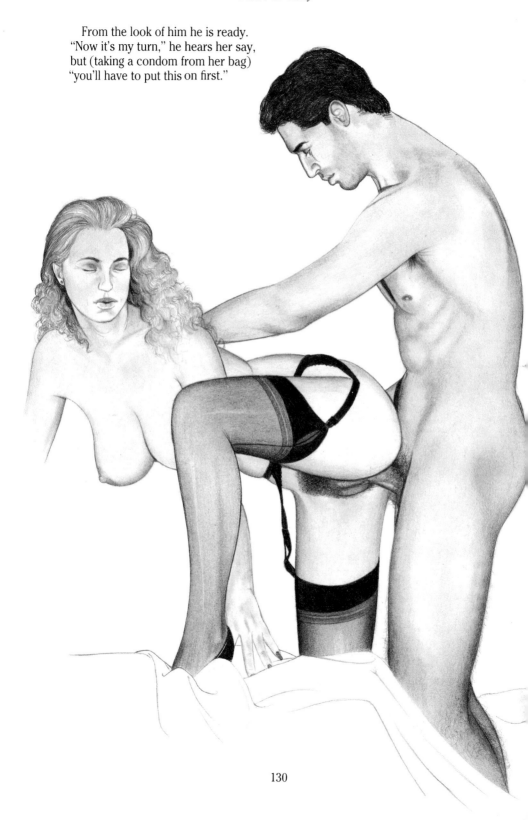

From the look of him he is ready.
"Now it's my turn," he hears her say,
but (taking a condom from her bag)
"you'll have to put this on first."

Claire's professional life is about taking risks and going out to get what she wants. She competes on equal terms in what was once, not so long ago, a man's world, making contacts and landing contracts outside her advertising agency, vigorously expanding and defending her territory within.

In social situations, by contrast, she is faced with a *status quo* in which, by tradition, the man makes the first move. If we believe what we read, however, men are increasingly keen for women to take the initiative. But the role of women was never completely passive; and there is some question in most women's minds as to whether men really mean they would like women to initiate sexual encounters.

It may be that deep down, both sexes prefer to play it the traditional way. Taking the initiative leaves a woman more directly open to rejection than in her stereotyped, passive role; indeed, men complain that if women put themselves on the line as often as men do, they might be more sympathetic to male approaches. Women counter this by asking if he thinks flirting is easy; that can involve putting yourself on the line, too. Better the risk of rejection that you know, than the one you don't.

In order to make 'cold' sexual contacts work, both men and women need to be assertive in their approach, but what ranks as a direct approach by a man to a woman can make men wary if practised the other way round. Her part is confined, traditionally, to initiating eye contact, smiling at him, and leaving the rest up to him. Faced with these signals, most men think they are taking the initiative, poor fools. If you really want to set things moving, you need only wink and turn your head away. He will probably knock over three tables getting to you; or hide under one of them.

But although most men and women prefer relationships to start in the traditional way, many men welcome a woman's initiative once they reach the bedroom. Being made love to is rather special, as women know. (And so, men will tell you, is being the lovemaker.) It seems a pity not to sample both roles from start to finish.

Claire's motives

But there is taking the initiative, and taking the initiative. Unlike her male counterpart alone in a strange town, it would never occur to Claire to hire a companion for conversation and/or sex. Experience has taught those who have tried it that an easy way to go broke is to set up an escort service or a massage parlour, even a high-class one, offering sexual services to women. Why?

Being able to attract a man is a measure of a woman's success. Paying someone to do it for her suggests she is no longer attractive or desirable to men. (Women know that men are not very fussy who they fuck; it is surely an undesirable woman who cannot find *someone* prepared to give her a ride.) Where is the pleasure in paying to prove to the world that no man would consider a freebie with you? Failure is certainly not Claire's scene. Instead, she allows Tony to pick her up.

Why Tony?

He has at least three things going for him: he is young, good looking and self-confident. An experimental study of blind dates has shown that for both women and men, initial attraction to strangers is largely based upon physical attractiveness and not upon similarity of attitudes. No other aspects were found to count, and people had formed their first impression within four minutes. But Claire does not respond to every good-looking young man that comes along. So why this one?

In one sense, Tony is a familiar element in Claire's life; or should we say a 'common' element. She is used to organizing the likes of Tony: they fix her car, deliver her mail or arrive on dispatch bikes to take her urgent packages. Tonight, Claire is indulging in a bit of slumming that is more typical of men. In bygone days, upper class men sought out the serving wench, or the wild gypsy woman for their unbridled sexuality. The Victorian gentleman going after the flower girl, or the American plantation owner forcing himself upon one of his female slaves, was supremely confident that the animal heat of these women was a mark of their low breeding. They could be had in ways which were not acceptable with respectable women. Coupling with inferiors permitted such men to give freer rein to the aggressive aspect of their sexual emotions.

Prostitution fantasies and realities

Prostitution fantasies are not uncommon among women. Claire's, like those of many other women, revolve around being examined, appraised, done to. They make her the centre of male attention. As the men line up, put their money down and enter her, she has a tangible measure of their lust. Fifty dollars a trick, and just look at them lining up. Was any woman ever so desirable? These fantasies also reflect that old and deep-seated anxiety that her sexual desires make her a bad girl. However, the self-degradation involved in these relatively tame fantasies of prostitution is usually mild compared with that of other sorts of fantasies or ritualized activities – see **Connie & Lloyd**, pages 187-190.

Deep down, Claire wonders if somehow she might slip into becoming a prostitute; but she need not worry. She was not abused as a little girl; no one called her a slag, or treated her like one as an adolescent.

She did not have to run away from an unloving home, or drunken parents. She was not driven by economic necessity, as are most pros. Claire did not have her first experience of sexual intercourse at 13+, as do half of those that become prostitutes. Their sexual precocity was a sign that these girls were using sex to seek any proof that they were lovable.

Claire's fantasies don't include the hassles and hazards of being on the game, including sexually transmitted diseases and violent abuse by the tricks who cannot get it off straight away. In many countries, including Britain, the hassles of street-walking also include arrest and detainment; call girls are legal in Britain, whereas in the United States the only legal form of prostitution is in brothels such as the Mustang Ranch in the state of Nevada, and there, only in counties with populations under 300,000.

A bit of rough

Tony is not a man to every woman's taste, so what is the attraction of a bloke who comes third in an Elvis look-alike contest? He is not about marriage, or safety, or sensible shoes and clean white underwear or good jobs, or prestige. He is not someone you take home to your mother, or out to meet your friends.

The attraction is of the outrageous kind. Who wants a one-night stand with Mr Nice Guy? If you are going to do it, you might as well do it in style. Safe sex with the accountant in the next office never had this potential.

Picking up a bit of rough is sexy because it is so risky. What would Daddy think? Tony is just the sort of man to drive Daddy wild with jealousy, which is exactly what Elvis himself did to the parents of the generation that worshipped him. Fuck Daddy.

One of the dangers of sex for a woman is the likely loss of her 'reputation'. But with modern loosening of the controls on female sexuality, reputations are harder to lose. She is not going to do it by slipping into bed with Roger Respectable. She needs to be spotted with the likes of Tony to set tongues wagging. Make something safe, and there is always someone ready to escalate the risks.

Satyriasis and nymphomania: the myth

The terms refer to an insatiable desire for sex in man and woman respectively. The satyrs of the Greek myths were men above the waist; below they had the appearance and sexual appetites of goats. You are more likely to have heard of nymphomania than satyriasis, and this is because the alleged condition has more social and psychological significance. While a man is supposed to be randy all the time, a woman behaving in the same way must be exhibiting some defect of character or morals. Thus, Chaucer's Wife of Bath fucked each of her seven husbands to death, inherited their money, then took on a succession of young studs for her greedy pleasure. A nymphomaniac is obsessed: no man can satisfy her. She is out of control, a handmaiden of the devil: mentally ill, and not so long ago, it was excuse enough to keep her locked away in an asylum. Not only that, but once in the asylum she could be subjected to a clitorectomy. The nymphomaniac's image undermines a comforting 'truth': that women need love, not sex.

The double standard of desire, like other aspects of sexuality, has a long history. The Chinese Emperor Yang-ti had 4,000 women in his court. True, Tzu-Hsi, the Dragon Empress, had 4,000 males in her entourage, but since some were eunuchs it would seem that Yang-ti still had the edge (although we are not told how often he visited each of his ladies). But there have been many more Yang-tis than Tzu-Hsis. If a man says he has to seduce every woman in sight, we are more inclined to think of him as a 'bit of a lad' than mentally ill. Instilling a fear of nymphomania is one way in which society controls the sexuality of women. So, as she reaches out for pleasure and approaches the self-abandonment necessary for orgasm, a little voice whispers in Claire's ear, 'Am I liking this too much? Isn't this a bit degrading?' Away flies the orgasm. Maybe you want to consume him, shout out in pleasure, burst into tears of joy, or bay like a wolf to the moon, but can you admit such need?

To a man, a nymphomaniac might be any woman who wants sex more than he does. The label signals his fear of the mythical devouring vagina: the one with teeth. It also helps him come to terms with the impossible demands of the male stereotype: that he is always ready, willing and able.

How often is too often?

Claire's fear of liking sex too much is irrational. Like other natural pleasures, sex is largely self-limiting. The Roman Emperor Elagabalus offered a large portion of his treasury for the man or woman who could resuscitate his flagging lust. Sexual over-indulgence has occurred among the bored upper classes of several societies, but it takes the form of forays into variant forms of sexual activity, not in an increase in the frequency of normal activity that follows from the irresistible pleasure of sex. Obsessive sexual activity over an extended period is a sign of something lacking, not of over-indulgence.

When dieting becomes anorexia or eating becomes bulimia, illness is relatively simple to define. Abnormal frequencies of sexual behaviour are much more difficult to assess. Abnormal tends to be what the other person does.

With how many and how often does Claire do it? Not often enough? Sometimes? Excessively? She has not told us, but the statistics tell a useful tale.

These days, the median number of partners a woman has in a lifetime is eight, a man 16: more than double the figures for 1974. As the age of marriage continues to rise, we suspect this figure will remain at a level which would shock the 1920s man in the street. In a recent survey, women reported an average of just under 5.5 orgasms per week from about four sexual encounters: considerably higher than Kinsey's 1940s figure of about 1.5 weekly encounters. Elsewhere, the average married couple is claimed to spend 50 hours a year on sex and 2,000 in front of the TV. There is a great deal of variation; some couples are happy with considerably less of both. At the other extreme, a few men report up to 17 orgasms in a single day. In the Devlin survey, Susie from Leeds topped that daily figure by an orgasm or two, but she does so continually. Through the combined efforts of husband, lovers, and her own nimble fingers, she achieves a steady 140 per week. Even with Susie excepted, the women of Leeds must be thinking of England with commendable enthusiasm, since they are raising the national figures, with a weekly average of 5.9 orgasms in 4.8 sessions.

Seriously, though, the best guide for each of us is that 'abnormal' is reached when any one aspect of our behaviour, sex, eating, orwhatever, interferes with normal life, health and happiness, recurrently, or for a prolonged period. Most of us have occasional sexual binges, the weekend in bed with a new lover, when we qualify for nymphomania (or satyriasis) by anyone's standards. We doubt that this is a problem; worrying about whether it is, might be.

For sex alone . . .

To some people, Claire's casual sexual pleasuring may seem improbable: for them, sex (especially sex for women) can only be enjoyed within a loving relationship. While we would not want to deny that love adds something very special to sex, we do not agree with the old saying that women endure sex for love, men love for sex.

For the vast majority, sex can be separate from a loving relationship. It is every time we masturbate. (If you ignore Woody Allen's quip that, "Masturbation is making love to someone I love".)

It has even been suggested that when masturbation is the main sexual activity during development – as it is for almost all adolescent boys – it teaches that gratification can be separated from loving. It also offers urgent satisfaction, secrecy and perhaps a little guilt. Whatever society has said, those who masturbate nightly soon learn that you do not have to love someone in order to feel sexual pleasure, and that urgency and a feeling of being outrageously naughty can augment that pleasuring.

For most women, though, such lessons go unheeded. A woman's sexual lessons are more likely to be learned through her encounters with men, her first pleasurings occurring as she lies with someone she loves. After all, less than one in four women reach orgasm before they are 20, and many do not masturbate until much later than this.

The Casanova Complex

Claire is not Tony's first one-night stand. In fact, like a number of good-looking, self-confident men, Tony has had a pattern of conquests. In its extreme form this becomes the Casanova Complex, so called by author Peter Trachtenberg. Casanova can take on many guises: the boy next door who spends his endless nights in hot pursuit of any woman; the embittered divorcee who sees each new woman as an adversary; or the bachelor who collects beautiful women like so many butterflies. They share an obsessive, forever unsatisfied, need to pursue women.

Several different bestiaries have been compiled to describe the various sub-species of Casanova. In one such, there is Don Juan (God's gift to women); the Operator (the control freak); the Notcher (counts his scores); and the Rollerover (in and out). In another, we have the Hitter (any woman will do); the Drifter (he can fall in love for minutes at a stretch – James Bond is the archetype); the Juggler (self-explanatory); the Nester ('Let's live together for at least a week'); and the Tomcat (Frank Sinatra working his way through his list of Hollywood lovelies).

Casanova's lifestyle seems to satisfy the stereotyped male need for variety, yet Casanovas find it unsatisfying. They appear to be using women to fill a hollowness in their lives. They need the thrill of the chase, the feeling of mastering a new creature: they are excitement junkies. If their supply of women dries up, they become anxious and depressed, many of them turning to drugs and alcohol for relief. Trachtenberg suggests that sex may be the only way Casanova can ease his crippling disquiet and feel complete. He suggests that men like Tony do not fuck for love or even pleasure. Sex is mechanical, the men themselves talk about scores, body counts, grading themselves on technical proficiency and number of orgasms.

Perhaps the transient wholeness Casanova may feel when he has sex is dangerous because it could give women too much power over him. Because women are unconsciously threatening, it is safest to love them and leave them, before he begins to see them as individuals and they establish a claim on him.

Sexual politics

Tony, cocky and arrogant, needs to be the boss in the bedroom. His arrogance is a cover for his insecurities, which have been underlined by Claire's status and accomplishments. For some men, being in control is crucial to alleviating their doubts about masculinity. A few fellows of this ilk insist on the missionary position. They must be on top, quite literally. And her pleasure? Well, if she cannot manage to get off with a stud like him, there must be something wrong with her. The female companions of these men are given no choices. And while Tony's attitudes constrain the woman he is with, they also deny him the pleasures associated with being passive. See **William & Francesca**, pages 74-79.

Another form of control is exercised by the man who throws himself

The tactful way to derail a locomotive: you will put him on, and off, his stride.

into contortions to make her come, carrying on for hours if necessary. Having plenty of practice, they are good at their job. If, like Claire, you are interested in straight cock for an evening, you could do worse than finding one of these sex mechanics. Leave your interest in a long-term relationship at home.

Mastering Tony is a challenge to Claire's ego; after all, she is a woman thoroughly experienced in power politics. Fortunately for both of our players, Tony is more flexible than other Casanovas, and Claire is able to derail him.

Derailing the locomotive

Stop! Wait! What is in this for me? Men like Tony often need derailing. There is an old myth that men cannot stop once the juices flow. The excuses go like this:

Men are driven: But so are women. There is no perceptible difference between the sex drive of men and women once it is aroused. If orgasm feels the same, is it unreasonable to expect orgasmic equality?

A man who is stopped gets 'blue balls': We have yet to see anything approaching azure. Certainly, they may ache: but denial usually does. The testes don't have special juices which build up if he does not ejaculate, although they are bigger when he is aroused (and so are her ovaries: did you hear her complain of pink ovary syndrome?) Blood makes balls bigger and blood escapes through the veins in the usual way. The balls produce sperm – and then only a drop for each ejaculation. The fluid comes from the prostate and Cowper's glands, within the trunk. 'Blue balls' are probably caused by muscle tension in the pelvic floor, which some women can feel too.

Idols

We asked a man we know to describe his ideal woman. Without hesitation he provided every loving detail, from the tip of her toes to the crown of her head, including the colour, texture and distribution of her pubic hair. The description was so complete that we assumed it was from life; in fact he had never met her. Needless to say he is still looking.

Looking for an ideal is fruitless.

Getting lucky

Claire got Tony, and vice versa. But how can we get so lucky? Mercifully, there is no magic formula, but we think much comes down to attitude. First, you have to believe you deserve love; until you love yourself, it is hard to imagine anyone wanting to love you. So, improve your self-esteem. List all your good points (physical) in obsessive detail; and all your strengths (of personality). Add to this positive list all the things that are 'not bad', then look it over. Are you making use of all your advantages? Having got the positive picture in focus, move on to the negative. List your bad points.

Look at both lists. Is the positive one longer? If not, are you sure you have all your good points on it? Ignore all the negative things you cannot help, such as short legs, and re-examine the list. Are there any weaknesses you can improve upon? Work at it. Even small changes help boost your confidence. We are all good enough for someone to love us. Start the ball rolling by liking yourself – different from the empty self-confidence of Tony, Casanova and friends, and indeed of Simon in **Simon & Willow**, pages 162-175.

Getting it

Do you get the partners you deserve, or only the partners you think you deserve? We suspect that those who think they are worth having find themselves in popular demand. Who ever bought the brand which advertised itself as pretty good for an off night?

Confidence works. If you feel you are worth caring about, you are in the mood to try your chances on the helter-skelter of love. If not this one, pick up your mat, climb the steps and start again. Don't think she is 'too good' for you, or that he is only 'waiting until he finds someone better'. It is arrogance to assume that you are the only one who can make that judgement. If someone wants your company, at least give them credit for being capable of making up their own mind.

Feeling shy

We all do on occasions. Some people feel shyness more intensely, and in more situations than others. It is said that shyness is a type of vanity: the shy individual is saying to everyone out there 'If you want to know me, you make the effort. I'm too tied up in my own problems to get to know you'.

Whether or not this is true, it is not very helpful. It takes courage to go out there and face a rebuff, and few people do it with a completely easy heart. People are worth knowing. We suggest that you keep this in mind and that you remember 40 per cent of people rate themselves as shy. It is quite likely that you will be starting a conversation with someone as shy as yourself. They will be grateful you are making the effort. Focus on what the other person is saying, rather than your own insecurities. As you concentrate on them, you will find some, or perhaps much, of your own shyness disappears.

Eye contact

Being sexually assertive means checking your body language, and making sure that the messages you send are the ones you want sent. Take a look at **Robert & Jenny**, pages 24-25 if you need guidance.

Eye contact is probably the most important signal. Hold it for about five seconds in every 30; much longer, and it is threatening. In between meeting her eye, don't look over her shoulder: this gives the impression you are bored. What most people prefer is a look that flits back and forth, meeting the eye before looking away. To some extent, sexual encounters break this rule: few of us ever hold each other's

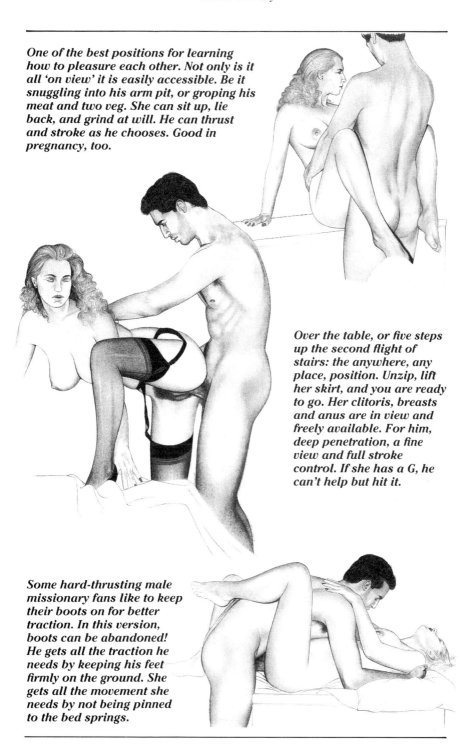

One of the best positions for learning how to pleasure each other. Not only is it all 'on view' it is easily accessible. Be it snuggling into his arm pit, or groping his meat and two veg. She can sit up, lie back, and grind at will. He can thrust and stroke as he chooses. Good in pregnancy, too.

Over the table, or five steps up the second flight of stairs: the anywhere, any place, position. Unzip, lift her skirt, and you are ready to go. Her clitoris, breasts and anus are in view and freely available. For him, deep penetration, a fine view and full stroke control. If she has a G, he can't help but hit it.

Some hard-thrusting male missionary fans like to keep their boots on for better traction. In this version, boots can be abandoned! He gets all the traction he needs by keeping his feet firmly on the ground. She gets all the movement she needs by not being pinned to the bed springs.

141

gaze as long at any other time. Slightly longer eye contact is the simplest way of saying 'Yes, I am interested'. If you have any doubts about how to do it hire a few videos (romantic stories, not porn), and watch the experts.

Body language
Being assertive also means standing straight, not slouching, holding your head up and not mumbling into your beer. However you feel inside, looking confident quietens the nerves. Don't go in too close at first. People like their space. As you become more intimate you can, of course, move closer. Given that standing apart looks aloof, you may want to know exactly how far apart you should be. But it is impossible to specify. There are such enormous cultural differences (Swedes will keep a greater distance than Italians) that the only sound advice is to take a look around the room: how far apart are all the other couples? That is the distance to aim for, only back off from it slightly at first greeting. If you notice the woman standing or walking close to you, it is a very good sign.

Touching is another body sign with great cultural variations. In café society in San Juan (Puerto Rico) people were seen to touch each other 180 times per hour; in Paris 110; in London 0. A touch in London has much more of a sexual connotation than a touch in San Juan.

Relaxed is better than tense, and a few non-sexist jokes thrown in when the conversation lags will amuse her and relax you. Relaxed is better than intense, too. Looking at her and touching her is enough to get across the message that you are interested. It is unecessary to enquire after her taste in kitchen wallpaper within the first 15 minutes, or to discuss your relationship with your mother on the first date.

You can always try buying her a drink without asking, or paying for one when you see the barman pouring it (ask the barman or the waiter to tell her you have done so). If you see her at a dance or in a club, chat her up for a few minutes before asking her to dance. It will hugely improve the chances of her saying yes.

Between her breasts
Claire takes Tony between her breasts, and thereby indulges in safe sex on this first encounter with a stranger. And she insists on a condom before any further activity.

If the vagina is the primary and the mouth the secondary, the breasts are surely the tertiary site. If you want to do it 'à la Claire' with the woman lying on her side, the breasts need to be quite large. Make a tunnel by wrapping them around the penis and pull them together by holding the nipple between the thumb and the side of the forefinger.

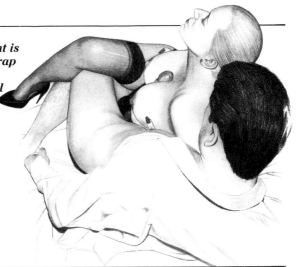

The essential requirement is breasts big enough to wrap around a penis. If you climb on top, gravity will help in marginal cases. If she crosses her legs and holds her nipples between two fingers, she can probably be excited enough to go almost as soon as he comes.

Or let her do it for you. We think some nipple work and lubrication are necessary: rolling and squeezing for the former, vaginal juices, saliva, KY or butter for the latter. (Body oil and face cream work, but don't taste as good if she needs sucking to orgasm after he has come.

If her breasts are small, it will work better if she is on top. Other positions worth trying are 69, or with him sitting on a chair and her kneeling.

There are plenty of other little spots that can be used for occasionals. Armpits, between the legs, thighs, even the feet. The best is surely rear entry femoral: at least for her. She lies prone with her legs crossed, he approaches as for flattened doggy, but rather than going into the vagina, he moves between her labia and up to the clitoris.

Age differences

Claire is the older: reversing the traditional pattern, which we suppose made sense economically: when he needed someone to work his fields, a fit young wife was the sensible choice.

In the days when only men sowed wild oats, it was wise for those who had to remain virgins to marry as early as possible, especially when she lost marriage value, even when raped.

None of these factors now hold. Sexually, the coupling of an old man and a young girl never made a great deal of sense. A man is at his sexual peak in his teens and twenties, a women in her thirties and forties. After that, both decline into old age. So the obvious sexual match is young man, mature woman. But women often see the slowness of an older man as a bonus: his very incapacity to come fast and furious is amongst his major sexual attractions.

THE LAST ANNIVERSARY

Joe & Sue

It was their 15th anniversary; but the celebration had to be over lunch. He had been married for 27 years.

It had started in the usual way, two people working closely together, somehow putting his family ('Anne and the kids') at a distance. Neither had intended to get 'involved', but somehow it had happened.

They had gone back to a nearly empty office, late in the day. As they came through the door, his mouth had closed on hers and he had taken her against a filing cabinet. She remembered the excitement of hearing distant voices. Knowing that he shortly had another appointment. The race. The shyness when it was over. She had turned away from him as she had adjusted her skirt, embarassed now at having to face him.

He had been driven on by the contained desire of several weeks, fuelled by bathtime fantasies of her breasts filling his mouth. Her perfume that morning as she adjusted the papers on his desk. Buttons and zips had been a barrier, but he had humped her against the wall like a 17-year-old.

She had expected him to say, "Are you sure?", to be slow, gentle. But he did not, had not.

He had felt powerful. The inner force in his imagination became the inward force in the thighs squeezing around him. He had meant to give pleasure as well as to receive, but the excitement of thrusting into her had been too much.

It had been too quick for her, he knew. He had slipped his hand down and taken her breast in his mouth saying, "I'm sorry, Sue, let me make you come." But it couldn't work that way, not at that point, not exposed in his office. Not with the sounds of colleagues' footsteps in the hall. The thrill of being entered by him had been followed by disappointment. She had built so much into her expectation – the looks, the body language, the 'accidental' touches. But he had said, "Next time for you," and she had known he meant it.

Fifteen years ago today.

* * * *

144

Like most long-term lovers, they were comfortable together, but because opportunities were infrequent, each time was special, and this made the sex particularly good. She stayed with him because it was so good; it was so good precisely because it was illicit.

Why did he go on? For him there had never been one woman. There was his wife; there was Sue; there had been others here on the office sofa.

Today, Joe sits on that sofa. Sue is on the floor in front of him, her head resting on his naked thigh. She has discarded her skirt and stockings and opened her blouse. He watches her hands coaxing his erection.

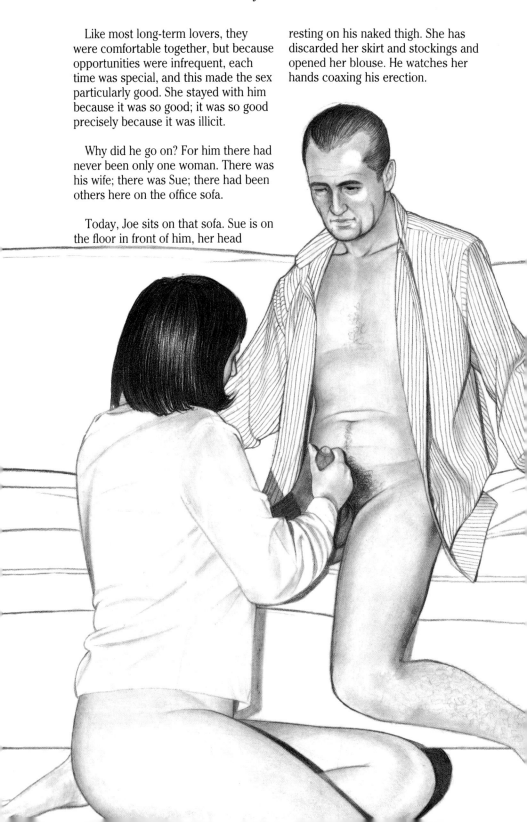

Joe is not the only man in her life, but she has come to depend on him. When they are dressed, in office 'mode', she asks his advice about this man or that who happens to be in her life. Today, she feels a little guilty imagining she is with the latest of these men. But then she kicks herself metaphorically, reminding herself that she owes Joe nothing.

He strokes her hair and holds out his arms. She comes into them, lowering herself on to his erect penis. He says, "Going to the seaside?" – the tag line from an old joke about having sex in a crowded railway carriage.

His fingers seek out breasts. He feels the flow. It was always good with her.

She lies forward, bringing her legs up around his head. Long, slow, squirming; the way she likes it.

Joe is lying on his back, Sue face down between his legs: the X position. For the – what is it, 2000th time? – he observes the modest roundness of her bottom, the birthmark on the right cheek, the delicate red fringe of pubic hair surrounding his entry of her.

How had he got himself into this situation? It had been a flirtation, but somehow she had turned it into a great love affair. He was fond of her, very fond of her. But the bottom line was Anne and the kids.

Sue knows it is better not to see him when her mind is elsewhere. Something is in the air today. She closes her eyes and squirms. She imagines men running across the hot sand to her. Closing her eyes she sees three of them, naked with huge erections. She wants to tease them, wants them to see her here, making love to Joe. To watch as they excite themselves.

Suddenly, she wants Joe to take charge. "Let me see you," she says. She raises herself to a sitting position, rotates on him and lies back.

The shudder creeps up on her. He has moved up; her legs are around his neck. He pushes down hard, thrusting deep. He is in control. "Joe, oh Joe, my lover."

His control slips away. He should be prepared for her animal craving but he is not. He feels the relief of not having to control. Waves of sensation crash over him, choice gone, past caring about anything else.

For 15 years he has brought her to such peaks. She cries softly.

He wasn't expecting that. Each time it happens, he is lost so quickly. He is usually, well, so good with words. "Sweet Sue," he says. "Don't move."

Sometimes Sue has wondered how it will end. Will the firm transfer him? Would his wife find out? Anyway, it was 15 years, possibly the best years of her life, and there was no point in thinking about the future, even if she was 39 now. "I'm getting cramp," she says. "I'll make some coffee."

After she has gone Joe feels guilty. He knows he must soon tell her he is accepting early retirement.

Despite the guilt, despite his own low opinion of what he had been doing all these years, they were good together; there was no price you could put on that; it had been a major part of his life. He was going to miss her; going to miss them all. He was not sure how he would cope with monogamy, or how to make it otherwise. Still, better not spoil their anniversary. He'd tell her tomorrow.

Sue and Joe are part-time lovers. He has a wife and family, she sees other men. In that sense, it is an open relationship in which neither expects to be faithful to the other. One presumes, since it has been going on for so long, that this suits them both. Some mistresses would like to be wives, but Sue would not. Her affair with Joe was not unusual when it began; many of her friends had had fleeting relationships with older married men. However, unlike some of her friends, Sue is not going to let the relationship be permanent. Not for love of Joe. She is not foolish enough to think that there is only one man out there, nor is she sure that if there were, he would be called Joe.

Sue is the first to admit that Joe is a convenient excuse for never making a commitment.

We can only guess at her reasons. Her parents' unhappy marriage? A strong desire not to have children? A tendency to avoid change of any sort? All play their part. Probably, above all, she prefers relationships which are a little unreal. A 15-year affair with a married man has to be lived in a sort of dream. One which makes the dreamer comfortably oblivious of the devastation that discovery could bring to her lover's life, and to her own.

Does she feel guilty? Not any more. When Joe's children were small, she felt the odd pang, especially if Anne called after a lunch-time session. Now she reassures herself that if Anne really wanted to know, she would surely have discovered the affair by now. In this she may well be right. After 15 years, she feels she has a right to a little of Joe.

Sue and her kind

There have always been women like Sue. We used to think that they had no choice, but that was when we thought women could not help falling in love, and men could not help taking advantage. Women can certainly be foolish, and men can certainly exploit, but most affairs were probably not entirely men's fault. Of course, there were economic reasons for women to get involved with men, and indeed, some were bought or lured into sexual slavery. But others, like Sue, must have chosen this way of life. Today, they are joined by a new class of single women: those in their late thirties and early forties who leave long-term marriages. They have been described as '40-year-old women avoiding remarriage'; their ex-partners as '45-year-old men searching for replacements'.

Both seem to find what they want. A large proportion of newly divorced men remarry within two years. Many women remain single.

It is not surprising. Many men find it hard to care for themselves after years of home comforts. A man has made a huge investment in his marriage, not only financially, but psychologically. Wife and family

150

provide his main emotional support system. Work and the family come first. Compared with his bachelor days, there is little time left after their demands are satisfied in which to keep friendships in good repair, and social life running smoothly. To a great extent, the woman now takes over their social life; and she, in common with most women, has many more 'emotional' friendships with her own sex than the average man. If a break-up comes, he is likely to feel far more cut adrift than she, who can fall back on girl friends and the social circle.

Joe and his kind

Why does the affair suit Joe? When asked if he loves his wife, Joe invariably says "Yes," and means it. She is a friend; the mother of his children and provider of home comforts. She is also his social anchor. To separate his life from hers would isolate him from everything but his working environment. Joe tells himself that his marriage is far from ideal, and there is truth in this, but it is nonetheless a convenient way of coming to terms with his affairs.

In the beginning, he added that he could not leave his children. Now they have left home, he admits there is more to it than that. Even if Sue had been the great love of his life, he would have found it difficult to leave the security of his wife and family. Since she is not, it has never crossed his mind. His excuse? That Sue likes things the way they are, and so does Anne. He is right.

Anne and Sue have shared his life, each comfortable with her role. But both relationships lack sparkle. Anne and Joe are still occasional lovers, but the sex has always been better with Sue. Sue shares his work, but the friendships are always better with Anne.

Jealousy

If Sue could love Joe without ever feeling a pang of jealousy as he and Anne share the high days and holidays, the 15-year romance would, from her standpoint, be ideal. In the beginning, Sue occasionally asked for details of his relationship with Anne; later she realized that the only way to cope with this sort of affair was to block his wife from her mind. She never asks him about his home life. He has learned not to volunteer anything.

Of all the emotions, jealousy is the most painful and potentially destructive. Grief, rage, and self-loathing come together with a force that dispels reason, caution and common sense. No one is immune. As children we felt rage at the rivalry of a new baby, had tantrums while our mother talked to a friend, and hit the child who took our toy even if, at that moment, we had no intention of playing with it.

Jealousy is never logical. We can build an innocent phone call into a

151

major crisis, yet fail to see the most blatant evidence of infidelity. In principle, one might say that jealousy is childish, and that adult relationships should always be open; but in practice this is no help. Once jealousy takes root, it grows.

Can't live with him – or without him

As Joe knows, it must all come to an end some day, and in a way, Sue has been waiting for this to happen. There are many reasons why relationships drag on. Sometimes there is a fear of commitment, sometimes she is holding on to Mr Nice Guy while looking for someone more exciting. Sometimes the attraction is strong, yet deep down both lovers know that living together would drive them to distraction. Opposites may attract – but they cannot always share the same roof.

There is little point in sitting back hoping a partner will change. The only mind which can be changed is your own. *You* can be more decisive, more flexible, and more committed. There is no point in hoping your partner will be any of these out of the goodness of his or her heart. You can sit down and ask yourself exactly what it is that you want. If it is the *status quo*, you must accept, as Sue does, that it will always be like this. If it is not, you have to decide what you really want from the relationship. Then your only option is to demand it, and face the consequences, including ending the affair.

Check list for the dependent:

- *Do you hate going anywhere alone?*

- *Do you hate going back to an empty home?*

- *Do you feel more important when you have a partner?*

- *Do you hate to admit there is no one special?*

- *Do you hate being the only one without a mate?*

- *Do you think there is a Mr Right?*

- *Do you want to be married more than anything else?*

'Yes' to all seven, and you are severely dependent.

Check list for the needy:

- *Do you feel depressed or change your mind when others disagree with you?*

152

- *Do you always say 'Yes'?*

- *Do you always fit in?*

- *Do you often say sorry?*

- *Do you think needing someone makes you happy?*

- *Do you envy married friends?*

- *Are you easily hurt?*

- *Would you sacrifice your life for someone?*

- *Do you always keep people waiting?*

If you fit this pattern, you probably love from a sense of need, and this is to love from a position of weakness. Keep shouting 'Exploit me', and someone will surely oblige. If you want to be treated as an equal, you must be able to stand alone. No one can ever *make* someone else love them.

Out of Joe, Anne and Sue, Joe, unlikely as this may seem, is probably the most dependent. His 'props' are well in place, but imagine how he would feel if Anne and Sue both went under buses on the same day. Sue, by contrast, is a good example of someone who has managed to shake free from the reins of dependence and need.

Marriage – in theory
Why, at bottom, did Joe and Anne marry? Up until say, two generations ago, marriage was a public contract making sex legitimate, its primary concerns, property rights and kinship. It protected a woman's virtue; if she had sex outside marriage, she was not socially respectable. As society's attitude to female virtue relaxed in the Fifties and Sixties, this fundamental motive for marriage shifted to the need for security. Today, that need is not so widespread: women have property, substantial incomes. Yet people still marry.

An exclusive sexual relationship between a man and a woman is, of course, the basis of a family. Being part of a family is the connecting thread that helps sew us into the patchwork of our culture.

If we are to keep the quilt in its traditional form, most of us have to live in families. If too many patches unpick themselves, there is no quilt, at least not a traditional one. There may be a new type of cultural quilt made from single-parent families fringed with free males, but that is a fundamentally different form of bedcover, one whose warmth we have yet to test over a significant period. It is because many of us doubt the value of the alternatives that we see the old quilt of monogamy in a rosy hue.

Marriage – in practice

Joe doubts that the new quilt would suit him, even if he does make sorties out of the marital bed. He is typical. The majority of men are unfaithful within the first two years of a relationship, and have more than one partner. Given these figures, it is not surprising to find that 40 per cent of single women, such as Sue, have had affairs with married men. We do not know Anne's history. If she were typical, she would have waited longer, then taken a lover. Five years into a relationship, between 40 and 70 per cent of men *and* women have had other partners, or so surveys suggest. For some, it is a foretaste of separation and divorce, for most it is not.

Why monogamy?

Most wives try to turn a blind eye to their husbands' extra-marital wanderings, but until recently a wife's affairs were a different matter. Her fidelity was essential, because in western society, like many others, monogamy was the way a man acknowledged his children. If no one else had access to her, the children were his and no more need be said. By contrast, the man who was unknowingly duped into raising another man's child – the cuckold – was a figure of merciless fun. Because of men's terrible fear of being the cuckold, because they have always promoted ways of publicly claiming parenthood of their children, it is fair to assume that this is a very basic male need.

Saying 'It's mine'

Men promote their claims to parenthood by maintaining a society in which to question a child's paternity would be absurd. The most extreme example is surely the harem. The Ottoman sultans kept their women in a special part of the household protected by up to 500 black eunuchs. No women who passed through its doors ever came out again.

Another way of saying 'The child is mine' is to make a statement of social responsibility, as parents do when they adopt children. In some primitive societies, where monogamy cannot be guaranteed, men make an elaborate public statement of 'social' paternity when a child is born. In some tribal societies, men even go into a form of labour, known as couvade, which includes stomach pain and cramps. As he feels the birth pains, he is saying 'I'm having this baby too'.

A front entry position that stimulates her G spot; deep penetration and full 'stroke' possibilities (1.5 liter vagina optional). Her movement is limited. His has endless possibilities. Clitoral stimulation can be good. For her, it is 'O.K., force me to come' position. Good for conception too.

As marriages fail in ever-increasing numbers, and female infidelity rates rise, western society appears to be moving away from monogamy. Perhaps this is why men have begun to demonstrate their paternity in more obviously social ways. A modern version of couvage, perhaps. Not only are men in the delivery room, but they attend classes, assist in the birth (even sometimes cutting the cord), and later feed, change, and push the baby in the pram. (See **Rosie & Paul, Robert & Jenny**, pages 122-123 and 22-23.) We have moved from assured biological paternity to a declared social paternity. A system which can accept a much looser form of coupling.

Perhaps our belief in monogamy is part of that social statement: a way of stating a man's right to a continuing involvement with his children.

Affairs

Joe promised to "foresake all others", but never expected to be faithful for life. He would always be tempted, and would occasionally give in, as his father did before him. Our parents' marriage(s) are our models. With small variations, we often repeat their pattern. Infidelity may not be in the genes, but we inherit the tendency all the same.

If discovered, Joe would surely say: "Anne, it wasn't important, it was more about sex than love". But who could blame her for saying that this is just the problem?

Sex is part of the marriage contract: the public and private statement of a commitment. A body given as a symbol for a life shared. Primitive – but what else do we have?

Sexual interactions are the only interactions we regulate so strictly. We eat with friends, pee with strangers, grieve and share confidences with others. Even birth and death are shared with unknown medical personnel. If Anne told Joe not to share meals with anyone, we would say she had gone mad: if she said, "Stop fucking Sue," we would think her perfectly reasonable.

Now that most of us have a fairly wide sexual experience, we know that sex, even between happy long-term lovers, can sometimes be pretty banal. It rarely involves the emotional depth of caring for a sick friend, nor does it necessarily involve closeness, trust, love or even mutual regard. Mercy fucking ('Give it to me, I need it'), plain piggery ('On offer, so I'll take it'), and unenthusiastic obligation ('It's easier to say yes') are within the experience of most of us. Yet to marriage partners we still promise sexual exclusivity – and mean it. A measure of the importance of fidelity.

Not wanting to know

It may seem strange that after 15 years, Anne knows nothing of Joe's affairs. Perhaps she does not want to know. She may even unconsciously encourage Joe to look elsewhere, enjoying the 'free' evenings when he stays with Sue in town. For his part, Joe, like most men (and women), believes his partner is faithful.

There are, remember, advantages when a partner takes a lover, although we may not say so out loud. It gets him or her off one's back, and other positions you may favour less than him or her. Let someone else prop up her insecurities, and anyway, if she is out on Wednesday, he can watch TV and have a few beers. It feels like freedom, and as love's young dream vanishes, freedom is sometimes thin on the ground.

Long-term affairs

For Joe, the affair with Sue says, 'Despite all evidence to the contrary, I'm not really committed'. For Sue, it offers an odd sort of security, a regular lover on an occasional basis. For both there is the joy of a little illicit variety. Many women in Sue's position have children, but this rarely changes the basic set-up. Long-term affairs do not lead to marriage, in fact they often carry on through the upheaval of a divorce, new romance and remarriage. They are regular, uncommitted relationships.

Why are men unfaithful?

'Sex,' men say, but a recent survey suggested that 67 per cent of men rated sex at home as 'very pleasureable', while only 40 per cent of them claimed this for their affair. Sex may be all that happens in an affair, but it is hardly the reason why. Nor is it love. Very few men fall in love with a lover. She is a friend.

If the affair is not lust nor love, then what is it? For some, it is surely a rebellion; for most it is probably a confirmation that they are still attractive and lovable.

Why do women have affairs?

Married women give different reasons. Most say they feel alienated, emotionally separate from their partners. Affairs give an emotional basis to their lives. Others say it gives confidence and self-assurance, even independence.

Like men, some women claim the sex is better, others that it relieves the boredom of their lives. Some, foolishly, have affairs out of spite. ('I can hurt you too'.) Most do not look for (or find) love – although about 20 per cent fall in love during the affair.

Like the men, few are caught. And if they are, men forgive.

Is monogamy possible?

Love means not hurting, being unselfish and taking a partner's feelings into consideration. We confine our behaviour in the ways our lover demands, and in return ask that our partner confines his or hers. It is, after all, what social living is about. We might leave the garlic out of the casserole, or keep our bodies for each other. The important point is not the nature of the restrictions, but that they are agreed between us.

In principle, we may feel that an open marriage is a more mature relationship: in practice, few of us can live with it, or indeed see any point in it. If it is immature to select sex as the only restricted behaviour, most of us admit to that immaturity. Sex is the restriction because sexual jealousy consumes – like nothing else.

If only we had a bed right here

Under the Board Walk made it into the charts, but Joe's version, *Up against the Filing Cabinet*, is not the stuff of romantic songs.

Nonetheless, many of us have chosen some pretty strange places. Looking back at the back-alleys, driveways, planes, trains, cars and

She stands on one leg and tucks the other around him. Even more ornamental is the standing position where she wraps both legs around him and bounces up and down while he keeps the balance. Best when a smallish woman is swept off her feet by an athletic man (see Jack Nicholson in the movie 'Five Easy Pieces').

With her backed up against a tree in the park, it can be wonderfully decadent. Less like 'Mummy and Daddy' sex, more like an attempt on the north face. Movement is restricted, it is hard to get in and too easy to fall out. The books tell us that she adjusts the depth of penetration by moving her legs up and down, and that hands and mouths are free to attend to other body parts. But we have found it safer to concentrate on fantasy – unless you have a soft bed of leaves to cushion your fall.

waiting rooms in which we have taken our pleasure, it is surely the mood, rather than the place, which stands out in our minds. The combination of excitement and personal challenge. A feeling summed up for us by the French couple who said with enthusiasm, "How can one resist the British road signs which say 'Beware of soft verges'?" (*Verge* is French for penis.)

Quickies

The essence of a quickie is 'now or never'; and it often has to be done in an odd place at an odd time. Necessity heightens the race to the finish. The quickie is about your own pleasure, not pleasuring someone else; the archetypal 'zipless fuck', a showy thing. 'Look folks, I can come', even if there is only an audience of one.

Some say it works first time, but it is surely better after we have learned each other's short cuts to mutual orgasm. (See **William & Francesca**, pages 14-19.)

First time with you

Sometimes, though, there is too much at stake to really enjoy the first time. The excitement may carry you forward, the river runs inevitably towards the waterfall, but it is easily dammed. A sudden strange sound, a little nervousness, and excitement begins to die. As we approach the moment of truth, we are often plagued with performance anxiety.

Self-consciously, we flit from one erogenous zone to another. You pinch his arm, he pulls your hair. You notice a fly walking across the damp patch on the ceiling. It can be irritating to find yourself alone like this; he pumps merrily on; you want him to be exquisitely aware of your mutual pleasure.

To make the first time easier, acknowledge that waiting is a tease, and find a time when you can relax with a drink, a massage or a warm bath. It is good to discover each other's bodies without the anxiety of sexual performance. Some like to wash each other, others to dance, some just to lie together and talk.

How long will you take?
Who can say? Alone, most of us take two or three minutes. With a partner, those minutes stretch out, willingly and unwillingly. Women begin to lubricate within ten to 20 seconds, men become erect in three to eight. As to the rest, how can one measure? The average couple in a bed are probably unwilling to be timed by sex researchers, and if they did volunteer, who can say how 'average' that coupling would be?

Women usually take longer than men: anything up to 45 minutes from lubrication to orgasm. But some women come much faster. How couples deal with differences in timing is something that needs to be sorted out early in a relationship. Advice books usually remind men that 'nice guys come last'. It is a fair starting point, but you should always feel free to say "Go for it, don't wait for me," in the secure knowledge that your turn will come. Most women do not come consistently during intercourse anyway; she needs to know she can be brought to orgasm by hand and/or mouth if necessary.

It is not the time to be embarrassed about giving a few stage directions. Always having to come first can be as off-putting for a man as expecting to be left high and dry is for a woman. Sometimes she may be too self-conscious to go it alone. Asking an old friend to work away for an hour is one thing, asking a relatively new partner is another.

Sexual fantasy
Sue, in common with many women, regularly uses fantasy to heighten her arousal. Freud thought that a happy person does not need fantasy; it was not his only mistake. Many perfectly happy people know that practised day-dreaming is a great skill. It speeds the build-up of arousal, and provides an escape from anxiety.

When a group of middle class married women in New York were studied in the early 1970s, 65 per cent admitted to fantasizing. The most popular fantasy was of being overpowered. Many imagined themselves on a beach or in a car and over 40 per cent imagined themselves satisfying many men. These were no wanton libertines, but women married for ten years or more, describing lovemaking with their husbands.

Position X

Sue's favourite, Joe calls it, but this slow grind is probably near the top of every woman's list. Either in this position, or with the woman face-down and the man face-up, it involves complete penetration and little or no thrusting. Asked about their requirements for orgasm during intercourse, many women would, like Sue, order a good thick penis on which to slowly grind. The X position, or the woman-on-top, are hard to beat for this. Do it rear entry if you want to stimulate the sensitive vaginal area which lies just above the urethra – the 'G' spot or urethral sponge (see **William & Francesa**, pages 89-90).

Experienced women like Sue initiate sex in this position, but it is also a good learning-how position. She is in control, and part of the secret of coming during intercourse is in learning how to position herself to get the stimulation she needs, both inside and outside the

Possibly the best position of all for the mutual grind. Practice it enough and you might make it without any movement (if she has good vaginal control). The secret is to start off slow and to concentrate completely on what your body feels. Slow down until you are completely relaxed. (Massaging the hands and feet sometimes helps.) Let your orgasm take over. Not easy, and not for novices, but worth the training sessions.

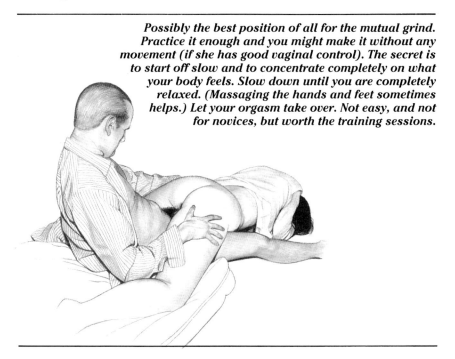

vagina. If he finds that a slow grind, and her excitement, is not enough to make him climax (and there is no reason why it should), let her take her pleasure and then roll over so that he can take his from the top. Many women find the missionary more acceptable after they have reached one climax.

Office romances

The office has overtaken the dance hall as the most popular dating agency. In the usual course of things, some dates progress to live-in relationships, but the workplace is rarely shared on a long-term basis with a live-in lover, so it is separate from the night-to-morning life of home and family; the quickie over the office desk, less threatening to his marriage. Like a cream cake, it is naughty but nice, and not necessarily harmful – or so he – and she – often like to think.

Not all advances from male work mates like Joe are welcome to women. Most experience sexual harassment in some guise. Although much of it is mild, some is not. There is an intrinsic power inequality between boss and secretary which men can (and do) use to sexual advantage.

Attentions you don't need

In an ideal world, men would not be sexual bullies, but since some are, a wise woman should be aware of the signals she gives in the workplace. Standard advice for those who wish to keep male attention at bay is:

- *Choose clothes that are smart, safe and a little dull, such as a suit or skirt in a neutral colour with a contrasting blouse. Avoid dresses, feminine or casual clothes and eye-catching colours such as red or yellow.*

- *Talk about work, not your private life, or his. If the conversation wanders, put it firmly back on to a work tack.*

- *Don't give the impression that you are available, even if this means inventing a boyfriend.*

- *Don't get into the habit of having coffee or lunch alone with him if you don't want his advances, and never ask for special favours, or agree to anything that might seem like a date.*

But, and this is an important point, if it doesn't stop, or prevent, his unwanted advances, you are not at fault. Warn him that his advances are unwelcome, and if he still persists, report him.

IF YOU WERE THE ONLY GIRL
IN THE WORLD

✦ ✦ ✦ And I was the only boy,
Nothing else would matter in the world
today ✦ ✦ ✦

──────────────── *Simon & Willow* ────────────────

If a person loves only one other person and is indifferent to the rest of his fellow men, his love is not love but a symbiotic attachment, or an enlarged egoism.

Erich Fromme

Simon

The trouble with package holidays is the people. I enjoy skiing but that doesn't mean I like skiing folk. Fact is, I find them superficial, always going on about trails and bindings and things. Sitting around the bar is not my scene. Early in the week, Willow and I could be alone off piste. We'd get breakfast while the night revellers were still asleep and be at the lifts first in line. Sometimes it was just the two of us alone in the whiteness. As soon as it got crowded we'd go down, back to the hotel room, shower, make love. In the evenings we'd lie together on the bed reading, her head resting on my stomach. The hotel food was indifferent, so after the first night we ate in our room. We don't need anyone else. I am everything to her, as she is to me.

Willow

I think it's sad the way couples seem to grow apart. Simon and I are like two people in the same skin. Some people would rather talk to total strangers than to each other.

Simon

Saturday we got driven off the slopes early by the weekend madmen with their dangling wine skins and coarse jokes, so we went for a walk. Fabulous. Willow makes me so happy. Then three idiots came careering through the trees shouting and hollering like it was a football game. Why go off piste if you can't appreciate solitude? We went back to our room.

Willow

Showering together is our special thing. First we soap each other, then we press our soapy bodies together, slipping and sliding over each other. Simon sings to me, and sometimes we harmonize. Folk songs and blues, mostly. He brings a towel to wrap me in. Then he rubs body lotion all over me. I love the way he touches me. Licking my toes and that nice bit behind my knees. I feel myself expanding. Like a bubble. I stretch out my arms and draw him in. He makes me real. To him I am everything.

Simon

I roll her over. Willow's breasts are small. I like them like that, not great fleshy bags. When I enter her it's like awakening. The hollow shell of pretended life disappears; I need her every minute of every day.

Willow

When Simon makes love to me our souls meet. We look into each other's eyes. Flesh of my flesh. Simon says he wants to know every moment that it is me. That's how I feel, too. It must be so impersonal any other way. The eyes are the windows to the soul, don't you think?

Simon

It's especially good when I place Willow on her back. I lie on my side next to her and touch her thighs, she spreads her legs. I am raised on one elbow so I can see everything. Little Simon, now, he's a pushy fellow. I hardly have to encourage him and he's clamouring at Willow's Door. I love to see Little Simon slip his way into Willow, he pushes her lips apart and open. Willow's Door gets so nice and round while Little Simon, he slides in and out so slickly.

Willow

I feel I am above us, looking down at us. I am both inside and outside the bubble that surrounds us. I see Simon slide gently in and out. So sensitized. Little Simon feels like fingers gliding softly across my skin. I know people talk about thrusting. But that must be sex. This is a love touch, a melt. I hear his breath quicken. I want him. I want him to come inside me, I love to please him, to give him everything.

Simon comes – a flourish of trumpets.

Oh darling, darling, sweet, sweet
Simon. That is what I always say as he
comes inside me. I love how we make
love. I am proud that I can make him
happy. It is the love and the closeness
that matters.

Simon and Willow are people in name only. They are struggling to enter each other's skin; where Simon leans, Willow bends. But they turn to each other in need as some turn to drugs or drink. If love is a commitment to mutual growth and development, two separate pillars supporting the bridge of a shared life, Simon and Willow are not lovers, but two desperate selves seeking dependency: they are addicts.

Both of them lack a sense of their own worth. Instead of self- sufficiency, there is self-deficiency or emptiness. Through Willow, Simon finds his value. In creating a self for Simon, Willow fills her own emptiness. But it is a fragile interdependency. When your reason for self lies in another body, there is too much at stake to allow that person to grow outside your control. Balanced in need, as Simon and Willow are, the relationship could go on; but more often than not, a couple's needs are less balanced.

Addictive love may be extreme, but it is not unusual. Many of us have the seeds of an addictive relationship within us. We can all be lovesick. A useful measure of health is flexibility, the ability to learn and to change; sickness is an inability to let go, even when sated. In time, the drug addict needs a higher dose; for Willow to keep Simon, she will have to give more of herself. Perhaps too much. Addiction is an attempt to control pleasure and pain, a fantasy which helps deaden the fear of loneliness and rejection. As relationships fall apart, many of us resort to an addictive way of behaving for the simple, and honourable, reason that we are afraid.

The 169th car

It is only 6.53 and you must not start counting for another seven minutes. You watch the clock. It watches you. You walk to the bathroom, adjust your hair and walk slowly back to the clock. The hand has moved on 50 seconds. You put on the kettle. It boils, so you take it off. You switch on the TV, flick through the channels and turn it off. And now it is almost time to start counting. One, two, three – but the cars are coming rather too fast. Better just count the ones coming from his direction. So you start again. 'Please, just let it be the next one. Please, I'll give up chocolate for a whole week. Please, I'll be nice to the parking attendant and clean out the car and tidy my drawers and . . .' Of course, you started counting too early.

And what happens when he finally gets out of the 169th car? You rush into the bedroom and hide your shoes. You count to 36 and pick up a lipstick before opening the door. You hug him, kiss him and smile; you say, "Help yourself to a beer, or better still, help me find my black shoes, then I'll be ready to go."

'In love'

It is a scenario familiar to anyone who has 'fallen in love'. Nothing is as important as the loved one. He or she distorts life, and, frankly, it is delicious finding him or her never more than two steps from your thoughts.

Even in the beginning of what may ultimately prove to be a healthy relationship, this 'in love-ness' is not normal. It is wonderful, dreamlike, overpowering; but even as we wallow, no one with any honesty expects it to go on for ever.

Obsessions, by their nature, overwhelm, and even as they happen, most of us know they are absurd, except perhaps when young and green. Lift the honeyed veil from your eyes, and she is quite ordinary. The essence of obsessive love is that we open up ourselves to hurt. We recognize that a lover has the power to harm us, and instead of running away, we embrace the demon. You are never so vulnerable as now, and little wonder love sends normal, logical people in search of miracles and magic, courting doom and disaster in star signs and fate. He loves me, he loves me not. F. Scott Fitzgerald described it as 'wedding your unutterable visions to her perishable breath'.

Time passes, and through the fog of passion a person appears. So you never liked walking in the rain, or birdwatching, or the taste of freshly roasted chestnuts? You never much cared for dark blond hair, or grey eyes, or rounded figures, or hairy chests, or people who sing flat? But those eyes, and those small breasts, are the only ones. As Simon says, there is no question that from now on that is how they should be.

While the falling-in-love process is a distortion of reality, it is common, and really no cause for concern, provided you are prepared to take your chances and to put it all on the line knowing she or he might disappear next week. When the worst happens, you will plunge into deepest despair; but you will let it happen. You can recognize that obsessions are part of human experience, and of their nature are uncontrollable. You may spend your nights and days wailing and getting drunk; but you don't spend the weeks before the finish controlling your partner so that there is no escape. As Simon and Willow do.

Their psychological problem is an exaggerated need for security: security that love is really like the songs in which they harmonize together, a tune that plays for ever. Like Peter Pan, Simon does not want to grow up into a world where idiots disturb the peace, and ski resorts get filled with skiing folk. For them, deep fears and inadequacies make the normal ups and downs of relationships impossible. Addicts need constancy: a steady supply of heroin, or whisky, or Willow. The constant drip of mutual devotion.

But wait . . .

It is easy for those who have learned to love in a healthy way to laugh at Simon and Willow; to feel smug. Women may feel outraged that Willow is happy to spend her life propping up Simon, (as women so often have); men may think him wet and wingeing.

Simon and Willow are *both* happy putting all their emotional eggs in this basket. It may not be our idea of heaven, but then most of us do not face the utter devastation Willow and Simon both feel when alone. Within this tight relationship, Simon gives Willow succour. Neither of them grow, but we cannot all be pilgrims. Before condemning love addicts, consider their alternatives. When deprived of an addictive relationship, the Simons and Willows of this world are more likely to turn to drugs and drink than psychotherapy or personal growth programmes. We doubt a bottle of whisky a day offers Willow more freedom, or Simon greater happiness.

Which does not alter the fact that addictive relationships are potentially dangerous: the players may well be addicted to drugs or drink as well as to love. They are never psychologically robust, and often desperate and self-centred. Such relationships can be destructive, violent and dangerous.

A definition of love

Love is the antithesis of addiction. Like chestnut trees, lovers spread their branches, mature and bear fruit. Standing together, each can admire the beauty of the other: strong and individual. The intimacy of lovers encompasses trust, understanding, independence, and freedom.

We cannot love from insecurity: we love only if we stand alone. We cannot love just one person in this world, because to love just one in such a wide world is to love only one's self. Simon's love for Willow is an enlarged egotism; without her love, his very identity would be threatened.

Check list for lovers:

● *Do you believe in yourself?*

● *Are you a better person for being in love?*

● *Are you friends? Would you be friends if you were not lovers?*

● *Do you have other interests outside the relationship?*

● *Do you feel that the relationship makes you a better person?*

- *Is the relationship part of your lives: integrated, not set apart?*

- *Are you possessive and jealous of the other person's growth?*

- *Do you want them happy more than you want them to be with you?*

- *Do you want to be indispensable to him or her?*

- *Do you build his or her pride at the expense of reality?*

- *Do you want to be his or her only friend?*

- *Is he or she your only friend?*

There should be six yes's: six no's.

Stepping stones to addiction:
1 I see: there is a powerful attraction.
2 I idealize. I am infatuated.
3 Songs tell a truth: romance blossoms.
4 I dream of eternal happiness.
5 Love is a compulsion: I am preoccupied.
6 Only he or she can make me happy.

Six steps out, and now the water runs deeper. The way back is diffi-cult, the stones are wet and slippery.

7 I have no choice; I must go on. I am dependent.
8 I become obsessive, jealous and possessive. Nothing else mat-ters. I deny myself.
9 I give everything, but I can't make it come right.
10 I am in pain: I cannot go on mentally or physically.
11 I jump for the bank, or I stay and face the inevitable emotional and physical damage.
12 The twelfth step is like the first. Turning, I see a new attraction, another love. And so I begin again.

Who are the addicts?
There is a school of thought which suggests that there are addictive personalities, and that it is only chance that Simon turns to Willow in-stead of booze. There may be something in this: there is even a ten-dency for addiction to run in families; but most people agree that addiction can also be learned.

It often stems from childhood deprivation. Like most addicts, Simon and Willow grew up in disfunctioning homes. Which does not mean they were deprived of money; they were not. They lacked an environment which taught them how to feel and control emotion. This is how it might happen.

Lessons in love

Babies are dependent on their parents to make life safe and secure. There is a special name for the love between a baby and its care givers: attachment. As the name implies, attachment is something we cannot help; it is love without question. Indeed, parental love is often totally forgiving, and normally lasts a lifetime. No wonder that those without self-esteem crave such love.

Most children gradually grow out of their obsessional baby love, forming attachments, and love relationships, with siblings and friends. They accept they must share their mother with husband, brother and sister. In time, they are probably relieved that the obsession is broken and the cord lengthened. From friendships, children learn that love is not automatic; from family, that it can be tested to its limits. They see people quarrel and then kiss and make up, love and laugh and then become angry and happy in turn. They learn that people can come together and move apart; the pattern serves as a model for later relationships. There is no need for sacrifice, or escape. No need to cling, because love does not suffocate or harm.

In a disfunctioning family, a child has instead a model of emotional abuse. Disfunction is often linked to alcoholism and other addictions in the parents. A man retreating from the excessive demands of a drunken wife casts his children adrift, loving no one. Faced with this, the child can withdraw, or cling more tightly to the wreckage. The pattern she uses to cope with parental rejection often continues for a lifetime.

As society changes and families move from one community to another, disfunctioning families become absorbed in themselves, and isolated. Keeping apart from the neighbours hides her bruises, and, in any case, what do neighbours say to a man who beats his wife, or a woman who is always drunk? The children are also isolated, and suffer the further deprivation of having no models but their parents, which may be one reason why addiction is such a serious problem.

But neediness is not only rooted in childhood. The child growing up fat and spotty has needs which may not be filled. The child growing up different – in colour, creed or outlook – may find it difficult to feel loved. Growing up with a basic lack of self-esteem is the root cause of many addictions.

Love in the bathroom

Sometimes it is good just to squeeze into the bath or shower together, just like Simon and Willow, and soak, and talk, and wash each other's feet. One at each end means someone gets the plumbing in their back, but it hardly matters.

At other times, one of you can sit on the side of the bath and soap the other. The soaper plays skin games, gives massage. The soapee just laps it up. Of course, there is a natural lingering on all the sexy bits, and a cooling off period called 'soaping the more mundane'. Eventually, of course, none of it is mundane, and then, since most domestic baths are simply too small, and bathroom floors too hard, the only course is to dry each other and race into bed.

Heartbreak

Willow is saddened that lovers grow apart; she is doubtless familiar with all the potentially destructive emotions that go with the experience:

● Like ringing them up at three in the morning, not saying a word, then agonizing over the thought that they will start to make love, and hoping he can't get it up and she can't come.

● Like hoping she snores and has fat thighs.

● Like thinking that you never really liked men with hairy chests.

● And maybe your heart *is* broken:

● Because it is impossible to believe that you will never again feel the coarseness of his curls.

● Because you find yourself dreaming about walking together, and saying how silly you were to part.

● Because you cannot think her bad, or get her out of your mind, or want anyone else, or make love to anyone without anger and hurt.

● Because no other body seems right.

Mending a broken heart

When something precious like a heart is broken, there is no point in saying, 'Never mind', and sweeping the bits under the carpet. A lost lover needs a funeral. We need to tell people we hurt; if necessary, smash plates, shout, cry and stick pins in his photograph. It is right to get drunk and collapse in a heap on the bathroom floor, because unless pain is released, it will seep out over the years, damaging innocent bystanders.

A friend is someone who listens to your heartbreak and makes all the right noises. She, or he, is usually on your side, but sometimes is not. Even the heartbroken need a challenge. A friend is the one who can tell the truth – in a week or two.

Seven rules for sorrowing:
- *Throw away all his or her bits and pieces.*

- *Throw out all the songs you played while you made love. If you must, play them just once: just one orgy of sorrow and song, then directly into the bin.*

- *Take up jogging, have your hair done, buy a hat, get a massage. Start looking better than you ever did before.* Don't do it only because you want him to eat his or her heart out.

- *Picture her with curlers and an extra 30 lb – mostly on her thighs and chin.*

- *Picture him in a fairy costume with acne: whole body acne.* Don't imagine acne on his penis: better not imagine his penis at all.

- *Never ring him.*

- *Never fuck him for old times' sake, even in fantasy.*

Pop-song romance
There is an 'ideal' of love which sings daily from the radio and comes hot off the presses of a million books and magazines. While in our healthy selves we run from it, being in love makes popular songs seem profound.

- Listen to the propaganda:
  Just one look . . .
  That old black magic has me in its spell . . .
  Can't help falling in love . . .

- No wonder we feel there is no choice. In its spell, we become rash:
  Why don't you take all of me?
  It's now or never . . .

- We behave badly:
  With the girl of my best friend . . .
  Young girl, get out of my mind . . .

- We make unreasonable demands:
  Stand by me . . .
  Don't sit under the apple tree with anyone else but me . . .

- And we accept unreasonable demands:
  As long as he needs me . . .
  And tell your friend there with you he'll have to go . . .

- And we give too much credit:
  You make me feel like a natural woman . . .
  Only you can make the darkness bright . . .

No one is exactly to blame for the lunacies committed in the name of 'love' as defined in pop songs; but we are responsible. You can say no to unrealistic love, just as you can say no to drugs.

There *are* no spells, only songs about love potions. Whatever the songs say it is not right to suffer – or die – for love.

The message of pop-song romance is that this is the elixir of life. And it is not just pop songs. Many of us were raised to think sex should not be mentioned, except with a smutty giggle, and that romance was the stuff of a real relationship. He will be a prince. She will wake up. We just have to love enough.

She takes

And what does a woman such as Willow take from these images? The suffering; the devotion; the essentially female power base that moves behind the throne. She takes the view that through Simon she is whole. To be without a man is to be no one, and thus she is in danger of becoming a woman who loves too much.

Women who love too much

Women of Willow's type commonly find themselves in unhappy and destructive relationships which cannot and do not work however hard they try. The less the relationship works, the more the obsession grows. If a woman is prepared to excuse his moodiness, temper, anger and indifference because of love, the price is too high. When he fills her thoughts and conversation, and her hold on life is through him, she has lost touch with reality. When she believes she can change him, she is fatally deluded.

When a relationship stops meeting your needs, get out. When you know he does not care, yet want and need to keep him, say goodbye.

Who needs to be told? But often we are afraid to act – because however destructive a relationship, our self-esteem is bound up in it.

He takes

To a man such as Simon, raised never to express emotion, the feeling of romantic love is a heady drug. To love, to suffer and love again:

each is an aspect of a cycle which licenses him to wallow. Indeed, the actual process of falling in and out of love can become addictive: like a humming-bird, he flies from flower to flower, sipping. He is addicted to beginnings and endings; he avoids the growth and commitment central to healthy relationships.

Avoiding commitment

If loving too much expresses her fear of showing the masculine assertiveness within her, avoiding commitment expresses his fear of the female part of him. It is a predominantly male problem. At one extreme, men exclude women from their lives, at the other, a man acts to diminish a woman's power over him. As a boy, he wanted to surrender to his mother and be like her; but society told him in no uncertain terms that he must be a man. Now he fears this fragile maleness may be swallowed up or suffocated by her femininity. That if he lets go he may surrender to femininity.

The truth about Little Simon

'Little Simon' is a nauseating euphemism, typical of Willow's lover. To Simon, and to the world, his penis is more than a badge of his masculinity; it is frequently equated with it. Even his sexual feelings are somehow depicted as centred here.

The images commonly used to describe the penis are big, strong, hard, forceful, aggressive. Yet the penis itself is spongy and soft; even when erect, it is surprisingly small. The largest erect ones are shorter than the span of a woman's hand. The most obvious aspect of the male genitalia is their vulnerability. The erection that fails to rise, or shrinks rapidly and finally at the sound of an opening door. Few penises have much staying power, or come again as quickly as their owners would wish. They are not weapons, automatically shooting out streams of bullets. The semen, for all the fuss of ejaculation, is but a teaspoon of fluid.

Seeing it as 'Little Simon' separates the penis from the man, the penis-weapon apart. Down there, hard, without tenderness, love, or beauty, it is so utterly inappropriate that sometimes women cannot help but laugh.

Little wonder, then, that male insecurity about their members runs deep. Some men even imagine it is smaller than it really is, and most men (even the well-endowed), think it relatively small. The average woman with of eight partners during her lifetime, is in a better position than him to make comparisons. Worrying. Standard advice to women is to say it is about the biggest you have seen – if, indeed, you say anything at all.

Lazy loving for a sunny afternoon, complete with a view; one of the endless variations on the rear-entry theme. Like all rear entry positions, it goes straight for her G. The feeling can be intense. Her body is freely available to his hands – and to hers.

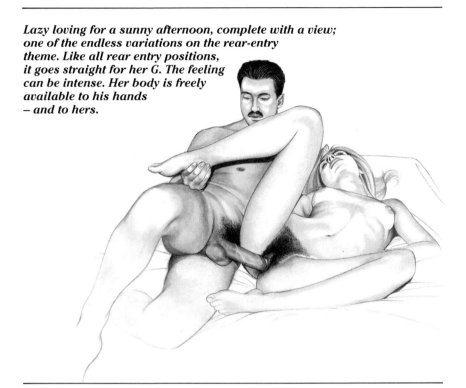

Conditioning

Long ago now, a Russian scientist rang a bell and placed a little meat powder on a dog's tongue. After repeating this a few times, he found that the dog's mouth watered when the bell sounded. Pavlov called this phenomenon conditioning.

Once upon a time, in a bed somewhere near you, a woman lay in the morning sunshine sucking a risen, if spongy, penis. It was not particularly large or hard or aggressive. It was just a regular sort of thing. As she sucked, the man moaned and her loving of him grew. Watching the penis in her hands, and sensing him in her mouth, she knew this was pleasure and that it was good. We do not know her name, but the experience is readily identified: it is conditioning.

That she finds his genitalia desirable – even beautiful – has more to do with conditioning than man-made imagery to describe their nature. She loves the way they grow, the feeling as they do, the sight, the smell. Not their 'power'. For many women, the way they love the penis simply reflects the way they love the man; her view of his masculinity, painted with her own brush; why else can women so readily take on the flotsam and jetsam of men?

BOUND TO PLEASE

— Connie & Lloyd —

Lloyd, a 34-year-old radio disc jockey and Connie, a 29-year-old dance teacher and aspiring country and western singer, sat on the couch opposite us and talked about the answer to a question that has plagued thousands of otherwise happy couples: Is there sex after marriage?

"After eight years," Lloyd confided, "we felt as if someone had turned down our sexual thermostats."

We asked if either of them had ever considered the quick fix of an earlier time: seeking excitement outside the marriage. Lloyd shook his head emphatically. "Nowadays screwing around is just plain stupid," he said.

"It's even more dangerous emotionally," Connie added. "We didn't want to destroy our relationship."

Lloyd looked at his wife with a sparkle in his eye. "Okay," he said, "everyone knows that time can curb the excitement. But we've discovered ways to put life back in to our sex life. Variety is a powerful aphrodisiac. We play games."

Connie spoke up. "Sometimes he gets a call at the office from Rock'em, Shock'em & Suck'em telling him that a new girl will be waiting for him at home." She pulled at the hem of her short skirt. "Other times, I just surprise him." We must have looked intrigued because Lloyd leaned forward to elaborate. "Let's face it, Connie knows all my buttons and how to push them."

"And I do." Connie grinned. "I love to drive him absolutely crazy."

* * * *

177

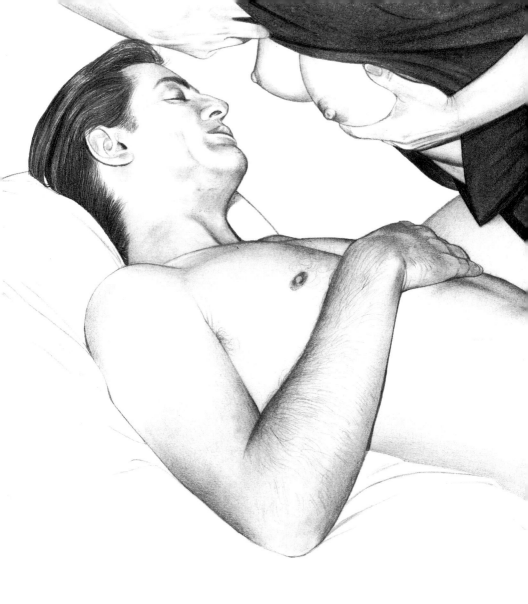

Connie awoke before the alarm went off that Friday morning and cuddled against Lloyd's muscular body. His warmth and scent aroused her and when she reached down she felt his erection. He moved in his sleep as she stroked him, but the alarm rang and it was time to deal with breakfast, getting Kenneth and Barbara off to school and catching the bus to work. It had been more than a week since they had made love and the feeling of his hardness in her hand came back to her at moments all through the day. Lloyd had been surprised but pleased when he came home to find that the kids had been sent to his mother-in-law's for dinner and a movie. He trooped off for a shower and a nap with the impression that dinner was under way. While Lloyd slept, Connie changed into net stockings: panties would be unnecessary for this evening's activities. She put on a wrap-around dress that fastened only with a belt.

Lloyd was lying on his back with his hand on his crotch when Connie came into the bedroom. A good sign. She placed a pile of soft cords on the table and slipped her hand under his. Lloyd awoke most pleasantly to find his wife having her ways with his tumescent penis. He smiled at her sleepily muttering, "Is supper ready?" Connie leaned over him and let one breast fall from her dress. "Taste this," she said, rubbing it lightly over his lips. "Mmmph," responded Lloyd thoughtfully, his eyes closed and his mouth filled. Connie looked southward to confirm that the flag was indeed raised. Now confident that one appetite would supersede another, she straightened up, drawing her breast reluctantly from his mouth. "Hold that thought." She quickly tied his wrists together taking special care to catch his thumbs. Pushing him back on to a pile of cushions, she tied his legs spread-eagled to the bed posts.

Lloyd tugged experimentally on the cords. They did not release. He pulled harder, but he was still his wife's captive. She could do anything to him she wanted. "Do your worst," he challenged, then, as if it were a casual afterthought, "but if I say 'ice cube' set me free." What would she do? Answer: give him a foretaste of sensations to come.

She knelt on the bed, her cunt peeping out between her thighs and buttocks, hovered a tongue's length from his face. Her fingers slippery with oil, she held the base of his penis between her thumb and forefinger. A rapid stroke up to and over the glans. Lloyd bucked involuntarily. A thousand heartbeats later she stroked him again. His enthusiasm, which had begun to wilt, immediately sprang back. The sight and the smell of her, and the teasingly slow stimulation, were too much; he began to thrash.

Connie had wondered about the next part during the tango lessons she was giving the Gautiers. (How Marlene Gautier expected Maurice to tango was beyond her – still, it would pay for Barbara's music lessons.) Satisfied with the effect so far, she now knew how to play it. Pull out all the stops, bold and brassy. Connie turned on the tape deck and danced slowly to the open door. Holding on to the handle, straddling it with her legs and leaning back, she offered her cunt to the edge of the door. She humped the door jamb, her head thrown back, grinding her hips to the tempo of the music. Connie threw Lloyd a quick glance. Oh yes, his expression was intense, the flag was flying high. The rhythm throbbing in her head blended with the warmth between her legs; each liquid pelvic thrust . . . was . . . just . . . perfect. She was *on*. Caressing the handles as she pushed herself harder into the jamb, she crooned, "It's so hard, it feels so good."

Lloyd strained forward, watching her slip the dress off her shoulders slowly, seductively, revealing her breasts. Then she was standing beside him, one leg raised and resting on the bed. The smooth flesh of her thigh was dimpled by the top of the fishnet stockings, her belly and cunt framed by the garter belt. Looking down at him, she sucked thumb and forefinger, then rubbed her nipple.

She pushed her left breast upwards and licked the nipple with her extended tongue. As she raised her head he saw a thin strand of saliva between lips and nipple stretch and break. He thrashed again.

Connie unhitched the stockings, grinding slowly. "I want to be screwed. I want to be screwed deep. I want a big, fat cock rammed up inside me. Want to screw me, boy?" Kneeling above him on the bed she cupped and stroked her cunt, spread herself open for him, and moved her fingers rapidly in and out. "Mmm, that feels good. I love a good finger fuck. I'm all hot and wet. I don't need you." She flicked her finger against his hard cock straining into the air. Lloyd twitched and groaned. It was time to refocus her attention.

"Lie still." Connie breathed hard in his ear, squatting to lower herself on to him. He was in her, her breast pressed gently into his mouth. His relief was only momentary, however. She raised herself out of reach. One hand slowly traced the outline of his mouth, the other lightly caressed his penis. It was dark and very hard, the veins twining round it standing out vividly, filled with a hunger that she herself had created and controlled. Connie kept turning her head for the pleasure of looking at the splendid contours as she kissed the hair on his belly and chest, continued to watch as she rubbed her cunt over his body. He sucked the palm she pressed into his mouth.

"Are you ready for me?" she asked. He nodded helplessly. "Please." She sat well up on his chest, the soft folds of her buttocks just out of reach of his mouth. Her ankles were tucked beneath his knees. She once again took the root of his penis between finger and thumb and, in a sudden quick stroke gave him pressure along its length. "One," she said. Glaciers ran down to the sea, mountains eroded away and she reached ten. Then another heavenly, excruciating stroke. This time she counted faster and pulled again, bringing him up, taking him closer. "Finish me, please finish me," he cried as she alternated long and short pauses. Each time he came near she stopped, waited until the possibility of release had passed. She did it, again and again and again, until his world was spinning and she could not contain the arcing explosion.

Even before he was down she untied him and held him like a baby between her breasts.

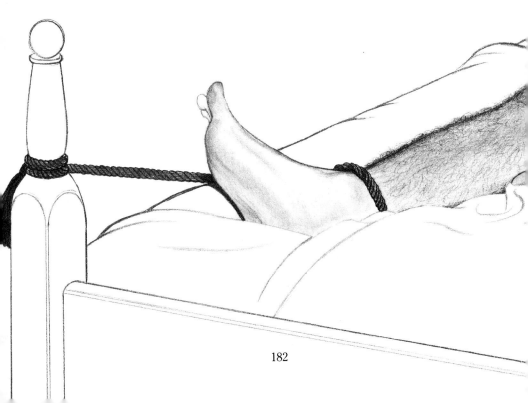

182

Connie, reaching down to feel Lloyd's erection as he slumbers, offers a trivial, but charming prelude to the excitements which follow later in the day. Or not so trivial, perhaps. For the memory of the erection in her hand acts as an erotic focus several times as she goes about her work: the seed, who knows, of the evening's virtuoso performance. As in **Larry & Wanda**, anticipation, however slender a thread, can twist itself into a potent spring. Moral: savour the little things.

Lloyd's erection almost certainly waxed against the background of a dream. Eighty to 95 per cent of men's dreams are accompanied by an erection which reaches its maximum about five minutes after dream onset, is maintained more or less continuously during the dream, and subsides in the ten minutes following the dream. Connie could not be sure what Lloyd was dreaming about, however, because erections occur with dreams of all sorts. But the strength of the erection is reduced with high-anxiety dreams, and, surprise, surprise, it increases with sexy dreams. As you would expect, sexy dreams are remembered better upon waking than non sexual ones. Women, incidentally, make sexual movements of their hips during dreams, and it is possible that they may lubricate, too.

The sure indicators of dreaming sleep are rapid eye movements (R.E.M.s). The accompanying erection, known in the trade as nocturnal penile tumescence, is monitored by a sex therapist in order to decide whether a man's impotence has a physical cause such as diabetes (see **Martin & Giselle**), or a psychological one.

'Geddem off, geddem off . . .'

Connie's striptease, which makes full use of her dancing skill, is intended, first of all, to excite her husband; but many women, Connie included, are aroused by fantasies of being watched.

Professional strippers, by contrast, perform not in an excited flush but tend to withdraw into their own private world. Some say that the professional stripper's trade makes good a need for male attention ungratified in childhood. This is borne out by a survey of 35 strippers, in which 60 per cent were discovered to have come from unstable homes with inadequate fathering. The women interviewed also estimated that 50 to 75 per cent of strippers were lesbian. For many of these women, then, the emphasis is on the tease, with no expectation of delivery. For them, stripping may even be a form of revenge directed at the men in the audience: 'You want me, but you can't have me.'

As is so often the case with sexual behaviour, the same act can be performed for radically different reasons. Connie's dance was for fun.

At the Moulin Rouge in Paris, amateurs disrobe out of sporting spirit. Ordinary women go up on stage to be introduced in their workaday roles ('Marie-Therèse is a secretary; she only started last week, but isn't she doing well?'). The same sporting spirit doubtless inspires the female British soccer fans who from time to time make a clean breast of it before the watching millions.

Different motivation again is found in the Friday night wet T-shirt contests popular among American collegians. Water splashed on to the material renders it clingy and transparent. The contagious excitement of the crowd, and urging on by friends, encourages women (who turn up bra-less) to participate spontaneously. The contests make overt and explicit the competition among women to be watched.

Yet another variation is the phenomenon of working class get-togethers in Scotland, where, prompted by certain numbers from the disco, stout middle-aged women will get up on tables and strip down to their corsets. Here, the audience's riotous laughter is a mockery of the whole process of striptease.

No clothes, equal opportunities

But if you regard men's delight in striptease as damning evidence of the male instinct to view women as a sex objects, think again. Striptease shows in which men are the performers take place regularly all over Europe and America. Women go in rowdy groups for girls' nights out; yells of "Bring out the men", and other less innocent suggestions, begin as soon as they are seated. Bank notes are stuffed into the strippers' G-strings. After the show, dancers find slips of paper with sexually specific requests nestling among their private parts, telephone numbers included. Some of the spectators hang about the stage door, hoping to make friends. The dancers collect most money in tips when club rules permit the women to touch and kiss them. G-strings are pulled off and the men are not infrequently scratched, pinched and bitten on the bum. A dancer in one club came to dread the finale in which he had to dance on a table, grabbed by as many as ten pairs of hands at once.

So much for the 'gentle' sex which wants emotional involvement as a prelude to sexual activity. True, the women who go to these clubs are not exactly the timid type; even so, they seem to be striking support for the argument that gender differences in sexual behaviour are largely determined by culture. The micro-culture of these clubs sets the stage, so to speak.

The turnabout is also complete from the men's point of view. The dancers use costume, make-up, and sexy movements to excite the audience – their tips depend upon it. Some of the men are then dismayed to find that the women treat them as sex objects.

Knot tonight, darling

Tying up your partner promises the exciting feeling of being in control; being tied can enhance your orgasm. Bondage renders sexual pleasure guiltless: you are overpowered and there is no way to resist.

For some, it is the symbolism that counts; loose tying is good enough for these folks. For others, struggling against the constraint will be important, and the bonds must be made thoroughly secure. But tie hands and feet comfortably so they have some possibility of movement. Too tight, and bruising will result. Spread eagled on the bed, arms and legs pointing to the four points of the compass, is the obvious way, but some people enjoy it better sitting on a chair with arms tied behind the back at the wrists and elbows. Catch thumbs and/or big toes in a loop for an extra *frisson*. Rubber or leather straps, soft curtain cords, or plain clothes line all serve well. Chains and handcuffs intensify the image of bondage, but can be painful. Insert pillows at judicious points for extra comfort. Most important of all, provide a method of quick release.

More extreme restraint can be achieved with a gag. According to one woman quoted by the 1960s sexologist Alex Comfort, a gag "keeps the bubbles in the champagne"; but being gagged is an acquired taste for most people.

Never abandon anyone who is tied up: muscle cramps can occur when restraint is prolonged more than 30 minutes. Choose a stop-game word, and honour it absolutely. Don't try it with anybody you don't know very well.

Tying and being tied may take a little getting used to, but they set the stage like nothing else for slow masturbation.

Teasing and slow masturbation

Connie shows how to do it for a man. For a woman whose orgasms are fairly reliable, the principle is the same but there is obviously more latitude in technique. Depending upon her preferences, or yours, stroke and kiss her mouth, breasts and vulva in combination. Penetrating her gently after she is tied will feed into her rape fantasies. Giving her head from below so she cannot see you will evoke her fantasies of anonymous sex. Play on these. Some women will appreciate being told how they look and what will happen to them, or what is happening to them, in graphic and delicious detail.

She may reach orgasm rapidly several times, but a different route to more intense sensation is to bring her close a few times, then let the

He trusts her enough to let her tie him up. She looks after him, and he looks up to her.

arousal subside without climax. Kiss and touch her elsewhere in the intervals. By this stage her erogenous zone may well extend from the crown of her head to the tips of her toes. Showing her your erect cock or rubbing it on her breasts will arouse her further; tease her with it. Slow, deliberately paced licking of her pussy will produce exquisite pleasure. Let her come for the final climax and untie her quickly.

As we have noted elsewhere, pain sensation is reduced by sexual arousal, hence rubbing can produce soreness that will only be noticed later. Using lotions or oils for lubrication makes sense.

Max and Sadie

Connie and Lloyd indulged in what the personal columns of certain newspapers and magazines call 'a little light bondage'. Bondage is not always so light; and it is one of the standard practices of sado-masochism or Sadie-Max as it is known in the porn trade. For some men and women, scenarios of controlling and being controlled are not an occasional bedroom game but a sexual way of life; they experience arousal and orgasm most easily or only if they are being manipulated and humiliated. Psycho-analists believe that something in their upbringing has convinced them that their sexual desires deserve to be punished. By incorporating fantasies of being punished as a necessary part of their arousal, they lessen their feelings of guilt.

Sometimes, therapists recapture horrific childhood scenes relating to particular fantasies. In the case of one teenage boy whose sadistic fantasies were directed against himself, it was discovered that at the age of four his mother had caught him masturbating. She ordered his sister to hold him down while she threatened to cut off his penis with a knife if he did it again.

Since there are relatively few women who will initiate sado-masochistic sex, men usually keep these interests secret from their wives. They go instead to prostitutes, who are accustomed to requests that they beat, whip, or step on their clients. One field study of New York call girls found that approximately 15 per cent of their clients (all upper middle-class Caucasian men) requested domination, usually in costume. Some would request specific scenarios and give the pros dialogue to speak ("I know what you were doing in the bathroom"). These experiences provide the men with a symbolic retreat into childhood or compensate for guilt about their own sadistic behaviour elsewhere.

The pros report that they reassure the men by telling them stories about other masochistic clients, and by saying that the activity is O.K. This allows the men to discuss their fantasies openly and to relieve sexual tension by acting out self-destructive or humiliating impulses (frilly knickers, babies' rubber pants and so on), which they cannot indulge openly.

Who's into Sadie-Max?

Sado-masochism must be a product of civilization, since it is unknown in primitive societies. The hair-pulling, biting and scratching by both partners during intercourse in less repressed cultures does not count as S. & M. since control and humiliation are neither intended nor perceived. Sado-masochistic responses were the single largest category in Nancy Friday's survey of men's sexual fantasies. However, this percentage is probably larger than its real frequency because of the strong needs these men feel and their limited opportunities to express them. Twelve per cent of women and 20 per cent of men surveyed report being aroused by S. & M. stories, but less than 10 per cent of either report having actually experienced acts which they consider to be S. & M.

Interviews with prostitutes in Washington D.C. suggest that those in political life indulge in extensive and extreme sado-masochism: an extension of power games into the bedroom. The difference between the prostitutes and rest of us is that when politicians do it to them, politicians pay for it; when the politicians do it to us, we pay.

Active female participation in sado-masochism is rare, but growing: witness the existence of at least three exclusively lesbian S. & M. clubs in San Francisco.

Clubs for sado-masochists

We believe in clubs for masochists, but only if persuasion fails. In the States, sado-masochistic scenarios are played out in the Til Eulenspiegel Society (straight and gay) and the Fist Fuckers of America (entirely gay).

The 'tops' are elaborately costumed in black leather and chains, while the heads of the 'bottoms' may be covered by leather hoods to increase their feelings of vulnerability. There are usually more who want to be 'bottoms' than 'tops' and it is even sometimes necessary to take turns at being the top. Tops can, however, get added enjoyment of the role by imagining themselves to be experiencing the humiliation being meted out to the bottom.

These games are co-operative, each player knowing and accepting his role; escape passwords may be agreed upon. A typical scenario would be for a leather-clad dominatrix to begin with verbal abuse ("You are filthy scum and deserve to suffer"), and then, contemptuously, to order the 'victim' to strip. The promised punishment is then administered.

Two thirds of 'slaves' prefer to be whipped and may arrive with an assortment of their own implements. Spanking with a bare hand is popular in Britain. A select few want to be 'tortured', for example by clothes pegs applied to tender places, or with drips of candle wax.

Rings threaded through the nipples are convenient to pull upon. Excretory acts such as 'water sports' (being given an enema) can provide particularly intense humiliation; and the 'golden shower' rams home the message that the slave is so far inferior to his master or mistress that even being urinated upon is a favour. With the proper mixture of arousal and humiliation, eight out of ten slaves can reach orgasm.

Transvestite

Here is another sideshow in the merry-go-round of deviant sex. It is an all-too-serious compulsion – not just a lark. At one extreme are those who confine it to the privacy of their homes, or to a club; at the other are those who feel so intensely that they are trapped within the body of the other sex that they eventually have a sex change operation.

Most transvestites are not homosexual or bisexual, and most are not, nor do they become, transsexuals. Another popular misconception is that they get a sexy thrill just by donning the other sex's uniform; only a small percentage find it physically exciting.

The need to cross dress may be acceptable to a 'straight' partner if it is occasional and confined to the home or a club. The problems start when he, or she, wants to go out on the town.

It would be unfair not to tell a prospective partner of your transvestite inclinations before he or she made a serious commitment. They must know the extent of your needs, and to what extent you are prepared to accept limits on your behaviour. Don't expect the security of a relationship to cure the inclination. Nevertheless, some transvestites are happily married, despite the strain imposed.

Female masochism

Sixty-five per cent of men who indulge in sado-masochism take a submissive role; 80 per cent of women taking part assume a dominant role. What if Connie and Lloyd had reversed positions?

Women with masochistic impulses do not routinely find outlets for these fantasies, but that they may find the real thing – in an actual, abusive relationship with a man.

To begin with, at least, there are several psychological factors which may draw them in. Many women find self-assurance an attractive quality in a man. For a few women, this attraction is exaggerated, as for example in the Stockholm Syndrome, named after an incident in which a woman fell in love with one of the robbers who had taken her hostage in a Swedish bank. For a woman with low self-esteem, being courted and controlled by an extremely dominant man appears to be confirmation of her desirability. The whiff of danger is an adventure. When his domineering escalates into aggression she may leave, but not if it taps a need to be humiliated.

The notorious recent American case of Hedda Nussbaum was an extreme example of real, rather than ritualized sado-masochism. Her man manipulated her psychologically and abused her physically, breaking bones. She thought of him as a god and returned to him even when the opportunity to escape presented itself. For men, masochistic impulses can lead to co-operative activities, which may be painful, but not life threatening. For women, they can be fatal.

Some of these same psychological elements may be found in battered women who persuade themselves that 'He needs me' and 'If I were better, he wouldn't hit me'. But what really makes most battered wives stay with abusive husbands are a lack of economic alternatives, social pressure from peers and relatives (including disbelief), a desire to protect the children and indeed threats from the men. Quite simply, men kill women who leave them: four thousand women a year are killed by their boyfriends or husbands in the United States.

Victorian myth

Early sexologists, including Freud, mistook female receptivity for biological masochism. One does not imply the other. Female chimpanzees, for example, actively solicit the attention of males. They do not seek out the most aggressive ones, but mate with the 'nicer' individuals. The Victorians assumed that sexual passivity was the natural response of woman, not recognizing it as a product of their own culture. They equated passivity with surrender.

Masochism

For many masochists, the anticipation of pain, and/or the memory of it, is more exciting than the pain itself. There are, however, boys whose masochistic feelings are so strong that they learn to have erections and ejaculations while being spanked – one of several reasons why corporal punishment is now a thing of the past in British boarding schools.

Similarly, troops of fourteenth-century pilgrims flagellated themselves across plague-ridden Europe in order to allay the wrath of God. Eventually, the Church recognized the eroticized nature of flagellation and banned it. Does this mean that any amount of pain can be converted to pleasure by an act of will? No. Toothache never becomes erotic. Skilled sadists know that if they venture beyond a particular slave's limit, he will not return for more. Masochism is about the rituals and sensations of punishment, up to a certain level, becoming a conditioned stimulus for sexual arousal; much as Pavlov's dogs could be taught to tolerate a specific, localized pain and even salivate in response to it, if it signalled food.

Sadism

This is commonly understood to be pleasure in the suffering of others; sexual arousal is linked to another's pain. There is probably more to it than this. The scenarios of ritualized sado-masochism suggest that an important aim is to gain control over another person. Making someone suffer is one dramatic way to accomplish this, but only one. So sadistic impulses are said to be at work when any means of domination is used.

A psycho-analist would say that the sadist is trying to get his own back for painful frustrations experienced in early childhood at the hands of powerful parents. Rituals involving excretion, for example, may reflect conflicts over toilet training. This form of delayed revenge only reassures the sadist temporarily, however, and must be therefore repeated again and again.

Individuals who act out ritualized sado-masochistic fantasies do not, with a few notable exceptions, commit violent assaults. However, some believe that similar sadistic impulses, at an unconscious level, are present in violent rapists. So, bedroom games with Sadie and Max should be approached with caution. There are real underlying emotions to be tapped here and they are not positive ones. Once again, the essential message must be: if one partner wants out, out it should be.

PAIN

MEETS PLEASURE

Kitty & Teddy

October 27th, 1988
Daddy bear needs Goldilocks,
to share porridge and much more.

November 9th, 1988
After what she did to your chairs?
Perhaps I could interest you in
Copperlocks, Goldie's furniture-
friendly sister?

December 10th, 1988
She'd answered 20 advertisements. He
had received 32 replies. They
exchanged photos and met one night at
'The Teddy Bear's Picnic'. The food
wasn't up to much, but it was hard to
resist under the circumstances.

March 11th, 1989
One thing led to another. Now Teddy
occasionally stays over on Saturday
night. Sunday, Kitty makes porridge,
amongst other things.

January 17th, 1990
They have been seeing each other for
over a year. He has come from work, as
he does on Wednesday, bringing
flowers and a bottle of wine. She makes
supper. After he washes up, they watch
a video and finish the wine. They would
probably say they were not 'in love',
though they have no other partners,
and haven't had since they met. It is
companionable, cosy. They are happy.

Here is Kitty coming out of the
bathroom, still damp from her shower.
She is wrapped in a towel, he stands in

his vest. Opening the towel she says:
"Shall we dance?"

They sing.
"Shall we dance?
Pom, pom, pom.
Shall we da, di, di da, di da di da
Pom, pom, pom.
And by chance . . . "

"Kiss me," Kitty says, and Teddy
pushes her gently on to the bed. She
smells of sandalwood. He reaches out
for a carnation and strokes her. Kitty
smiles. "Mmm, flowered."

"Or deflowered?" Teddy asks,
stroking the top of her thighs, creeping
up to her still wet triangle of copper fur.

She laughs because it tickles, and
tells him he'd have a problem
deflowering her with that. There is a
special current between them tonight.

Teddy studies the problem,
proclaims the flower not man enough
(his exact words are "Probably a wall
flower,") and turns her over.

Her back is so beautiful. Her wide
shoulders curve down to a narrow
waist. He traces a line with the flower,
winding back and forth across the
spine, moving slowly towards the
roundness of her bottom. The
separation between her cheeks
intrigues him. "Hmmm," he wonders,
not for the first time.

He flicks the flower around her anus. She squirms. "What are you doing back there?" she asks. He spreads her cheeks slightly and asks with some hesitation, "I was wondering if you would like me to penetrate you anally." She laughs, saying, "You funny formal teddybear. What a way to ask." She feels so relaxed with him. They have been together a long time. She says: "Let's see later, I can't start like that."

The idea is beyond the normal limits; it is stimulating. It lingers in the air as Teddy presses his hand between her legs, making circular movements with it, first soft, then firmly, in the way she likes. He glimpses her half smile as he slips his penis into her vagina. A few strokes, just to say, "Hello, I'm here," to feel her respond, "I'm glad you are." Then he carefully pushes a

moistened finger into her anus. Through the wall separating anus from vagina he can feel the pressure and movement of his penis moving inside her. It is a way to share her sensation. Occupying two of her body openings, he feels that he owns more of her, that she wants him to own her. The excitement between them is heightened.

Teddy feels the time has come and he withdraws. Kitty, sensing his timing, turns to lie flat on her stomach. "Promise to stop me any time," he says as he moistens her anus with vaginal juices. He pushes gently, waiting for her to relax. The sensation around the tip of his penis is very intense as he slips on the condom.

It hurts, as Kitty knew it would. She inhales deeply as he pushes. Thinking all the time that this is not pain, that by an act of will it could be pleasure. It seems an unlikely idea. If giving birth is like shitting a melon, this is like passing an orange.

As he eases forwards, Teddy feels his penis engulfed within her anus. She is dragging him in, while he waits passively for her anus to expand.

"Wait," she says. It is not pain alone. Like all places where pain and passion meet, it is an intense sensation. She is as open as a young bird gaping to be fed, knowing that he is violating her body space. It is something she can also feel with deep vaginal thrusting, or violent sucking of her breasts. It is not an everyday need. In the right mood, as now, it is extremely erotic. The pain is a barrier to pass, emotional rather than physical, like thinking about running a fourth mile while struggling with the third.

"You do it," Teddy says, moving the pillows behind him and half sitting. He expects her to come back on to him. Instead, she turns and squats, facing him, lowering herself gradually on to him while he guides her with one hand. Inside her, it feels tight and warm. His strokes are slow and short, anything longer and he would be ejected.

Kitty feels herself move through the barrier between pleasure and pain. She feels the sensations of the opening, feels him going into the void, like dragging, rather than a smooth flow, across a moist surface. Sweet pain. Her breath quickens as she see-saws. Pushing herself down on to him, then rocking forwards so that his pubic bone presses hard against her. Up and down she moves, until she is swelling, all edges gone.

He feels the heat flow through every part, tingling, waiting to explode. Life stirs. For a moment he is without breath, suspended as he withdraws from her, spilling on to the soft folds of her bottom.

He holds her, and as his hand moves into her vagina, Kitty feels her pelvic muscles tighten. She feels them gathering up the pleasure, gobbling it up like a deep vaginal kiss. She sucks, she chews, she swallows. A sweet pain,

almost too much to bear. The numbness overtakes her, like a shudder. The lines encircle her like iron filings on a magnet. She has fallen a million miles and is still falling.

Life goes on. Teddy, taking a tissue, wipes her bottom. He is struck by how oddly protective that act is, how close to her he feels.

Man is a social animal who cares about people. He evolved that way, living in groups of 20-200; his life is spent in the context of other people. We need them to care about us. We mind what they think, and what they think is that everybody needs somebody to love. Kitty and Teddy are no exceptions.

There is something comfortable about the whole idea of settling down: well, maybe not at 17, or even 27, but for most of us, sooner or later, it emerges from within. Yes, there are a few confirmed bachelors, and the odd Peter Pan who cannot commit. (In monkey troups, uncommitted males live outside the main group and borrow females when the boss male is not looking. Ethologists call them 'SF' males: it stands for sneaky fuckers.)

Coupledom may not be ideal for all of us all of the time, but it takes strong self-confidence to ignore the propaganda. And as society becomes increasingly mobile, the family unit is more and more prone to disintegrate. A partner is our best chance of a bosom pal: workmates come and go, neighbours likewise; but a live-in lover is there to share the good times and the bad.

Living like you should

When a man is doing what a man has to do, he shouldn't be alone. Nor should a woman. To be a spinster in Victorian England was regarded as, in theory at least, living death. In these heady days of independence and liberation, this should have changed, but the basis of social organization is still the couple, despite a high divorce rate.

Looking for someone

So, Kitty and Teddy go out to find someone. But finding a body to share, a friend to care for, is not always easy. Enter the market-place. Most couples meet at work or through mutual friends. A few meet at parties, dances, or bars. But when these have been tried, there is nothing for it but the inevitable classes, clubs and singles bars.

For the woman leaving a long-term relationship, especially if she has children, potential partners are thin on the ground, if one discounts the disgruntled husbands who inevitably crawl out of the woodwork. The solution for Kitty and Teddy, as for many, is to advertise, and to scrutinize the lonely hearts columns.

Thousands do this, not all of them ugly, unsuccessful or psychological disaster areas. Admitting loneliness takes a certain sort of guts. You may be desperate, you may be down, but you are not yet out.

In New York, an advertisement placed by a woman may bring 30 to 40 replies, one placed by a man, 60 to 70 (twice as many if he is a doctor). In London, you would be lucky to get 13. The most popular men are over 40 and professional, the most favoured women, 25 and attractive.

To meet the upmarket crowd in New York, you place an advertisement in the *New York Magazine*; the *Village Voice* is likely to draw more answers from the fringes. In London, *Time Out*, *New Statesman* and *Private Eye* cover the same ground. In the rest of the country, *Singles* magazine is used by a wide range of people.

If you want to know what advertisers look like, New York has a video dating service. In both cities, there are telephone dating lines, and, for the busy, high-flying New York executive, there is even a service which will find you a suitable mate from among top management: fee a mere $10,000.

It is said that four or five advertisements a year bring an adequate supply of potential partners. If you concoct a high-scoring message, friends can share the spoils. In any event, every night of the year on each side of the Atlantic, 4,000 hopeful individuals set out for a blind date. In spite of the occasional scare stories of psychopaths advertising for their next victim, a recent review of London advertisers showed it was as safe a way as any to meet a stranger.

The physical dangers may be slight, but wolves of both sexes are on the prowl. Some may look for sex, wrapped up in a 'long-term relationship', some for a long-term, supportive relationship wrapped up as sex.

Women, true to stereotype, complain that if they refuse sex he may never call again – and that if they do he may take the whole thing too casually. Because men by-and-large remain the predators in the singles scene, women are under pressure to hold off. They have a point. In one survey, more than half the men told women they cared more for her than they did in order to have sex.

But spare him a thought as he flees from her. Two children, part-time job, untrained, debts rising. Commend his caution as child support and alimony already dig into his own salary. His prospects are good, he liked her, but it is a big commitment to make after a few dates. And what of her motives? Women with men are less likely to have jobs than single women. She needs to protect the children from a steady stream of bed mates. In one survey, 25 per cent of women admitted using sex to bind men into a relationship. He can play the field; she probably would if she could, but as she gets older, her field grows smaller.

Lucky Kitty and Lucky Teddy; for them, the advertising has paid off.

Dropping your guard

When you were a child, and your mother came through the door, it felt good. Your whole body smiled with the experience of love and security. The child is without adult care or caution; but growing up means submitting to restrictions, attempts to please, controls. Only at times, and with certain people, do these controls disappear.

Tonight, Kitty makes Teddy drop those adult controls: she makes him smile all over, not just in response to sex, but to something more: love, security, happiness. Teddy has no name for it, but he knows what he feels and sees. He knows that as Kitty comes out of the bathroom, into the bedroom, they can become childlike, without adult reservations and wiles. This is the candid meeting of two children ready to play, with trust and without exploitation. It is a goal of all relationships, and would that more people who meet through lonely hearts advertisements could achieve this covenant, based on freely giving, and freely receiving.

So, they move their bodies together, and laugh and smile and find things funny that no one else can share.

Dancing

In public or in private, clothed or unclothed, lovers must move together, just as Kitty and Teddy do. It is good to do it until you can hardly bear not to go on, and have to rush into bed – and not to rush: to kiss and hold and press and squirm, and massage your body with hers. It is rare, is it not? A pleasure in itself.

If you must – and sometimes you must – you can enter her, still standing, from behind, as you sway together; or, from the front, if she wraps her legs around you in the manner of an Indian statue. Face-to-face as you do a slow foxtrot is for the well practised, and only really possible in high-heeled shoes, unless you are the same height. For most couples, a judicious balancing of leg length, and an acceptance of less ambitious foot work, is all that is needed. And then you fall, and laugh, and that probably brings you closer.

Flowers

Flowers have great potential as symbols of love and sexual sharing, but you need to know the folklore, and most of us get no further than 'Rosemary for remembrance'. For Teddy, the flower has another purpose. It goes before, testing the ground. Will she, might she? Kitty's answer comes in a squirm, a lingering emphasis of where he is. "What are you doing back there?" she might ask, telling him she knows what he has in mind.

Anal sex

In Kinsey's 1940s survey of the sexual behaviour of women, virtually no one had tried anal sex. By the 1970s, one in six had had it and in a recent survey in Britain one in four had experimented. Ten per cent enjoyed the experience. Most people agree it needs a special mood. They mention feeling very relaxed, as do Kitty and Teddy, or particularly erotic. It needs to be approached with gentleness and care, like Kitty and Teddy do. Anal intercourse is not for everyone, nor is it sensible to share it with a relative stranger. Remember, as far as the HIV virus is concerned, it is not just your current partner who enters you, but all of his partners, and all of theirs. It is suicidal to do it without a condom designed for anal penetration.

Positions for anal intercourse

Doggy style is the most obvious, and probably the most common. Men often report that women take up an extreme position, tilting their bottoms to meet the man. This may be a way of offering him more control. Most positions are possible, from missionary and woman on top, to spoons or standing.

The woman-on-top positions give her most control, and as she is the one likely to get torn, they are probably safest in the present climate. We doubt, however, that this fact is likely to influence anyone's choice.

Minor sexually-transmitted infections

NSGI is the most common disease passed by sexual contact. In men there may be gonorrhoea-like symptoms: discharge from the penis and problems urinating. If it goes untreated it can spread to the testes, prostate and bladder. A small percentage of men can go on to develop arthritic symptoms and conjunctivitis – Reiter's disease.

There are a number of minor vaginal infections. The most common are candidosis (thrush), trichomoniasis (Trich) and scabies (The itch); also *Chlamydia*, and infections of unknown origin, which cause inflammation of the cervix and vagina. They make intercourse – and often urination – painful.

Candidosis, or thrush, is a fungal infection, which causes an itchy swollen vulva and a curdy discharge from the vagina. Often there is pain on urination. Men may have a red, spotty penis and inner foreskin. There are a number of home remedies. Natural yoghurt works well: (introduce it on a tampon but don't leave the tampon in place for more than two or three hours). If thrush persists for more than a day or so, get a fungicide from the doctor.

Trichomoniasis is a parasitic infestation which causes a foulsmelling, greenish, foamy discharge which covers the vagina and vulva. It can be treated with a variety of drugs. Most men have no symptoms.

Scabies is caused by a tiny mite that burrows into the skin. It can be recognized by the thin dark burrowing lines which end in small dark lumps. It itches. It is easily cured – as is that other genital itch, pubic lice.

Chlamydia is a bacterium which acts like a virus. It can inflame the Fallopian tubes in women; in men it causes non-specific urethritis. Antibiotics usually clear it – though it may return.

For many, anal sex is first considered as an alternative to vaginal intercourse when a vaginal infection exists. But it is important to remember that the anus itself can be a source of infection. No finger or penis which has entered the anus should ever be placed in the vagina. Always wash thoroughly first. This is another advantage of wearing a condom.

Pleasure and pain

Pain hurts. If you feel pain you feel little else, as anyone knows who has suffered from toothache. But feeling pain is far from automatic. A man severely wounded in battle may be unaware he is hurt. Women giving birth at home often report less labour pain than those giving birth in hospital. Pain, in other words, is a matter of interpretation, at least in part. Increased arousal generally leads to reduced perception of pain.

Some people find roller-coaster rides exhilarating. A moderate level of fear is necessary to produce the thrill; but too much fear, or physical discomfort, will destroy it. In the same way, danger, physical discomfort or even some pain can intensify some people's sexual arousal. (See also the discussion of S. & M. in **Connie & Lloyd**, pages 187-189.)

Many women report that anal penetration is just too painful to give pleasure, others know that it can give pleasure if they are relaxed enough to get beyond the pain barrier into pleasure.

Feeling vulnerable

Pain also makes us vulnerable, and the experience of anal penetration reminds Kitty of her vulnerability. She feels like a young bird waiting to be fed; she has perhaps, a desire to be helpless, protected; or to take risks. She may also feel a desire for punishment.

But a woman's feelings of sexual vulnerability are not confined to anal penetration. Kitty also feels vulnerable during deep, vaginal thrusting, or violent breast-sucking. Men are stronger, and in that sense women are often at risk during sex. Although anal penetration is not just for those with sado-masochistic tendencies, there is an obvious attraction for those with such leanings.

Humiliation

A very few people are turned on by being called names, hit, or otherwise humiliated. A smaller number are turned on by doing the humiliation. For them, sex is about guilt and domination, which make the anal route particularly attractive.

Rimming

Kissing, licking and pushing your tongue into your partner's anus is a most enjoyable activity for some, and totally incomprehensible to others. We are conditioned into thinking the anus is disgusting. From an early age, lavatorial humour is an obsession – especially for the British: beneath the humour there is probably fear.

Silly anal games

Anal masturbation is another form of rear passage sexual activity. Doctors in emergency rooms who used to remove the nozzles of rectal thermometers are doing continuous business these days taking out broom handles, soft drinks bottles, toothbrush holders and, if you can believe it, the occasional light bulb. Other folk seem confused about just which end is supposed to be fed bananas, carrots, salamis, hard boiled eggs and turnips. Objects reaching high into the rectum, or entering the convolutions of the sigmoid colon can easily perforate the colon wall: be warned.

Dangers of anal sex

As AIDS spreads, it becomes more and more dangerous – unless you can be certain of your partner's history. But even within monogamous, long-term relationships, there is often a third person. Sometimes a fourth, fifth and sixth as well. One partner may be unaware of this.

That's the attraction

The stolen peach tastes all the better. Sailing in a high wind, or skiing down a steep slope is fun because it is dangerous. Anal sex attracts Kitty and Teddy because it is beyond the limits. The excitement is psychological. If it were sensible, few of us would do it.

Safe sex is practised by an increasing number of people, or so the sale of condoms indicates. But unprotected sex has not gone out of fashion, and we doubt that it will. Whatever is said about the dangers, we suspect that anal intercourse will remain on the agenda for some people.

If you are one of them, be aware that the vagina was designed to accommodate a thrusting penis, and nine months later to deliver a baby into the world. It is tough, stretches easily and as long as a woman is excited, is continuously bathed in a slippery fluid. Not only does this lubricate, it contains organisms which help protect her from infection.

The anal passage was designed to pass a soft, pliable substance in a fairly gentle manner. It is completely unlubricated, not designed for a dry, stiff and thrusting penis. The fine lining easily rips and bleeds.

Here comes a penis with a sexual history, heading for an unprotected zone. To do this with a stranger, or without a condom, is suicidal. To do it at all is pretty foolish. But some of us are fools, and the feeling, if you like it, is intense. If you must, the only way in is slow and lubricated.

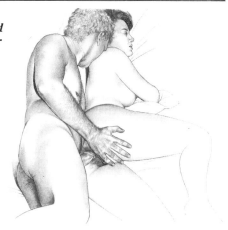

Even if initially lubricated, the membranes rapidly absorb most lubricants. Vaseline, which works well, should not be used with condoms because it weakens the rubber.

There are no friendly organisms to reduce the chances of infection. Catching a sexually-transmitted disease was always likely by this route. The particular danger with AIDS is that it seems to be transmitted in body fluids, blood particularly, but also in semen and possibly vaginal secretions. The ripping of the anal passage (and the fact that bleeding from piles and other abrasions is not uncommon) make it a far more dangerous space for a man to enter – or for a woman to receive a possibly contaminated body fluid at ejaculation.

One can protect from some of the dangers by using a condom: you need to buy ones specially designed for anal intercourse (they are described on the packet as 'Tough'), as the others are not strong enough; and by using a spermicide, which offers both lubrication and additional protection. The best protection is to avoid anal sex, or sex with strangers.

AIDS

AIDS is an illness, and one that is always fatal. It is not a disease: the virus which attacks the body does its damage to the immune system. You do not die from AIDS, but one of many diseases which the body cannot fight as a result of a damaged immune system. The most common are chest infections, Kaposi's sarcoma (a skin cancer) and brain infections which cause severe dementia (loss of intellect). The virus cannot be killed by an antibiotic. It is possible to slow down the progress of the illness, but as yet there is no cure. People who have the HIV virus do not always develop AIDS at once. In a long-term Californian study, 80 per cent did. That figure will probably rise.

Where did AIDS come from?

It is not altogether clear where AIDS started. The best guess is that it began in central and East Africa, and spread from there to Haiti. Haiti is a popular holiday spot with American gay men and from here it appears to have spread to the gay community, particularly in New York and San Francisco. From there, it travelled to gay communities in London, Amsterdam, Paris, the East and Australasia. Haemophiliacs in the U.S.A. and the U.K. caught it from infected blood supplies. Drug users got it from sharing needles with someone who was already infected.

Who has AIDS?

In Europe and the U.S.A. the majority of people with AIDS are still men. They include gay men, who form the biggest group, people of both sexes who inject drugs, and haemophiliacs who have received contaminated blood. This does not mean that men are necessarily more susceptible to AIDS, or that it is easier to catch it if you are gay. It simply reflects the way the disease is spread. Most HIV positive men are gay, and most of them only have sex with other gay men. If a man has had ten partners, and each of them has had ten in turn, and each of them ten more, his love lines stretch a thousand deep within the gay community. As yet, fewer heterosexual people in Europe and North America carry the virus, and since the virus is passed when people share body fluids, there is – at the moment – less chance of catching it in Europe from heterosexual intercourse. This could easily change, and the virus has already spread to the straight community. Some gay men are bisexual, others have shared needles while injecting drugs. A proportion of prostitutes in all big cities are drug users, and some can be expected to be carriers.

Although AIDS has not reached epidemic proportions in heterosexual communities either side of the Atlantic, it is nevertheless the biggest killer of young women in New York. At the moment, the chance of catching HIV from a woman in London is small, but growing.

A FEAST IN THE GARDEN
OF
LOVE
Larry & Wanda

Wanda lit the candles on the dining-room table with a sense of anticipation. As she moved about, her awareness of her body was heightened by the short black velvet dress moving against her thighs. She brushed away crumbs too small to be seen with a hand that lingered perhaps a moment more than necessary on the bare skin of her breasts.

The food she was preparing smelled delicious, her table setting was elegant, and the jet black vase was standing empty in the centre of the table waiting to be filled by the flowers Larry would bring. She pressed her legs together warmly at this thought of her husband. But with the sound of the key in the front door, she let out a small cry of alarm. She wasn't *ready*.

Larry breathed in the scent of the burning candles, a smell that suggested intimacy. He threw his jacket and the small rectangular package on the couch and loosened his tie. Wanda emerged from the bedroom, her hair freshly brushed, to find Larry rolling the TV stand in front of the couch. She

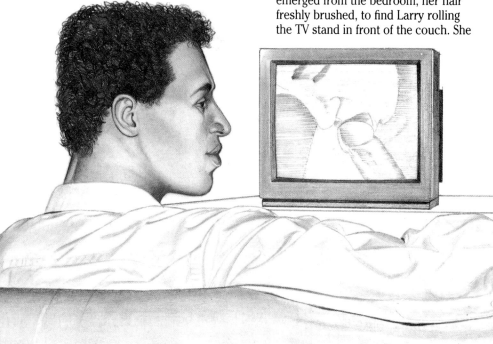

grimaced, but then noticed the dozen beautiful long-stemmed roses. She put her arms around him from behind and nibbled his ear, brushing the back of his neck with her breasts. Her perfume, Desire, was well named. Larry immediately felt himself get hard. He turned his head, caressing her nipple with his ear.

Wanda returned from the kitchen with two glasses of the wine they had reserved for a special occasion. On the tray were also canaps, sandwiches of smoked salmon, caviare and asparagus. Larry lay on the couch, Wanda sat in front of him on the floor feeding him morsels, taking only a bite or two herself. Larry was secretly anxious.

Would she try to feed him a big meal? He loved both eating and making love, but not at the same time. Didn't women realize that the man does 75 per cent of the work during sex? How could he be at his peak with his stomach full?

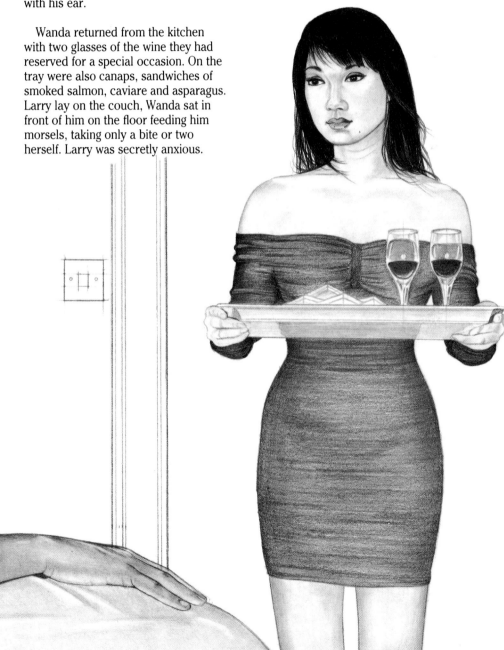

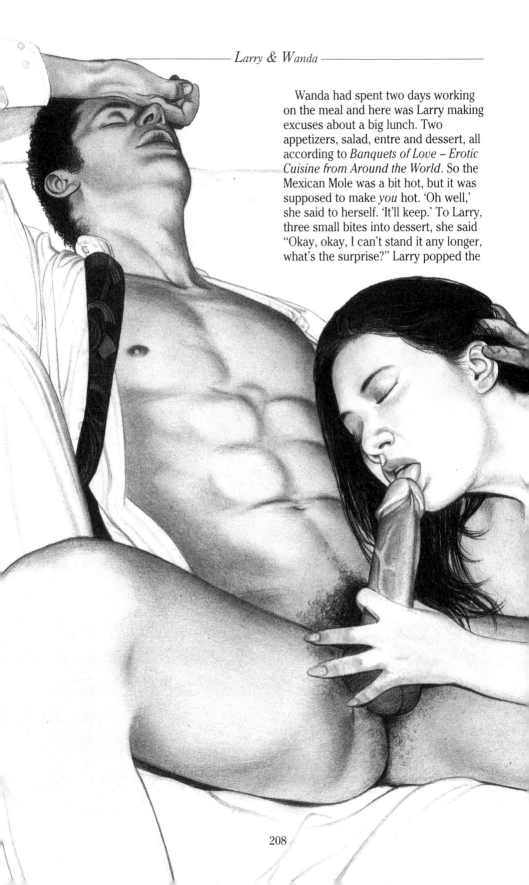

Wanda had spent two days working on the meal and here was Larry making excuses about a big lunch. Two appetizers, salad, entre and dessert, all according to *Banquets of Love – Erotic Cuisine from Around the World*. So the Mexican Mole was a bit hot, but it was supposed to make *you* hot. 'Oh well,' she said to herself. 'It'll keep.' To Larry, three small bites into dessert, she said "Okay, okay, I can't stand it any longer, what's the surprise?" Larry popped the video tape into the VCR and, as the title *Deep Tulips* writhed across the screen, gestured for Wanda to join him on the couch.

On screen, the credits were superimposed on a garden of sprouting organs. The penises were apparently in bloom this season, being carefully cultivated by female tongues and lips. This synchronized thrashing seemed too mechanical to Wanda, an opinion obviously not shared by her husband, who was enjoying himself, mostly with his right hand. He was mesmerized by Tulips herself, a pretty, if hard looking, blonde who was licking the reddish purple crown of Johnny Stalk's large cock.

Larry's excitement mounted as he watched her mouth following and accommodating the thrusting organ. She held the base of the cock in her hand and, with circular motions, took in more and more with each advance of her head. Larry's own cock was ready to burst. His balls were no longer hanging, but pulled up tight. He pulled Wanda's head towards his engorged member, pleadingly. Wanda, for whom fellatio on Larry was usually a favourite pastime, found herself reluctant to play clean-up woman. Recognizing Larry's need, however, she licked his shaft, first concentrating on the area below the glans and then took him into her mouth, swirling her tongue as far around as she could. Larry squirmed and moaned, his buttocks tightening. This was her signal to run her fingernails under his hard scrotum, a gentle scraping across his tightened skin which raised chills that travelled all over him. Larry came in Wanda's mouth just as he saw Tulips receive the creamy blossoming of Johnny's stalk.

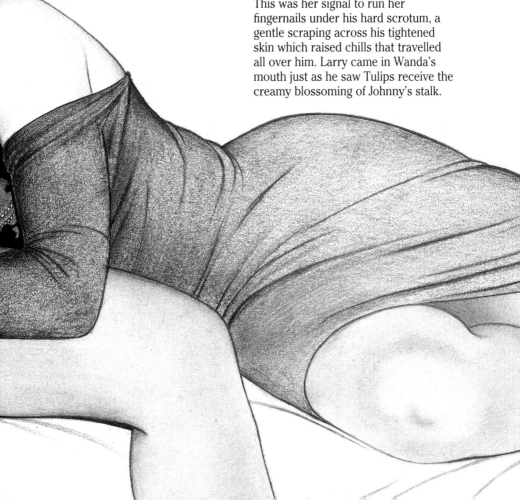

When Wanda raised her head, Larry was not gazing at her fondly through half lidded eyes as she expected, but was looking with glazed eyes at the screen where Tulips was now experiencing a vigorous tilling of her back garden. Enough is enough, Wanda decided, she simply wasn't going to swallow any more. "This video turns me off," she cried. "Why?" asked Larry, startled to attention. "Well, it's as if I'm not enough to turn you on." "Oh, honey . . ." Larry began, but the residual taste in Wanda's mouth reminded her. "The oysters!" And she was off to the refrigerator. Larry turned off the VCR.

Wanda returned from the kitchen with a tray of oysters on ice, and a wicked smile. "Let's play Hide the Oyster," she said. She sat back, pulling up her dress, hooked one leg over the arm of the couch and spread the other luxuriantly. Her smile was as wide as her legs. She plucked one of the oysters from the tray, held it up, and licked it. Larry watched with considerable interest as she spread her labia with one hand and then worked the oyster into her cleft with the other. He dropped to his knees in front of the couch and winked at his wife.

It took Larry some time to find the oyster she had hidden well in between her internal folds. Wanda aided the search by covering his eyes. For dessert, he nuzzled her pussy with his lips, then sucked her labia in and out. He alternated licks along the full length of her vulva with rapid tongue flicks of her clitoris. In the interest of thoroughness, he inserted his tongue as far into her as he could. He licked the inside of her labia as her excitement mounted.

Wanda was melting. The tightening of her vaginal opening told him that she was approaching orgasm. Three times the fine tremor in her legs indicated that he had brought her to the edge. Each time, he stopped, kissed her thighs, waited until her arousal ebbed slightly. The fourth time he continued licking and sucking, reaching up to rub an erect nipple. She writhed, shuddered, and cried out as she came.

Teasing time was over. Larry continued licking, his face between her legs, drawing her from peak to ecstatic peak, until at last: "Oh, stop, you could keep me going all night." Wanda pulled away convulsively.

He held her and hugged her. They both knew that their evening was just beginning.

Suppose you started to talk about yawning: feeling like yawning, thinking about yawning, maybe even watching people yawn. Do it long enough, and you are bound to yawn. Just as talking about your daughter's smiles will make you smile. It is the way you are made.

Talking and thinking about sex makes us, likewise, feel sexier. (See also **Robert & Jenny**, page 25.) Not only that, it feels good. This is Wanda's frame of mind as she prepares for Larry's arrival. Just as the smell of fresh coffee brewing, or the sight of the cake shop window is a pleasure in itself, thinking about sex is a pleasure, something we do for its own sake. Both Larry and Wanda have learned to make the most of this form of anticipation.

It is a bonus to know that dreams can be fulfilled when evening comes, but even without that promise, the planning can feel good. By contrast, think too much about sex without the opportunity to fulfil your plans and the pleasure turns to frustration. Which is, of course, why the breakdown of a sexual relationship can leave us feeling the way it does. The more we think, the more we want, the more we want, the more we think.

Acting out fantasies

To the extent that our sexual expectations are derived from the books we have read and the TV shows and movies we have seen, we want everything to go as perfectly as it does for the lovers on screen. Our beautiful idols plunge over cataracts of lust to fall gracefully into deep pools of ecstasy. Nobody gets an elbow in the ribs, or has to go to the lavatory at an inopportune moment, and everybody comes on cue. It is useful to remember that, in all probability, the flawless love scene you are watching was shot several times until the actors got it just right. The best laid plans of mice and men don't always produce the best-aid lovers. In Larry and Wanda's story, not coincidentally, neither character's plans work out quite as they hoped, but they enjoy each other anyway. Moral: *Go about it with a light heart.*

Food and sex

Larry's oyster has impeccable precedents. In Hungary there was once a courtship ritual in which a man would earn a kiss from his fiance by buying her a bag of apples. To love is to feed, not only for humans, but also for some of our animal cousins. When the great crested grebe courts his mate, he offers her a piece of pond weed. Better, perhaps, than the regurgitated fish traded by some other water birds. Mouth feeding was, and still is, a crosscultural sign of affection. In the West, concern about hygiene has led us to drop the habit, although it is hardly less sanitary than deep kissing. A pity. Mothers once naturally placed food between their lips for a child to take, as the child so reared would later feed his lover. In parts of Germany, boys chewed resin – rather like tobacco – and offered it to women as they danced. 'Come on,' the gesture said as they pushed it out through their lips: 'Take it'. If it sounds familiar, it is. We play like this – without the resin. It is called kissing. You may feel that the *Kama Sutra* goes one better by suggesting that wine be shared from the mouth of one's lover.

Love potions – how potent?

Food with aphrodisic properties abounds in folklore. Many ancient Greek, Roman and Indian aphrodisiac recipes call for nutritive foods such as milk, honey or ghee (clarified butter) into which was incorporated some delicacy representative of reproduction, say a bird's egg or a ram's testicle. Through the magical Principle of Similarity, aphrodisic powers have also been ascribed to plants or animal parts which resemble male or female genitalia.

More brutally direct was the Tartar recipe for stallion's penis which was to be separated from the stallion after the unfortunate beast had been provoked into full erection by the presence of a mare. Such foods were eaten to obtain sexual vigour or to raise the ardour of the object of one's desire. In seventeenth-century England, girls would knead a piece of dough, then hold it against the vulva. If the baked dough, retaining the impress of the young lady, was eaten by the man to whom it was presented, he would fall beneath her spell. In contemporary New York one can order biscuits shaped like genitalia from the Erotic Baker.

The last two options would have been much less trouble to Wanda than spending two days preparing recipes from *Banquets of Love*, but that is scarcely the point.

In reality, the physical effect of this or that food probably matters little, if at all; believing is more than half the battle. If we think it makes us sexy, it will. The magical Principle of Similarity is probably correct in that the strongest aphrodisic effect of food is through association and visual metaphor. Remember the dinner scene in the movie *Tom Jones*? How lustfully Tom and his girl looked at each other while deliberately licking and sucking their food, bits strewn wantonly on their faces and in their hair. Perhaps it is the very motions of eating that have made hunger a common metaphor for sexual desire. The sharing of food, the intimacy of eye contact, the thought of the evening to come, allow desire to build. But as Larry knows, too full a stomach draws a great deal of blood to the digestive system, making it hard work to sustain an erection, itself dependent on blood filling the spongy erectile tissue of the penis.

Oral lovemaking – precedents

Larry and Wanda are a state-of-the-art, 1990s couple, but don't be fazed by their apparent sophistication and inventiveness. There is nothing trendy about oral sex. Earliest historical records of oral sexual activity include its description in Chinese scrolls dating back to 200 BC, and oral sex is plain to see in sculpted figures on Indian temples.

Even as people did it, religious and secular authorities were proscribing it. Conventional intercourse was excusable since essential for procreation, but the mouth is no route to the womb (although the nun's wimple which covers the ears is explicitly meant to prevent impregnation by the aural route). So the medieval church declared it sinful and church and state punished it. Only a few decades ago, a spouse's demand for oral sex could be used in an American divorce case as evidence of mental cruelty and perversion. American state laws often consider oral sex as a form of sodomy even between consenting adults, and punishment includes a one- to 20-year prison term in Ohio and up to 30 years in Connecticut. In Georgia, the punishment could be hard labour for life; the priorities of Georgia's state legislature are suggested by the contrasting jail sentence of five years for having sex with farm animals.

The Kinsey Report data of the 1940s suggested that less than half of young unmarried men surveyed had received fellatio while less than a quarter of the women reported giving it, the difference presumably being due to the men's contacts with prostitutes. For women in the Kinsey survey, fellatio and cunnilingus predominantly occurred within marriage (50 per cent of all couples had tried it). By the middle to late 1960s oral sex had become substantially more frequent before marriage and the rates reported by men and women had become equal.

These days, it is being initiated at an earlier stage of sexual experience. For example, between 40-50 per cent of American high school students surveyed in 1982 reported it, up from 20-30 per cent in 1973. It is currently estimated that between 75-90 per cent of American and British married couples have experimented with it. Amongst younger couples little distinction is made between intercourse and oral sex. It is an everyday form of love play. Some couples, Larry and Wanda among them, regularly use it as a substitute for intercourse.

A large majority of men enjoy giving, and women enjoy receiving, cunnilingus. In recent surveys, 57-93 per cent of women report having experienced it, with the percentage increasing as one moves from short-term dating relationships into long-term marriages; 80 per cent of wives report that their husbands do it 'frequently'. One factor which has certainly influenced this is women's expectation of sexual plea-suring. Women take time to reach orgasm, and some men (particu-larly younger men) find prolonged intercourse difficult to sustain. Even if they can sustain it, a substantial number of women do not reach orgasm through intercourse. Cunnilingus can help solve both problems. In one survey 82 per cent of women who received it re-ported liking it. Almost all men (most surveys put it at over 90 per cent) say that they like being given fellatio and about three quarters of the women asked say they enjoy giving it (but possibly not to ejac-ulation). Most of the male dissenters mention fear of being bitten. Despite these generally positive endorsements, the second most common complaint in sex clinics is 'Why won't my partner give me oral sex?' This is discussed along with suggestions on what can be done about it, in **Eric & Judy**, pages 70-73.

Charms of fellatio

One fellow we know, desperate for oral attention from his girlfriend, tried to convince her that semen prevented tooth decay. Why is it that men find being sucked so pleasurable? For starters, it is passive. For most men there is no performance anxiety (Larry is typical of this type), no need to wonder if one is being a good lover; for some it is the highest form of pleasure and release. A few dissenters do worry about losing their erections and some are concerned about being *too* pas-sive: they feel that they should be *doing* something. Some worry that their partner's mouth is getting tired, or that she might choke. But for these reservations, there can be no doubt that men love it.

This form of lovemaking, like all others, has particular psycholog-ical meanings for the lovers. For most men, the symbolic significance of being sucked lies in the active role played by the woman and her willing acceptance of his cock in her mouth. It is their closest ex-perience of being made love *to*. For this reason, they would appreciate any sign that she really enjoys it, from getting her to initiate it to keep-ing at it until he comes, and swallowing the semen. Graffiti seen in a men's lavatory in New York's Greenwich Village asked, 'What is the difference between like and love? Spit or swallow.'

For a woman, the attractions of fellatio are very much in the giving of pleasure, Wanda being no exception. If she ever wonders whether or not she makes love to him as much as she might, this is one situa-tion when she feels sure. There is a delight in seeing and feeling the penis as it grows in her hands and mouth. There is the smooth feel as she kisses and sucks, and with these sensual pleasures there is, of course the power she has over him. But the liking does not extend to semen: Wanda usually takes it in her mouth only if caught by surprise.

Perhaps this is not surprising when one considers the biological purpose of sex: to impregnate women. While he may be welcome, his 'seed' may not be.

For aspiring cocksuckers

The ultimate expert on how a man is to be treated is the man himself, of course. To begin, some men like having the crown licked, others find this too intense. Licking of the underside, as Wanda does, particularly the frenulum (the wrinkly bit on the underside, just below the crown), is usually greeted with extreme enthusiasm. The infamous J, she of *The Sensuous Woman*, greatly recommended the technique of a tongue swirling around the tip of the penis after shallow insertion, just as Wanda does. Another technique to prevent gagging is to guide his penis against the inside of her cheek.

In the early 1970s movie *Deep Throat*, Linda Lovelace gained fame for her ability to take the entire length of an erect penis into her mouth and throat. Although she later renounced her title as porn queen, saying that her performance had been coerced, there were many men who would have been her willing partner and some women who admired her ability. Deep throating (also called skulling and Frenching) requires the same inhibition of the gag reflex as accomplished by professional sword swallowers.

You can try it if you want, but it is not really necessary. Think instead of the natural habitat of an erect penis, that is, inside a warm, wet vagina which provides contact for its whole length. You can make a warm, wet tunnel with your hands and mouth. Use long, slow, smooth strokes so the whole shaft is enveloped. The hands should pass over the skin, not tight enough to move the skin, especially if he is not fully erect.

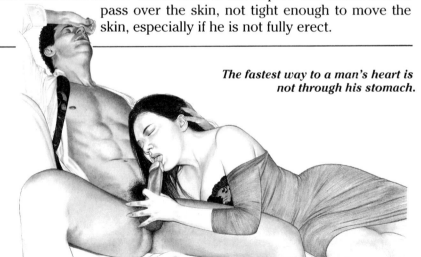

The fastest way to a man's heart is not through his stomach.

Holding his penis also gives you control. How much you take in your mouth does not really matter; most cocks are not that sensitive, and they cannot tell the difference between hands and mouth, especially when hands are wet with saliva or butter. If you can manage it, keeping your mouth slightly open around his penis can be excrutiatingly pleasurable. If there is room, covering your teeth with your lips is appreciated by those nervous about being bitten, but it does cause strain and fatigue.

More important than how much you take in is simultaneous stimulation of other erogenous areas of skin. Touching or lightly scratching the scrotum, as Wanda did for Larry, can be exceedingly pleasurable especially when it initiates or augments orgasm. Some men prefer stimulation of the anal region by stroking or the insertion of a finger. Arrange yourself, if you can, so that he has a clear view: for most men, part of the pleasure is watching you make love to him.

Fellatio variations

For those who don't like the taste of tube steak there is always the traditional whipped cream topping. For those who like to slide their hands over the shaft as they suck, a liberal pat of butter, or plenty of saliva work well. Or you could try 'fire and ice', in which the woman puts a few small bits of ice in her mouth before taking him in.

Cunnilingus

Women are slightly less enthusiastic about cunnilingus than men are about fellatio: 90 per cent of men and 70 per cent of women say they like doing it and like receiving it respectively. For a woman who likes this most intimate attention, it is among her very special pleasures. Surveys suggest that women reach orgasm more easily and quickly in this way and that it is a particularly efficient way to achieve a series of orgasms. If you are amongst the women who don't care for it, see the discussion following **Eric & Judy**, pages 71-72.

Charms of cunnilingus

Stimulating the clitoris with the penis has been likened to cutting a diamond with a chainsaw. Perhaps cutting the diamond on the bench with the chainsaw on the floor would be more accurate. The penis rarely goes anywhere near the clitoris. To stimulate the clitoris during intercourse, a woman has to position herself so that she can rub it on his pubis, or stimulate manually. (See **William & Francesca**, pages 84-85.) It is possible to come without clitoral stimulation. A tongue in the ear, or a suck of the breast can do it for her (as can a penis in the vagina); it is just easier, and more reliable, when the clitoris is stimulated. When she sucks him she gives exactly the right stimulation by providing a delightful wet tunnel to receive his engorged member. When he sucks her (and kisses, and nibbles) he provides the same delightful wet contact to just the right places. Oral love gives both partners ideal stimulus to a key 'switch'. Which is not to say that it is better than intercourse, just different.

Cunnilingus: do men like giving it?

Men's attitudes to cunnilingus are certainly tied very closely to their feelings about female genitalia. (See pages 57-58.) The attitude of some men towards the female epicentre can only be described as worshipful from the beginning. Others may be apprehensive on first descent, but are delighted by the actual smells and tastes; for them, like Larry, it is a rapidly acquired taste. In fact there are fewer bacteria in the vagina than the mouth. Men often specify that they enjoy kissing a clean vagina, which does not mean they want artificial sprays and female deodorants. Emphatically they do not. Indeed the message is clear: men like the way a woman smells and tastes. (See **Robert & Jenny**, pages 25-26.)

Men who like cunnilingus enjoy it for a number of reasons. The woman's excitement pleases them (moans, wiggles and other testimonies of pleasure are always appreciated). Their desire to give pleasure can find its ultimate expression in the spoken or unspoken request, 'Please come in my mouth'. Another major feeling is that this is the way to be most intimate with a woman. 'I would crawl all the way into her if I could' is not an untypical sentiment. Cunnilingus blends an extension of male macho (I have power over this woman) with a deep expression of the warmth and passion men feel for women. Some men revel in the direct animalistic qualities of the experience; the tastes and smells and the feel of her juices on their face. Indeed, male and female cunnilingus addicts are not unknown.

Care of the inner woman

As with other forms of lovemaking, a common mistake is to begin cunnilingus too directly. Larry sets straight down to it with Wanda, but remember, she has been anticipating this attention all evening, perhaps all day. Most women need to be moderately aroused. If there is no build-up, she may perceive cunnilingus as a demand. It is best to begin with manual stimulation and kissing elsewhere, before working down to her thighs and mons, finally nuzzling her clitoris and vagina. How women like to be stimulated varies enormously. It is best to ask, and if he does not, for her to tell him. Some women like direct stimulation on the tip of the clitoris, others find this painful. Some, like

Wanda, enjoy the labia being sucked, others nibbled. Some like the labia folded over the clitoris so that it can be stimulated along its length from the side. Many women find stimulation of the urethral opening (and along its path within the wall of the vagina) highly exciting. Multiple orgasms, such as Wanda experiences, are easiest from clitoral stimulation, although not always preferred. For many a single (or final) orgasm is easier if there is a finger pushed well up into the vagina. Not only do women vary in their wishes, they vary from moment to moment and occasion to occasion. There

Lickerty split is too fast for lickerty-spit.

is some evidence that emphasis on clitoral stimulation is appreciated pre-menstrually, while vaginal stimulation is preferred mid-month.

There are always those who would gild the lily. If you must, the vagina works better as a dessert tray than the penis. One man we know, not satisfied with whipped cream alone, adds cinnamon and chocolate chips to his vaginal topping.

The message of the statistics on fellatio and cunnilingus is, of course, that these are sexual techniques which can add greatly to many couples' sex lives. But such generalizations can carry no weight with those who have doubts about oral sex. For further discussion of other aspects of fellatio and cunnilingus, especially in the context of sexual problems and difficulties, see **Eric & Judy**, pages 70-73.

69

Opinions on mutual oral sex are divided. Some folks like to do it together, especially those who find the performance aspect daunting. Others like it single file, feeling they can better concentrate on giving or receiving pleasure.

Oral sex: communicating the desire

How can you tell your partner what you would like? Larry and Wanda have no doubts about each other's wants, but others may be embarrassed to make direct requests. But you can show him or her. Sucking

on your partner's fingers might suggest the idea (see **Robert &
Jenny**, pages 15 and 25) or leaving this book around opened at the
appropriate page.

Pornography and erotica

Why are Larry, and so many men, turned on by porn? Why are Wanda
and many other women turned off by it? What impact does it have on
the lives of women and men?

Do men ever get tired of looking? Do dogs ever get tired of sniffing
each other? Erotica is no modern invention. Sexual activity has been
portrayed on cave walls and by the statuary of antiquity. Each culture
has its own sexual corpus, from the Indian *Kama Sutra* (prior to 500
AD) and the Arab *Perfumed Garden* to Japanese pillow books featuring enormous genitalia. In the West, erotica began to be published as
early as 1470. It was not deemed dangerous to public safety by the
ruling classes when literacy was a privilege of the élite. Bans were imposed only when reading became relatively commonplace.

The consumption of erotic writing and films is largely, although not
entirely, a male preoccupation. Men collect magazines, movies and
tapes, not to mention nude pictures of old girlfriends. There is no
question that reading or looking at this material is powerfully exciting;
its use usually being associated with masturbation, or less frequently,
with intercourse. Favourite, highly charged, scenes can remain
etched in memory. The sight of semen on a woman's lips, for example,
is a familiar icon in pornography. The excitement this can cause in
male viewers is a classical example of a learned association, the
image implying that a cock has just ejaculated into her mouth. From
whence comes this power to stimulate? The answer, surely is that visual
images of sexual activity tap our empathic ability to share emotions:
think, for example, about wincing when you see someone in pain.

Such erotic empathy is part of our primate heritage: according to a
report in the Chicago Tribune of 30 May 1973, keepers at the Chessing-
ton Zoo in England showed their chimpanzees films of other chimps
mating in order to encourage breeding. It worked.

Women and porn

In studies, surveys and questionnaires, women universally appreciate
erotic material less than men. Understanding men's attraction to it
can be difficult when, like Wanda, you are turned off by the explicit
depiction of organs and mechanical sex acts of commercial porn.
Contrary to earlier thinking, however, research in West Germany and
elsewhere has clearly shown that women, like men, can be aroused by
visual erotica. In one experiment male and female responses to erot-

ica were quite similar (80-91 per cent of men and 70-83 per cent of women found them arousing). When erection in males and vaginal lubrication in females are compared directly, women actually respond to erotica more readily than men. The erotic empathy factor is strong in both sexes.

Is it that porn needs a more appropriate subject matter for women to respond to it? *Playgirl* magazine features nude men (albeit with strictly non-erect penises), but a large part of *Playgirl's* readership may be gay men. *Viva*, another magazine which featured this sort of material, folded for lack of readership. The market-place may be a dubious oracle for the divination of sexual preference, but women just don't buy visually explicit magazines.

Lesbians represent a 'pure' culture of female sensibility, just as the behaviour of gay men reflects purely male sensibilities. But is there a lesbian porn industry, as there is for gay men? No. The market-place equivalent to male porn is probably women's romantic novels, which are produced in floods. There is no evidence however, that these books are bought or used for explicit sexual arousal and masturbation. So there does seem to be a gulf between the sexes on this issue.

Part of the difference is certainly that many women object to the demeaning aspects of commercial porn, which men overlook. But it is also true that some women find even mild erotica such as female nudes, or even fully clothed couples embracing in romantic settings, give no pleasure. Although a woman may *get* aroused by it, she will not *seek out* this form of arousal.

Perhaps, as is frequently supposed, women really do need an emotional setting for sexual activity. That is, visual images of sex alone provide less than adequate stimulation. Alternatively, or additionally, pornography may evoke guilt and shame, or other negative emotions, which are overcome only in the proper, emotional setting for sex.

The romances written for women on both sides of the Atlantic have become more sexually explicit in the last few years, and perhaps this is a sign of moves towards erotica that will please women as well as men. Although Mills and Boon would have us believe that intercourse was just invented, it is now part of the romantic novel's formula and a female reader can expect a juicy bit every 40-50 pages. When Wanda read a recent American novel of the same genre, she encountered 11 episodes of intercourse, five of cunnilingus and four of fellatio.

The development of egalitarian, female-oriented, sexually explicit visual erotica in which the emotional response of both partners is given a fair hearing, might, who knows, displace the current misogynistic lot and provide enjoyment equally for women and men. The erotica in this book is intended to be just such a coming together.

URNING OFF, URNING ON

Martin & Giselle

Giselle

How many families have seven kids these days? Well, I don't know many. My mother had seven in as many years. That includes two sets of twins. After that she gave up sex. For 20 years. You can imagine the tensions. Never kissing and hugging in case it would lead to something more. They were passionate people, for God's sake. I can remember mother's irritation, father pacing about like a caged animal. For 20 years while I was growing up there was no sex in our house, unless they did it alone. There was an ethos of 'Don't touch me'. I remember how my friends kissed their fathers, and how mine stepped back. You see, I should have known. I should have understood. My mother never talked about sex. She didn't tell me I'd have periods until I started. Then she only talked about keeping clean and not taking baths. Later she told me it was cheap to give yourself. But hell, who wants to be the only virgin in the class? I needed love and I found that sex came with it. You've heard about those girls who do it for cuddles? That was me. I loved candlelit dinners, the words 'I love you'. Sex I endured: through one marriage and seven boyfriends.

Then I met Martin.

Martin

That year she had a lump. It was so scary; I couldn't imagine life without her. I'd been feeling pretty ill myself. Diabetes. Then at work, sales were down, people in my department were quitting, it was a mess. It was one thing after another. So when it began to happen I told myself it was stress. Like most guys, I've had an occasional failure. It even happened the first time Giselle and I were together. Embarrassing at the time, but you just back off for a while and everything is fine.

Giselle

He was always so giving and gentle. He would let me come in his hand or mouth. I mean, that's how we often did it. He liked to make me come and I never complained. Not after the wasteland years. Then I gradually began to realize that it was happening less often and it was usually without penetration. I felt rejected, deficient, less of a woman; that something was wrong with me. After he'd gone to sleep I would cry.

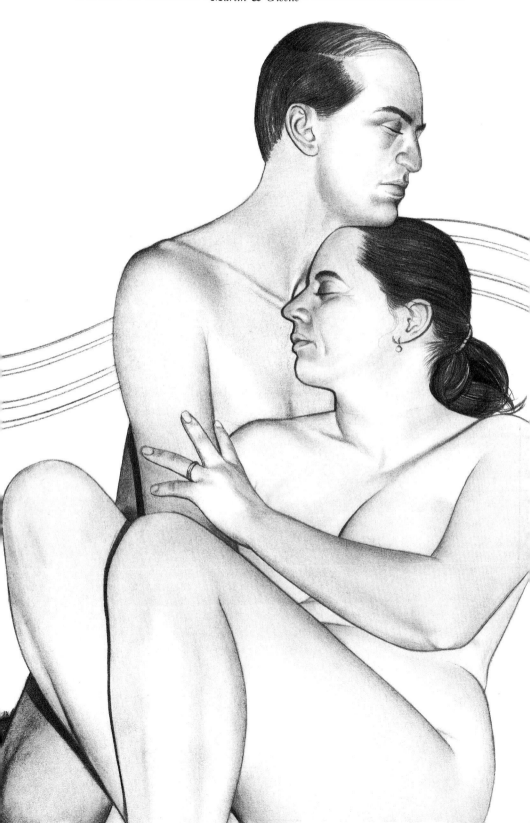

Martin

After a few months I knew something was wrong, but I didn't want to say it out loud. The easiest way was to avoid the situation. So I stopped kissing her because kissing made me want her. Wanting her and not getting hard made me angry. I hadn't realized it before, but my definition of being a man meant having a good hard on. I was depressed a lot of the time. I picked on the sales people, but mostly I would work late, come home saying I was tired, eat and go to sleep. I felt righteous about that, at least I was trying to do something right. If I came home early I'd pick a quarrel so we'd go to bed too angry for sex.

Giselle

As he became quarrelsome I started to think he must have someone else. He was trying to avoid me. For weeks I searched his pockets for clues to 'the other woman'. I rang every number he jotted on the telephone pad.

Martin

I did think of finding someone new. I wanted to believe it was Giselle's fault. I recounted to myself all the things she did that turned me off. Well, actually, she does snore. It was the possibility of failure that stopped me from approaching another woman. Eventually she suggested we go for help.

We paid a visit to the sex therapist, we tried marriage guidance and psychotherapy for good measure. It was overkill, I know, but it worked in some ways, by bringing us close again.

But it didn't give me the power to have an erection.

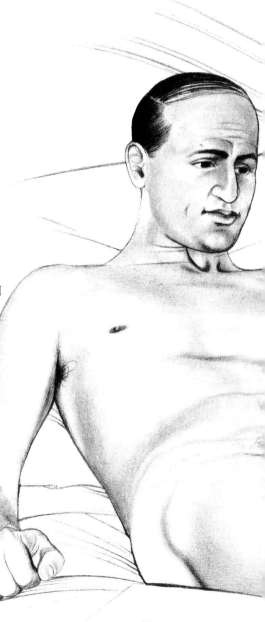

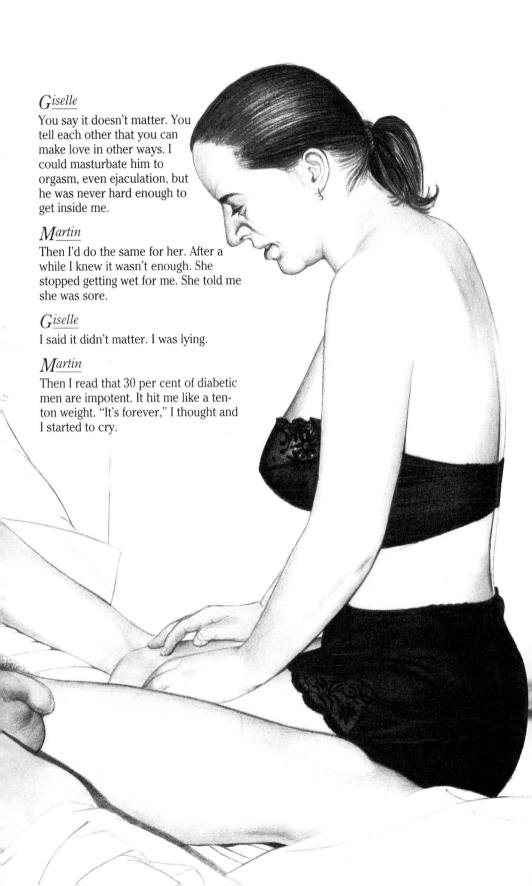

Giselle

You say it doesn't matter. You tell each other that you can make love in other ways. I could masturbate him to orgasm, even ejaculation, but he was never hard enough to get inside me.

Martin

Then I'd do the same for her. After a while I knew it wasn't enough. She stopped getting wet for me. She told me she was sore.

Giselle

I said it didn't matter. I was lying.

Martin

Then I read that 30 per cent of diabetic men are impotent. It hit me like a ten-ton weight. "It's forever," I thought and I started to cry.

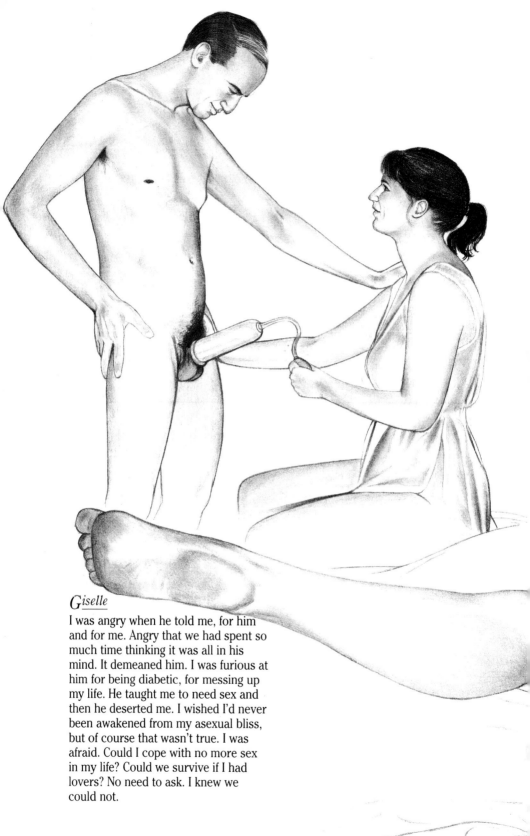

Giselle

I was angry when he told me, for him
and for me. Angry that we had spent so
much time thinking it was all in his
mind. It demeaned him. I was furious at
him for being diabetic, for messing up
my life. He taught me to need sex and
then he deserted me. I wished I'd never
been awakened from my asexual bliss,
but of course that wasn't true. I was
afraid. Could I cope with no more sex
in my life? Could we survive if I had
lovers? No need to ask. I knew we
could not.

226

Martin

It wasn't the end. Identifying the problem as diabetes a new beginning. My penis was there, my blood was circulating. The only problem was getting the two together.

Giselle

We had fun trying out the gismos. Sucking him up with a vacuum and putting the ring on to keep the blood inside. It was good to the hungry eye, to see him big again, even if it was wobbly and didn't stand up. After a year, who's looking that close? After he's inside, who can tell?

Martin

We tried PEP too – that gave me a four-hour erection. It was wonderful at the time. In the end we settled for an implant.

Giselle

Now I can say "Switch yourself on Mike, come on, knock my socks off."

Martin

"And I do."

227

Sex is (more or less) all in your mind, and your mind is all in your brain. In order to fully understand the ups and downs of Martin and Giselle's love life, you need to appreciate a few essential details about that single most important sexual organ.

The brain does not have one 'sex centre', but several different mechanisms for sexual experience and expression, scattered about the grey matter in the skull, and in the bundles of nerves running the length of the spinal cord.

The cortex, which forms the surface of the brain, is crucial for the highest levels of planning, movement and sensation. When Giselle is excited by Martin's sexy look, cortical areas at the back of her brain, which specialize in the recognition of emotional responses, receive and interpret the signals.

Similarly with touch. Each part of the body is represented on a 'map' laid out in the middle of the cortex. When Martin touches Giselle, neurones (nerve cells) in the cortex representing that particular area of skin become active. Neurones in his hand are activated, too.

The genitalia have their own special place on this map. Stimulation of this area produces sensations that feel as if they come from the genital region. However, they don't *feel* sexy; that is the work of another part of the brain.

The limbic system

The bits of the brain that make Giselle actually feel sexy are probably the limbic system, located partly in a lobe which lies like the thumb of a boxing glove at the lower outside edge of the brain. In animals such as monkeys and rats, stimulation of the septal region of the limbic system produces erection and ejaculation. Humans receiving stimulation here in the course of operations have reported sexual sensations. One woman experienced orgasm.

The middle managers

If the limbic system and the cortex are the higher executives, working on the floor below are the body's sexual managers: the hypothalamus and the pre-optic area next to it. They lie in the base of the brain, above the roof of the mouth, implementing directives handed down from above. When Martin becomes aroused by Giselle, the neurones in his pre-optic area fire vigorously. The pre-optic area in a man is larger than in a woman (one of the few neurone groups in the brain which differ between the sexes) and seems to be especially important for male sexual behaviour.

The hypothalamus supplies hormonal materials to the pituitary, the master hormone gland. It is pituitary hormones that drive the men-

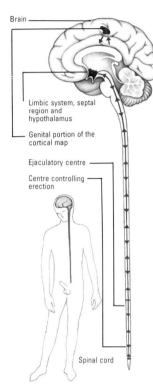

Brain

Limbic system, septal region and hypothalamus

Genital portion of the cortical map

Ejaculatory centre

Centre controlling erection

Spinal cord

Erection and ejaculation
– the plumbing and circuitry

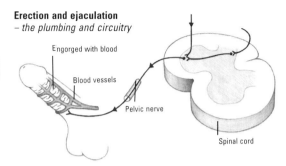

Engorged with blood

Blood vessels

Pelvic nerve

Spinal cord

Erection and blood flow

Erotic impulses descending from the limbic system of the brain are transmitted through the pelvic nerve and result in increased blood flow to the penis. Its spongy areas become engorged; the blood is trapped there; the penis stays erect.

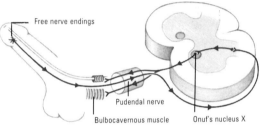

Free nerve endings

Pudendal nerve

Bulbocavernous muscle   Onuf's nucleus X

Sensation

Free nerve endings, typically in the highly sensitive glans, transmit sensations through the pudendal nerve to Onuf's nucleus X in the spinal cord and back again (through the pudendal nerve) to cause contractions of the bulbocavernous muscles, important during ejaculation – see below.

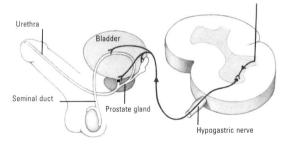

Urethra

Bladder

Seminal duct

Prostate gland

Hypogastric nerve

Ejaculation

Sensations from the penis travel to the ejaculatory centre in the spinal cord and from there through the hypogastric nerve to close off the bladder. The impulses also drive semen from the testes into the seminal duct and on towards the prostate gland where it mixes with fluids. With the help of contractions of the prostate, the mixture then moves on towards the penis. Contractions of the bulbocavernous muscles (felt by putting a finger in the anus) force it up the urethra and squirt it from the tip.

Above When a man gets aroused, various stimuli, including sexy sights, smells and sounds, and of course sensations coming up from the penis, activate regions of the spinal cord, and, within the brain, the limbic system and the genital portion of the cortical map. The erotic quality – the sexy feel – of these sensations comes from the limbic system, particularly the septal region and hypothalamus. These parts of the brain in turn help to mastermind the sex act by sending appropriate messages back down the 'main wiring' of the spinal cord to the centres which control erection and ejaculation.

Above right and opposite
To complete the action, three distinct mechanisms have to operate.

strual cycle in women and control the release of testosterone from the testes and adrenal glands in men. The hypothalamus also co-ordinates the hormonal output of the pituitary with the actions of the autonomic nervous system, the set of nerves which regulates heart rate, blood pressure, sweating, engorgement of blood vessels, lubrication. erection and ejaculation 'automatically', without conscious effort.

The operatives

Cortex, limbic system and hypothalamus produce actions of the body, sexual or otherwise, by sending messages down the long nerve tracts descending in the outer ring of the spinal cord. These messages may be relayed onwards from 'outposts' in the 'lower depths' of the nervous system to specific places where they are needed. One such relay station is Onuf's Nucleus X, in the spinal cord just above the small of the back. Highly important for sexual function, it controls the bulbocavernosus muscles lying between scrotum and anus. In the days before his diabetes became severe, Martin occasionally amused Giselle by making his penis rise and the tip expand just by squeezing his bulbocavernous and ischiocavernous muscles. Her amusement was mixed with pleasure if he squeezed when he was inside her.

Giselle's mind

Giselle has all this basic machinery for doing what comes naturally, and it is in perfect working order. So why, in response to Martin's changed behaviour, did she dry up and turn her back on sex when it was so important to her?

Giselle's childhood, we suspect, is a mainstream example of how upbringing can affect sexual attitudes. Growing up in a family which avoided physical or emotional contact that might have led to sex taught her from her earliest years that sex meant tension, and that feelings which could be expressed through bodily contact were to be ignored. With an education like that, it was not easy for Giselle suddenly to give her body in love. To make this step took some courage; then to be denied physical expression once more brought a bitter harvest of repressed anger and tension, much of which she redirected at the unfortunate Martin.

Giselle's experience is all too common, yet it is but one example of a blighted attitude to sex. Many ingredients go into the baking, or rather the spoiling, of this cake, and they mix in different ways. Whereas almost all boys masturbate, only some girls do, suggesting that major differences in male and female sexual behaviour start early. Sisters reared under the same roof can have wildly different attitudes to sex, suggesting that differences in biology may account for some of these variations. Natural testosterone levels may be a factor. All women have some circulating testosterone, secreted by their adrenal glands. Women who are given extra, as a treatment for certain diseases, and recently for sexual dysfunction, have increased libido and enjoyment of sex. Extra female hormones, such as oestrogen, turn no one on. A woman with a naturally high level of male hormones may have a high sexual motivation. Differences in blood flow to the pelvis are another possible factor (see **Paul & Rosie**). Differences in experience should not be ignored, though: the shameful child abuse and adult rape figures in the U.S. and in Europe must account for many a woman's sexual problems. One in four women has been the victim of attempted or completed rape in those societies. Being raped, whether as adult or child, leaves a woman feeling guilty and afraid of sex.

Turned off

Many women sometimes, and some women all of the time, experience no pleasure in having a man inside them; they feel suffocated by the weight of his body. They are unpleasantly tickled, rather than aroused, by a touch on the body or a tongue in the ear. They are intimidated, turned off, or simply uninterested in sex.

In the same British and American survey, the major problems reported by women were in getting and staying excited (20-48 per cent) and in reaching orgasm (46 per cent). Some women experience orgasm as a sort of pelvic hiccup. Ten to 15 per cent report being unable to reach orgasm at all.

Remedies

For many women, a complicating factor is their unwillingness to communicate their needs and fears to men, coupled with the feeling that if she turns him on, it is her duty to do something about it.

The sensate focusing technique as practised in **Andrew**'s wooing of **Meredith** remains probably the best antidote to this predicament. It teaches each side to become aware of the other's needs, and it commits no one to anything until both want it that way.

Other problems arise when women are ignorant about their bodies. Sexual awareness must to some extent be learned. For some this is a question of discovering how to masturbate (see **Gwen & Jack**). For others it is a matter of learning how and why they turn away from sexual arousal.

If coming to terms with your body is a problem:

• Think about the last time you were aroused. What produced the excitement?

- Try to produce that arousal in yourself. It is safe to do this.

- The last time someone aroused you, did you unconsciously push him away? By deed? By thought? How did you do this? Why?

- Find a time when you will not be interrupted for an hour or so and masturbate using any technique that suits you. There is no pressure to reach orgasm. Concentrate on feeling good about pleasuring yourself. The point of the exercise is your pleasure.

- Once you can masturbate to orgasm, or even before, show your partner how you take your pleasure. You may feel self-conscious; patterns of a lifetime don't change overnight. Try guiding his hand to do the things you usually do. Don't expect immediate results. It may take months before you learn how to climax with him and even longer to gain the confidence to show your pleasure to your lover.

- Focus on finding pleasure in his body and allow him to find pleasure for both of you in yours. Mutual masturbation can be very loving. It never was, and never should be, something you do only when the 'real thing' is not available.

- When you do have intercourse, a side-by-side position is comfortable and allows you to move freely and to see each other. Rear entry is also an option – it gives both of you access to the clitoris; and some women find that not seeing their partner gives room for fantasy. Don't be afraid to masturbate during intercourse. Feel free to put his hand, or your own, down there to stimulate the clitoris.

- For some, desire never overcomes the problems and fears of being with someone else. Even when the couple work on the problems together, the best that can be achieved is a state of loving acceptance. In such cases, further progress usually comes after psychotherapy or counselling.

Pain on intercourse
The causes are usually physical, such as lack of vaginal lubrication, common after the menopause, or vaginal discharge. Usually, the problem is short-lived; if it continues, you must see a doctor.

Vaginismus
Some women's vaginal muscles go into voluntary spasm when penetration is attempted. If it happens after penetration, this can mean the

pain and embarassment of both partners being packed off in tandem to hospital. There is usually a psychological cause. These women have difficulty accepting their vagina, and/or his penis; or they are terrified of getting pregnant. Sometimes the problem is a response to early sexual abuse, or to rape.

Treatment is difficult and not always successful. The woman must be taught gradually to accept penetration: first with one finger then with two; later with a vibrator, and eventually with a penis. Lubrication is always needed and penetration has to take place very slowly. Exercises play a part. She needs to learn how to exert voluntary control of her vaginal muscles: how to squeeze and relax while he gently pushes forward, progressing a centimetre at a time until he is inside.

Martin's problem

When the sight of Giselle causes a gleam in Martin's eye, his hypothalamus relays the good news down the spinal cord to his penis via the pelvic nerve. In the pre-diabetes days, the activity of this nerve dilated the pudendary artery to his penis, increasing blood flow there. One of the disease's main effects is degeneration of the arteries, so that dilation becomes gradually less efficient; blood no longer rushes into Martin's penis to fill the caverns within the shaft and especially within the glans, which is why it becomes so large during erection, and why its colour during arousal is reddish-purple. For the erection to be maintained, the blood has to be trapped. Instructions for this are transmitted through another autonomic nerve, the hypogastric; it also releases the trapped blood afterwards.

When (again, in pre-diabetes days) Giselle actually touched Martin's penis, the glad tidings were carried via his pudendal nerve and up the spinal cord, along nerves of the autonomic system; it by-passed his brain and directly increased his erection by reflex action: he didn't have to make any conscious effort; his penis had a 'will of its own'. Milliseconds after this transmission through the autonomic system, the same information ascended to his brain by a separate, non-autonomic transmission, and was consciously experienced as an erotic touch. In diabetes, there may also be some degeneration of the pudendal nerve.

The existence of these two separate pathways explains why stroking the genitalia is a doubly good way to encourage an erection, particularly in older men whose responses are slow.

Ejaculation

The intensity of ejaculation varies widely from man to man and from time to time. Sometimes it is a localized, brief, genital pulsation, some-

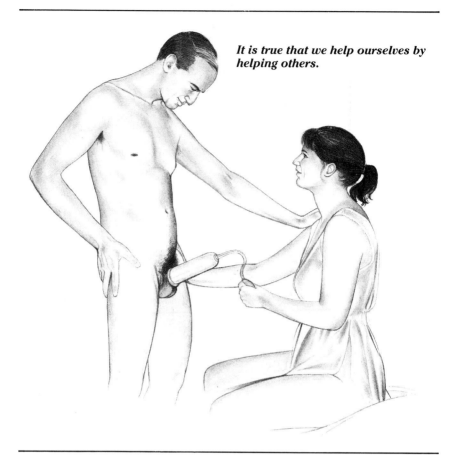

It is true that we help ourselves by helping others.

times a series of whole-body movements, like an epileptic fit, lasting for minutes. The refractory period, the time it takes before he is ready for another go, also varies from minutes to days.

In Martin's and in most men's experience, ejaculation is almost always accompanied by orgasm. They are surprised to learn that the two can be separated. There are men who have trained themselves to become multi-orgasmic by forestalling ejaculation while still experiencing orgasm; which implies that ejaculation is responsible for the refractory period.

How do these men manage multi-orgasms without squirting? Ejaculation is set off by neurones located in the middle levels of the spinal cord. But the associated sensations, notably the conscious, pleasurable experience of orgasm, happen in the brain. Multi-orgasmic men have found a way of suppressing the 'lower' ejaculatory centre in the spine while retaining the 'feeling' in the brain.

Too soon

However, the ejaculatory centre in the spine is not entirely independent of the brain. The brain's sensitivity can alter, which explains the common problem of coming too soon, after just a few seconds of penetration, or even rolling on a condom. Sex therapists may squabble over whether less than ten or under five seconds counts as premature ejaculation; the men themselves are in no doubt that they have a problem. A benign cause is excess enthusiasm: just being very keen for a girl can make you fire off uncontrollably. Should it happen more than once or twice, try these:

• Rubbing on anaesthetic jelly before sex.

• Masturbating solo to orgasm, quarter of an hour or so before sex, can also reduce sensitivity. But you have to know your refractory period and time love-making appropriately.

• Develop control by asking her to stroke you very slowly, with the firm understanding that intercourse is not to follow. Make a game of maintaining the erection for as long as possible without orgasm. A coating of baby oil or KY jelly can make it seem closer to the real thing. Learn to recognize the feeling of immanence – of being about to come – and when it occurs, stop her for a few seconds; then start again.

• Also try squeezing the frenulum, below the glans, as his excitement mounts. This slows ejaculation by engaging the bulbocavernous reflex. If he does come, you both relax for a while and try again; he'll be less sensitive second time round.

• In later sessions, graduate to penetration, but staying motionless inside her for intervals of one, two or five minutes. It takes a few sessions to get results from these techniques, and it is essential for the woman to be helpful, not impatient or critical.

Truly persistent hair-trigger trouble usually indicates deep-seated anxiety. If he needs to be reassured that she really likes and wants intercourse, she can talk about her desires ("I like the feeling of you inside me") and fantasies. If his concern is about his ability to bring her to a climax, then he or she can stimulate her nearly to orgasm before penetration.

Sometimes premature ejaculation is cured, only to be replaced by retarded ejaculation or complete inability to come. This is the province of a qualified sex therapist.

Temporary impotence

Finding yourself with an especially desired lady can, infuriatingly, lead to failure of erection just as easily as premature ejaculation. What distinguishes experienced from inexperienced men is not the occasional lapse but a calm recognition that the problem is temporary. If the momentary deflation puts you off pleasuring her with hands and mouth, fill the meantime with hugs, kisses, silly talk and tickling. They will reassure her, and you, that you have it in perspective.

Permanent impotence is psychologically devastating. Before the cause was discovered, the thought of being impotent brought Martin to a cold sweat. He felt he was losing control of his body; that the centre of his manhood was failing. Continuing impotence can be part of vicious circle in which anxiety on one occasion leads to impotence and even more anxiety on the next. Women often see lack of erection as lack of desire. This is utterly wrong. For her to feel hurt or depressed in such circumstances is as helpful as trying to douse a fire with petrol. Both sides should remind themselves that:

- Impotence is usually a symptom of something else. The most common something else is diabetes.

- It is also a common symptom of hardening of the arteries and/or heart disease. If the latter is problem, try intercourse in the least demanding position – her on top. Active muscles have to compete with the penis for blood.

- Nerve damage caused by injury to the spinal cord, or by diseases such as multiple sclerosis, which affect the pelvic and pudendal nerves, are another major cause of impotence.

- Impotence is also a side effect of recreational drugs such as nicotine and alcohol. It is also induced by a large variety of medicines, from radiation treatment for pelvic cancers to treatments for nasal congestion and high blood pressure. The ulcer medication Tagamet (chemical name cimetidine), possibly the most prescribed drug in the Western world, can produce impotence. So do anti-depressant drugs.

- Priapsim – involuntary and often painful erections that can persist for hours – is caused by damage to the veins which drain blood from the penis. Impotence can result. The condition is associated with certain blood diseases.

- Occasionally, impotence can be the first, and, for a while, the only sign of a pituitary tumour. This is readily treated, and the impotence entirely cured.

Psychological causes of impotence

Childhood experiences: A boy who has been sexually abused or who has been told that he will burn in hell for his sexual feelings may well be scared of fire and brimstone under the bedclothes. Misunderstanding of sexuality are a less obvious, but equally crippling cause. A man sees that the penis goes in big and hard and comes out little and weak. On a rational level he understands the physiology of erection perfectly well, but at a deeper, emotional level, he writes the equation *vagina = death*.

For other men, semen is dirty; they are afraid to come inside a women for fear of soiling her. In these cases, impotence is a way of avoiding the symbolic dangers of intercourse.

Long-term adult situations: Some cases of impotence can be traced to feelings relating to the man's situation in the adult world. A chronic sense that the other lads get more sex and do it better can ruin his style. Anger at his wife, repressed over many years, can take the form of impotence when he climbs into bed with her; he is fine if he hops under the covers with another woman.

Current events: Guilt over an illicit affair, low self-esteem due to a failed relationship, major stress at work and long-term depression are all proven causes. A man venturing into a new relationship after the death of his partner may have problems because he feels guilty of betraying the dead woman's memory.

Reading the signs

There is probably a psychological cause for impotence if the onset is sudden; if it follows a crisis such as the death of a loved one; if it only happens with some partners; if you have erections during masturbation but not during intercourse; if you have erections at night lasting more than a minute (this has to be established by medical test).

There is probably a physical cause if onset is gradual; if you don't have erections under any circumstances – during masturbation, or sleep; if impotence is not cured by relaxation, taking a holiday, sensate focusing or a change of partners.

These signs are only intended as clues: don't play doctor. Impotence is occasionally a warning sign of serious disease. If you have been impotent for more than a couple of months you should suspect a physical cause and must see a doctor.

Tests include monitoring of night-time erections, and a check on the functioning of the nerve supply to the penis.

Remedies – drugs

An injection of yohimbine combined with testosterone can work well for mild or moderate impotence. It works by making good a lack of chemicals ordinarily secreted by the autonomic nerves.

Injections of papaverine directly into the penis can work for some men. It increases blood flow to the area; you feel a sting and erection follows within five to ten minutes. Some find the injection unpleasant; the erection may last for several hours, which may be dangerous. The treatment is not recommended for those with a variety of medical conditions, including heart and liver disease, and alcoholism.

Remedies – external devices

Chinese cock rings, for enhancing erections, have re-emerged in modern medical guise as devices for sucking blood into the penis and trapping it by a ring around the base – what Martin and Giselle call the gismo. They tend to be offered as a first option when it is still uncertain whether the impotence is physical or psychological (though availability and indeed doctors' enthusiasm for them vary internationally). The suction is applied using a type of sheath. The result is a firm, rather than an erect, penis. Martin and Giselle had some fun with it, but such devices can make spontaneity impossible, and some men find they make ejaculation uncomfortable.

Internal devices

An implant may well be the 'ultimate' solution, once physical impotence is proved. The apparatus varies: it may be rigid or hinged, and some are bent into the required position. The one eventually responsible for Martin and Giselle's salvation consists of two inflatable rods implanted surgically in the spongy parts of his penis. They are inflated by a little pump buried in his scrotum; it draws fluid from a reservoir in his abdomen. A button on the pump deflates the penis when it is no longer needed.

Less can be more

Impotent men can sometimes reach orgasm. Orgasm does not depend on an erect penis – it just makes it easier and quicker. Even without treatment, some impotent men have active and useful sex lives. For a woman who prefers mutual masturbation and oral sex, a man with erection difficulties can be a Godsend.

Happily ever after?

Of course, regaining an erection is only a start. There is rebuilding to do inside and outside the relationship. Men don't talk about their im-

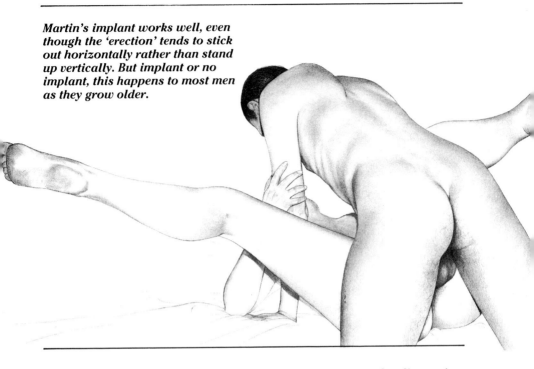

Martin's implant works well, even though the 'erection' tends to stick out horizontally rather than stand up vertically. But implant or no implant, this happens to most men as they grow older.

potence, and women don't want to shame their partners by discussing the problem with girl friends.

The couple may blame each other not for the problem itself, but for the physical coldness it causes. Even if she understands the problem at an intellectual level, she may find his withdrawal difficult to cope with in practice. 'Why can't Martin say he loves me any more? Why doesn't he put his arms round me?' The answer? He can't because those gestures remind him of what he and Giselle can no longer share. 'What is the point of the embraces', he asks himself, 'if they lead no-where?' And: 'I'm not the man I used to be; does she still care?'

Some men feel another partner might solve the problem; some women may feel this too. It may indeed bring release, but often this is momentary.

For both, guilt makes things worse. He may say 'If she were more lovable' (not as fat, not as dull) he would feel more desire; and then feel guiltily disloyal. If she suspects these feelings, her self-esteem comes under fire. Guilt on one side and poor self-esteem on the other puts a relationship under intolerable strain. Even if the physical cure works, some of the psychological overtones may remain; patience and determination to see it through are needed to regain loving and sexy closeness.

L THE OVERS

Andrew & Meredith

1 Meredith

Before I met Andrew I'd had two other lovers, but the sex had been pretty hit or miss.

2 Andrew

She had this air of innocence when we met, wide-eyed and soft. I was glad that we could skip the uncomfortable steps of sexual initiation. I wanted to show her what intimate pleasures could be; to teach her.

3 Meredith

We'd been together a few times. He's a bit stuffy, but very sweet. He suggested a picnic and I thought, why not?

4 Andrew

As we walked through the woods, I had to look at her again and again; each time I looked I had to touch her. I kissed her shoulders and stroked her hair; it was a dark honey colour.

Accidentally-on-purpose, I brushed her breast. When I stopped, pulled her close to me, and ran my fingers over her silken triangle, she drew in her breath, and trembled.

5 Meredith

"Come lie with me," he says, spreading the rug. His eyes hold mine, his voice is gentle. So I do. The leaves above me are changing colour, just touched by autumn, but the sun is warm. What do you call that? Indian summer. "In Russia," he says, "they call this 'Women's summer'."

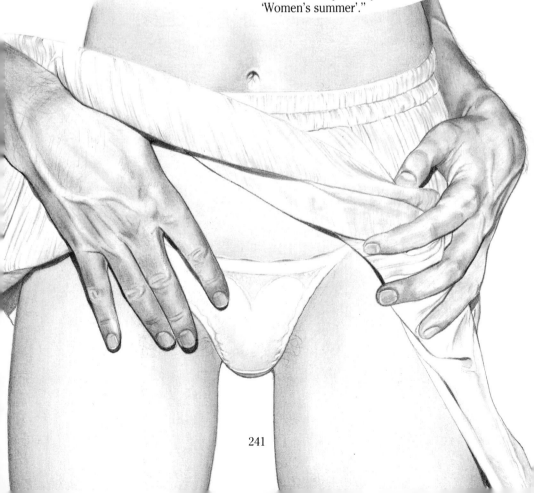

6 *Andrew*

I take her hand and stroke it. "Every part of your body has a special place, a place that calls out for touching. Where is the special place?"

7 *Meredith*

I close my eyes and say, "A little to the left, near the middle finger." "So where?" he asks each time as he touches a new area – my arms, my shoulders, my cheeks, my lips. His hands explore me. "And how?" he says, first touching me with his fingertips, then running his nail lightly across my skin.

8 *Andrew*

I raise her ankle in my hand, stretch her leg and flex it, marvelling at the curve of her calf, the fineness of the hairs. I kiss her bare thigh. "There or here?"

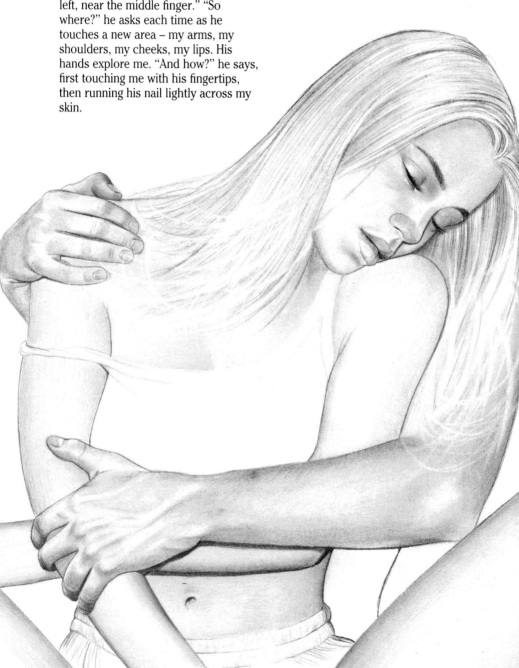

9 *Meredith*

My nipple is between his lips. He says,
"Now I can lick." And he does. "And I
can kiss or suck." He does these too
and I grow light.

He says, "I am going to take your
breast completely in my mouth." He
does, and somehow I feel the
pleasurable contraction down in my
vagina. He moves away. His mouth on
my breast has heightened my longing
for him. I want him to touch me again,
kiss my nipples again. I move my
breasts towards him. He smiles at me
and takes me in his mouth. Asking him
comes so naturally, yet I have never
asked for any particular caress before.

Suddenly I want to kiss him, to love
him. I had always thought that a man
was a man. His body hard, secure,
something to hold on to, not something
to need for itself. Not something to
excite the eye as he excites me now.
Until this moment, when men have
touched me, I have closed my eyes and
escaped. Being touched felt safe,
relaxing. Their entering me was a
passive pleasure, like lying in a warm
bath, like sunbathing. Needing to have
this man is new.

10 *Andrew*

"Imagine me inside you. Do you feel empty? Would you like me to fill you up?"

11 *Meredith*

I close my eyes, imagining him inside me, sucking at the emptiness. My need for being filled grows.

12 *Andrew*

"Take my hand and put it between your legs," I say into her ear. She does. "See, you have control. Now, cross your legs. Relax. Again. How's that?"

13 *Meredith*

It is good. Reaching down to my vagina he touches, caresses, opens me a little. I am very wet. He puts his fingers under my nose. "Don't you smell good?" I do. I have never smelled so good before. He says, "I am going to touch the inside of you," and my thighs open of their own volition.

14 *Andrew*

"You can stop us any time."

15 *Meredith*

I knew that. Thoughtful, but not necessary, not even remotely necessary. Suddenly, I feel the need to have him take charge, to finish things off. I have never felt this need to pull a man into me before.

16 *Andrew*

"I am going to enter you."

17 *Meredith*

The promise alone excites me more. He is pressing on my most special place, talking to me. I am following his words. Penetration takes ages, a thousand women's summers. He is so gentle. The energy which waited in all the places he has touched breaks free. His moving in me sucks it down, so that it gathers between my legs, in my clasping of him inside me. The loving instructions in my ear disappear into a rich, growling voice.

18 *Andrew*

"Take me into you, eat me up."

19 *Meredith*

Men have said it before, but somehow the analogy has never seemed right until now. I *am* hungry for him. I seem to move, upwards and outwards, until I am drifting.

20 *Andrew*

I am moving inside you. We are moving together. My role as guide has slipped away. My heart is thawing out. We are linked and moving so closely that I feel we are transformed. Your body seems new, soft, precious.

21 *Meredith*

"Andrew." The arching of my back, the hot pulses between my legs are uncontrollable. The intensity is unbelievable. I am fainting into the rainbow. "Andrew."

22 *Andrew*

"Oh God, yes, please come, please." Let me give you this pleasure, this release. Now I can't stop, I can't hold back any more, I am so deeply inside you, the most incredible warmth is flooding through me. I'm melting. "Hold me."

23 *Meredith*

I hold him tight. My fear is growing: it is like suddenly finding that everyone can read your thoughts. I know at this moment that this is the one I will remember all my life. I know I have given him a power over me. Can I trust him?

24 *Andrew*

"Lie on top of me. I need your weight on top of me to keep me from floating away."

"I love you. I really do."

Whether or not Andrew and Meredith live happily ever after we shall never know; which is fitting because no one ever does when they start a relationship. We must all take our leaps, if not in the dark, at least in the twilight of uncertainty. Even if it were possible to predict a happy outcome for a new relationship, or the reverse, we doubt that anyone would act on this better judgement. Not least of the charms of falling in love is its irresistability.

Moreover, most of us accept that this supremely fickle, impulsive, mysterious experience as the only satisfactory basis for a long-term commitment to another human being; a commitment which can just as easily ruin ones life as be the making of it.

Sex Life began, in **Robert & Jenny's** story, with speculation on the mechanics of sexual attraction: the powerful forces which bring the sexes together in the first place, sometimes, literally, from opposite sides of a room. It continued, in most of the following stories, with discussions, from various points of view, on how to keep relationships together, indeed how to make them sing.

It is fitting that with this last story – a simple tale of falling in love, where the partners are not, on the face of it, particularly well suited – we should come full circle: to reflect once more on falling in love – the cement which bonds the sexes.

Echoes

Why do you fall in love with one person and not another?

Of course, there is no straightforward answer; if the reasons for falling in love could be neatly analysed there would be dozens, perhaps hundreds; they would be different at different times in our lives; and they would change from person to person. Even if science suggests that sexual love is just another biological impulse, explicable in terms of human motives, and survival of the species, the impulse still depends on such a cocktail of different causes that it must amount to a mystery, and, moreover, a new mystery each time it happens.

Mysteries cannot be explained away, but we can at least try to define their essence. We believe the essence of falling in love is echoes; that the pattern of love relationships follows those which have gone before, like a song re-sung in a different key.

Your current love has echoes of your previous loves: the catch in her voice, the insolent expression in his eyes. You have seen them before; you loved them then, and you love them now. Maybe the echoes come down from childhood; perhaps from earlier generations.

The patterns of love affairs can often be seen repeated from one generation to the next, so that a child will recreate the essential power

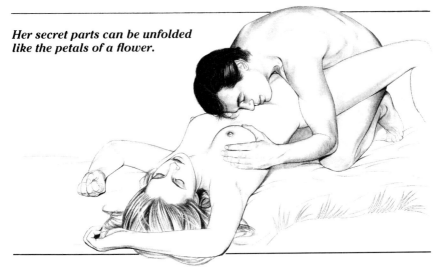

*Her secret parts can be unfolded
like the petals of a flower.*

base of the parents' marriage. This may not be so simple as choosing someone like one's mother, but of mimicking some fundamental aspect of the relationship. A man whose father was at the beck and call of his mother may, for instance, choose a woman who is very close to, and dependent upon, her father. The child of an alcoholic often chooses a partner destined to follow the same path. Perhaps we hope to solve in adulthood what as children we could not.

When you look at her, do you see a ghost of a smile in her face which is like the one that you saw leaning over your cot? Or could it simply be a face that reminds you of a carefree childhood?

The search

If the trigger of love is a ghostly memory of something that gave you happiness and reassurance, the drive that fuels the falling-in-love process could well be another basic drive: the Odyssey – the instinct to search out the homeland, to return to what is ours by right of birth.

Each of us seeks our other half; within every individual there is a man, and a woman, longing to be found and fulfilled. (If you want a literal explanation of this androgenous view of the sexes, see pages 101-103.) In love, we seek, therefore, to balance these forces, and love is so compelling because it has the power to complete us. The cliché cannot here be avoided: a woman needs the hardness of a man, just as a man needs the softness of a woman.

Security

We seek to complete ourselves; and, psychologists generally agree, we also seek to recapture the wonderful security of a our mothers'

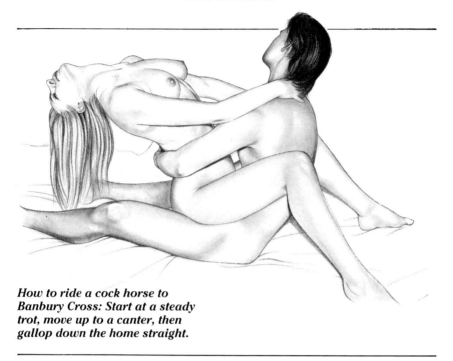

*How to ride a cock horse to
Banbury Cross: Start at a steady
trot, move up to a canter, then
gallop down the home straight.*

love. Our first taste of love was, after all, highly seductive: it came because of who we were, not what we were. The instinct to bond, to live happily ever after, probably owes much to the inevitable loss, as we grew up, of mother love.

Inevitability

Another aspect of falling love which the afflicted have always noted is a feeling of inevitability. Love sometimes knocks for six; sometimes it grows (and is no less strong for that); but somewhere along the line, there is the feeling that this person is extraordinarily familiar and inevitable; that they are designed (destined?) to have an impact on your life. Everything that concerns them and their existence automatically concerns you; indeed, you have an in-built understanding of it, and *vice-versa*. With this knowledge follows an urge to protect. And you find yourself telling him, or her, the most personal details of your life within minutes of meeting; or at any rate you feel you could; or perhaps, depending on your type, you feel no need to talk at all. Nothing needs be said, all is understood.

A dedication

Falling in love relies not only on childhood echoes; it can make us children again, giving a child's faith, and a child's zest for life. The excitement you feel as you approach his or her door is first cousin to the thrill of anticipation when as a child you contemplated the presents under the tree, waiting to be unwrapped.

Christmas comes but once a year; relationships have the potential to be better: there forever forever to be unwrapped, a renewable resource. This book is dedicated to that belief.

If you find yourself asking 'Am I really in love?' reflect on the near universal truth that love is not a passive thing. It can be seen. Its glow is produced by the migration of blood to the body's surface, puffing out breaasts and ear lobes and faces. The heart beats; sometimes, like Meredith, you tremble.

It unlocks feelings which lie dormant. You see and hear things as if for the first time. You want others to see you like this: renewed.

The loving touch

Andrew and Meredith seem to conform well to this pattern of falling in love. Andrew's technique in wooing Meredith, with its reliance on touching and holding, echoes the childhood importance of physical contact. Simply touching creates an atmosphere of physical closeness, as important for many as the physical act itself.

His touch is gentle and undemanding, his quest for the place she especially loves to be touched a treat he invites her to lie back and enjoy. His pleasure is in giving pleasure to her. He has learned, as we all must, that good sexual relationships depend on being ready to give *and* just as ready to take.

His technique is, in fact, based on sensate focusing, used by sex therapists to help couples with sexual problems, but it is of course ideal for the first time lovers come together physically. It is based on the principle that there should be no pressure to complete the sex act. If the pressure is off, both sides can learn, fully, and at leisure, to express the pleasure they feel in receiving caresses. Only after discovering, or re-discovering, the pleasure of giving and receiving is genital touching allowed.

Postscript

We have tried, in selecting these stories, and in writing the interpretations which go with them, to say something about the many sides of love and sex in a society whose underlying attitudes towards them have been transformed, over the past two decades, by feminism, and by A.I.D.S.

In his poem *Annus Mirabilis*, Philip Larkin neatly summed up the sexual revolution which went *before* feminism: the heady one of the swinging 1960s, linked in peoples' minds as starting more or less at the same time as the release of the Beatles' first LP. He saw it as

A brilliant breaking of the bank. A quite unlosable game.

By which he meant that neither sex could lose from giving sexual love freely; that the simple act of free love (now described as permissive behaviour) liberated the sexes at a stroke from the life-denying wrangle for the wedding ring that stood in the way of sexual enjoyment.

Hindsight has taught us that the reality is different: the game of sex and love is still just as easy to lose as the wrangle over the ring; and now there is the spectre of AIDS.

Telling a woman how she feels to you makes her ear her most erotic orifice. Here he is, talking his way into it.

So why do we go on doing it? Because not to do so would be absurd; to live without the joys and challenges of love would be a pale shadow of life.

After getting Andrew and Meredith's story, we asked them to try and wrap up for us, in the fewest possible words, what they saw in each other. Here are their responses, interpreted and re-written:

Meredith: '. . . *So what is he like, this man of my waking dreams? Let me look at him with your eyes if I can. I think he is perhaps rather ordinary. Not the stuff of your passion. Because he is my lover, I see him differently. He wears my rainbow like a ring.*

Andrew: '. . . *So what is she like, this woman who disrupts the careful order of my life? Whose very way of being churns my soul? She is like a hundred women you will see today, and pass by. Yet she is one in a million to me because she is the one in my life. The surprising pleasure of her familiar smile renews my rainbow.*'

If there are to be last words on this, of all subjects, one can surely excuse them for being a little purple.

252

INDEX